The Terrorist Recognition Handbook

The Terrorist
Recognition Handbook
A Manual for Predicting and Identifying Terrorist Activities

MALCOLM W. NANCE

Illustrations by Maryse Beliveau

THE LYONS PRESS
Guilford, Connecticut
An imprint of The Globe Pequot Press

For Lt. Col. Patricia Horoho

Printed in the United States of America

ISBN 1-59228-025-0

Book design by Casey Shain

1 3 5 7 9 10 8 6 4 2

The Library of Congress Cataloging-in-Publication Data is available on file.

CONTENTS

Part Two
Identifying the Terrorist Group and Its Cells

Part Three
Detection of Key Terrorist Activities

Preface

On September 11, 2001, the world witnessed a horrific act of terrorism. Three thousand eighty-three people from more than eighty countries lost their lives in the hijacking and subsequent crashes of four airliners into the World Trade Center towers, the Pentagon, and a field in western Pennsylvania.

Stunned and horrified, Americans began asking themselves, "How could this happen?" Television provided myriad bewildering and conflicting answers. In the days that followed, more questions arose as the skyjackers' association with Usama bin Laden's al-Qaeda terrorist network came to light. How could such catastrophic attacks be planned and carried out right under our noses? Are there more cells in the United States planning further attacks? What will come next? Over the years it became apparent that terrorists from more than one organization had infiltrated the U.S. and used it as a base camp for ideological training, recruiting, and fund-raising as well as a target rich with opportunity. Al-Qaeda made use of the United States' freedom and liberty—but it is not the only group. Immediately after the al-Qaeda terrorist attack, another one occurred, this time by a person believed to be an American citizen possessing biological weapons from U.S. military stocks. As if that weren't enough, antigovernment and neo-Nazi organizations in the country praised the destruction of the World Trade Center and attack on the Pentagon. America's worst seemed to take heart in the daring and simplicity of attack.

In the aftermath of September 11, 2001, billions of dollars are being spent by the United States and many other countries to ensure that a tragedy of such magnitude never happens again.

- Funds are being allocated to tighten up immigration flows at airports, borders and seaports.
- The FBI, CIA, and Homeland Security agencies are slated to buy integrated multiagency computer databases and fund tens of thousands of new intelligence analysts.
- The Transportation Security Agency is investing in new luggage-scanning machines and thousands of new federal officers.
- The Bush administration has urged the hiring of thousands of security guards and the creation of the Department of Homeland Security.

When all is said and done, more than half a trillion dollars may be spent so that we can feel good about our ability to stop terrorism. Unfortunately, these measures may not be enough.

Over-reliance on technological fixes such as computerized face-recognition programs, metal detectors, or explosive-sniffing machines may catch some suspects at certain checkpoints. However, they may also create a false sense of security, allowing security professionals to become blind to obvious human indicators that are right in front of them. With tens of thousands of people being brought into the new national game of anti- and counterterrorism, one critical component is still lacking: basic knowledge about terrorists and their operations.

The single best method of defeating terrorism is educating our military, law enforcement personnel, first responders, and security professionals (as well as the public) about how to recognize the roles and motivations of individual terrorists, their cell systems, and the street-level mechanics of terrorist operations.

During 2002, as the hunt for al-Qaeda worldwide was beginning, the following suspected terrorism incidents involving U.S. citizens or residents occurred: Two soldiers from Fort Benning, Georgia, were arrested for taking three hundred sticks of Emutrench ammonium nitrate explosives, bundling them into bombs, and storing them in a remote area of the base; an American man and woman from the supremacist group Racial Holy War's (RAHOWA's) White Order of Thule were arrested in Boston for planning a terrorist campaign; two Pakistani men were arrested in southern Florida for planning to attack power plants; a man was arrested dressed all in black, commando style, infiltrating a Florida power plant with weapons and caught planting a small explosive device; a doctor was arrested in Florida for planning to blow up fifty Islamic centers; the head of the Jewish Defense League was arrested for plotting to blow up a mosque in Los Angeles . . . the list goes on and on. The story to be told here is that all of these are examples of terrorists, and all conducted activities that led investigators to preempt their attacks.

Since 9/11, intelligence, military, law enforcement, and security professionals in particular have been seeking answers to a few singular critical questions: What exactly do we need to look out for? And how can we prevent further attacks? Few consistent answers have emerged.

The Terrorist Recognition Handbook attempts to provide some of the answers that have eluded professionals so far. *TRH* is primarily aimed at new terrorism and intelligence analysts, military people, law enforcement officers, and other security professionals tasked with anti- or counterterrorism duties, who need a solid understanding of terrorism in order to detect and predict attacks. We believe it will prove immensely helpful to those in the homeland security field—even members of the general public as well. The book will address the following questions:

- How can terrorist operations be detected before they occur?
- What types of terrorist organizations operate globally? Can their members be profiled, and if so, how?
- How are terrorist operatives developed and motivated?
- How do groups organize for their missions?
- What resources do terrorists require for planning and preparation?
- What basic intelligence tools can the counterterrorism officer use to predict potential attacks?

The book's central point is this: Terrorist operations are observable, their preparations can be detected, and attacks can be stopped before they begin.

Acknowledgments

This book was completed with the help of a dedicated staff composed of friends. The bulk of my thanks go to Lisa Hughes, a brilliant intelligence analyst and cartographer, a competent shot with a Glock pistol, and a very good friend. My appreciation goes out to my peers John "Brad" Michael—a great terrorism instructor and my critical information link to the world as we battled the fires at the Pentagon crash site on September 11; without him, we would never have known a fourth aircraft was coming our way—and David Mitchell, the antiterrorism officer for the U.S. Naval Air Forces, and Nicholas North of SAIC, two of the world's most unrecognized terrorism experts. The invaluable staff of the Special Readiness Services made this book possible, including Kathleen Stanley, Rajika Jayatilake, Tony Daza, and Brooke Trahan, our senior intern. The bulk of the research was carried out by our outstanding intelligence watch officer interns from Georgetown University, American University, George Washington University, and the University of Maryland: Dallas Frohrib, Meredith Hamilton, Michael Keller, Benjamin Michener, Graham Sugarman, Jason Kichen, Lauren Terzenbach, David Worn, and Francis Yoh.

Special thanks go to the people who edited and provided generous input and guidance, including the renowned al-Qaeda expert, Dr. Rohan Gunaratna; Margaret Poethig of the Washington, D.C., Metropolitan Police Department; Mark Overton at Naval Special Warfare Group One; Sheri Fatout and her husband, Aaron, of the University of California, Berkeley; and Assistant Deputy Director of Information Ron Huberman of the Chicago Police Department.

Special acknowledgment goes to my friend Robert Young Pelton, the renowned author, adventurer, and chronicler of the battle at Mazar E Sharif (and Sir Richard Burton look-alike); Jeff Herman, my literary agent; and Jay McCullough and Tony Lyons of The Lyons Press, without whom this book would never have been. Special thanks go to Maryse Beliveau, who provided the illustrations, and to SRSI's former chief of staff Beverly LaRue, whose traumatic first day at work for my terrorism consultancy was September 11, 2001.

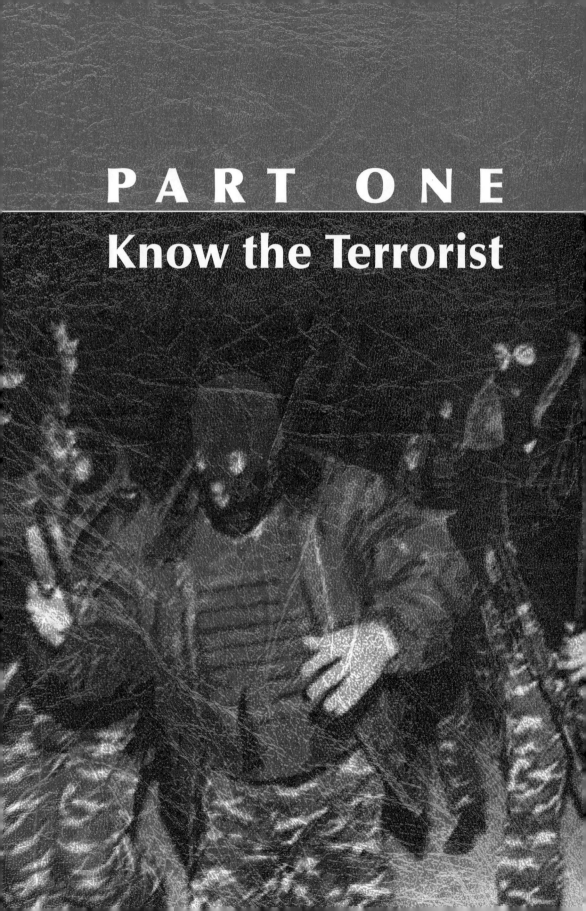

PART ONE

Know the Terrorist

YOUR MISSION: CRITICAL AWARENESS

Criminal investigators spend years studying criminal behavior to better understand and counter crime. The field of terrorism is no different. It is a specialized subject that requires serious study, and requires that those in the front line of defense be as knowledgeable as possible. Today's police officers, security managers, and customs officers have received most of their terrorism education in short briefings, or simply via magazines or television. In the coming years, security professionals may receive more specialized training and education on terrorism—or they may not. This book is intended as a resource for those who realize that they need to begin their own terrorism education today.

The most difficult and critical component of terrorism education is learning how to recognize and predict an attack. Those responsible for homeland security need to be well versed in terrorist attack pre-incident indicators (TAPIs). TAPIs are behaviors; they are actions terrorists must take before they can carry out an attack. In the law enforcement and intelligence communities, some TAPIs may be referred to as behavioral science or "profiling." For example, Secret Service teams are trained to watch individuals' behaviors—as well as their race, age, sex, or appearance, which are secondary indicators. The Israeli airline El Al has used this behavior-recognition approach for decades and is generally successful at stopping potential terrorists from skyjacking its airliners.

Until recently the United States has had a much less diligent attitude toward security—and terrorism in particular—than many other countries in the world, but we have since learned. Why even more diligence? First, America is a huge nation with a higher level of domestic freedom than domestic security; and second, the United States is a declared target of future terrorist attacks. The devastation caused on 9/11 may, tragically, only inspire others to continue the trend.

All members of the anti- and counterterrorism community need to seek answers to these questions:

- Who represents a threat?
- What options do those people have for carrying out harm?
- How might they carry out an attack?
- Most important, what behaviors can be observed when they are preparing or ready to act?

These questions will eventually lead to observable behaviors and actions of terrorists and their supporters.

For example, if terrorists want to disperse a chemical weapon, they must first acquire and move the chemicals; locate and stock a safe location; select a target and observe it; deploy a delivery team and support them; create a dispersal system and move it to the target. All of these actions are detectable to the trained observer. Before we can detect terrorist activity, however, we must first change our perceptions about who terrorists might be.

Adopt an Intelligence-Based Approach to Antiterrorism

Understanding and countering terrorism requires adjustment in perspective. Security professionals need to respect and understand terrorists, recognize the pre-incident indicators of terrorist activities, and competently analyze intelligence information.

1. One must learn to respect the terrorist's capabilities: You don't have to agree with terrorists in order to recognize their abilities and understand them. Terrorism as a political tool may be abhorrent; however, you need to identify and recognize the grievances of a particular terrorist group and—for lack of a better word—respect the intelligence and tenacity they use to perform terrible deeds. Why were they motivated to take up their cause? How effective are their tactics? If you disregard a demonstrated capability, or dismiss their ability to analyze weak spots and work around them, because you think terrorists are inferior, you may create a blind spot in your security. To get an edge on terrorists, you must learn to see the world from behind their mask.

2. Observe street-level behaviors: Learn the terrorist attack pre-incident indicators of a terrorist operation in the works. No matter how clever terrorists may be, they're not ghosts. Terrorists and their support personnel must perform certain behaviors in order to carry out their plans. They have specific roles and duties, many of which are observable to the trained eye.

3. Analyze source information: Basic analysis must be applied to any data or evidence collected by integrating intelligence assets, using computerized analytical programs, or just asking the right questions. Clearly, as we learned in the September 11 attacks, without cross checking the data and applying common sense the analytical process breaks down.

Field officers must make every effort to match the observed or suspected criminal behaviors with terrorist intelligence. Analysis does not have to be a long, drawn-out process. Even the simplest key-word associations comparing known intelligence to known capability can find potential TAPIs. Prior to September 11, the words *Usama bin Laden, al-Qaeda* and *pilot training* in the same sentence should have spelled out *suicide skyjacking* to most people who worked the al-Qaeda mission. All of these words were found in one FBI agent's report prior to the attack. Al-Qaeda's global capabilities, matched with Bin Laden's personal animosity toward America and a previous skyjacking for this purpose by a group associated with al-Qaeda (the skyjacking of an Air France airliner by the Algerian GIA in 1994), should have made even the coolest intelligence analyst spill his coffee and issue a dire warning. Several did just that.

These key steps—respect, observe, and analyze—represent an intelligence-based approach to predicting terrorist actions. With a few exceptions, the intelligence-based approach is surprisingly new to many law enforcement agencies; stereotypes and heavy reliance on technology still dominate our security perspective to a great degree.

Avoid a Stereotype-Based Approach to Antiterrorism

Why do we stereotype terrorists? Let's look at a basic fact: America is new to terrorism. We have a hard time understanding who would carry out such acts, and so to answer our own questions, we create stereotypes of "the terrorist" in the absence of facts. Some people see terrorists as incompetent cowards who can't stand up to us; others consider

Stereotype-based views of terrorism don't help us fight the threat but blind us to it.

them brilliant but suicidal bogeymen who can't be stopped. Until September 11, the predominant image of a terrorist in many people's minds was a cartoon character carrying a big bomb with a lit fuse.

In educating members of the armed forces and law enforcement, I often hear terrorists referred to as "crazy rag-heads" or "camel jockeys." One senior member of the U.S. House of Representatives, in an oblique reference to al-Qaeda, recommended arresting anyone with "diapers on their heads." These attitudes may have contributed to our intelligence community's focus on finding the stereotypical terrorist while the atypical ones operated with complete impunity within our borders.

But there is another damaging stereotype at work: that of the current counterterrorism effort. Some inflamed political rhetoric has created an inaccurate stereotype of how fast and effective the "war on terrorism has been. Americans now believe that we can stop terrorism by sending out our military forces to get them, "dead or alive." That may be true to some extent, but not entirely. Terrorism cannot be defeated in a grand war. Trying to preemptively hunt down every person in the world who might carry out or participate in an act of terrorism is akin to trying to hunt and catch a few specific ants in Texas: a nearly impossible task.

> **Terrorism against America can only be defeated through careful intelligence collection, surveillance, and cooperative efforts among law enforcement and intelligence agencies.**

Terrorism against America can only be defeated through careful intelligence collection, surveillance, cooperative efforts among law enforcement and intelligence agencies, and resolving the root complaints of the terrorist-supporting population. One thing is certain: We may not get every operative, but we can stop key people at critical junctures before an attack occurs. This book will assist you in this effort.

Defensive Action: The Detect, Deter, Defend (3D) Doctrine

Your role in stopping terrorism is to learn how to use the information presented in this manual to see terrorists, make terrorists stop their planning, and/or stop terrorists as they attack. The U.S. government's force-protection doctrine is based on the "3D" concept of "detect, deter, and defend." It is a highly effective concept that can be applied to the homeland security community as well.

You, as a professional, will *detect* the terrorist act in its planning stages through intelligence collection; use the intelligence-based approach of analysis; and take aggressive action to *deter* an attack before the terrorists leave their safe house. These are the fundamentals necessary to *defend* our nation from attack.

But before we can truly use this process, it helps to know a few things about the terrorists themselves.

2

WHO THEY ARE: IDENTIFYING TERRORIST OPERATIVES

If You Know the Terrorists, You Know Their Plans

Who are terrorists? What is the single most important thing you should know? There are many terrorists, and they come from diverse social and economic backgrounds. However, the most important thing you should consider is this: The intention of the terrorist operative is to use simple but bold, innovative actions to defeat your security and to render high technology useless.

This mode of operations, called "asymmetric warfare" or "technology judo," is the terrorist's profession. Terrorist operatives always consider the use of the most appropriate and lowest-end technology, best innovation, and exploiting any limits their target may have. However, these actions can be predicted and observed. Terrorists operate between the cracks of technology and laws, yet they must operate somewhere. They cannot hide in a safe house with the curtains drawn all day. Even that is an observable action that should draw suspicion.

Terrorists do not apply any rules or values to their operations other than what will enable them to gain publicity for their cause and hurt the enemy. If you attempt to get a fix on them with stereotypes of cultural traits, they will adopt the ones you don't suspect in order to carry out a mission. For example, more than one of the 9/11 skyjackers were seen in U.S. nightclubs. No American would think they were devout religious extremists given this behavior. In fact, they were using a simple technique to throw off government surveillance. The oldest rule of terrorism is in effect: "Do whatever it takes."

Rule 1: Anyone Can Be a Terrorist

- To fight them, get inside terrorists' heads and learn their tactics.
- Terrorists do not have capability to counter conventional military force except on their own terms.
- You must recognize the unusual activities that indicate an attack is planned or is under way.
- Looking for one specific group may blind you to seeing the hundreds of other groups that may gain the expertise and skills equal to a group such as al-Qaeda.

POLICE NATIONALE, MINISTRY OF THE INTERIOR, REPUBLIQUE DE FRANCE

Basque ETA terrorists (left to right): Pikabea-Uglade, Turrillas-Aranceta, Santesteban-Goikoetxea, Zabula-Muguirra.

Who Are Terrorists?

It is a generally scandalous notion that terrorists must be treated with anything but contempt. In fact, that is one of the views that blinds us. Terrorists must be respected for what they are: determined, ruthless human beings who use death and destruction to meet their goals. If you underestimate them, they will inevitably surprise you. You do not have to like terrorists. But you must respect their capability and their ability to realize their deadly objectives. Here are some key things to know.

Terrorists Are . . .

- **Human beings**: Terrorists are not automatons as depicted by Hollywood. They are human beings with emotions, feelings, and concerns. These emotions are channeled into lethal action and often bring innocent people within their definition of "enemy." If you ignore them as people, you may witness the horrifying determination of human intelligence.
- **Revered within their culture/ideology:** What may be an evil, horrific deed to you or me may be a respectful and honorable act to someone else. Don't judge terrorist actions by Western values, no matter how horrible the acts; ignoring their perspective will blind you to the terrorists' potential for future action. Have professional respect for a foreign culture, a strange philosophy, or a disagreeable ideology and use it to identify ways to predict and stop their acts.

- **Rational in their actions**: Terrorists are rarely insane. They are generally intelligent, clear thinking, and rational. In the heat of an attack, they harness the human ability to overcome obstacles and attack with clarity and with ruthlessness. Westerners who observe this ruthlessness may view it as "insane."
- **Well motivated:** Terrorists use personal motivation to carry out the deadly acts necessary to demonstrate their determination.
- **Mentally justified in their actions:** Terrorists view the necessity of the mission as justifying any act necessary to meet their goals. Murdering women and children, attacking nurseries, blowing up hundreds or thousands of people can always be justified in the mind of the terrorist. For the terrorist, the end justifies the means.

Some Facts About Terrorists

• Rarely are terrorists insane, though their acts may appear insane.

• Terrorists are human beings who care about their families, ideology, and cultural values.

• Terrorists are usually very well organized when ready to attack.

• They rely on seemingly random acts of violence to inculcate fear.

• They may fail in the attempt but have won when they gain your attention.

• If you know terrorists' options, you can beat them.

• Terrorists fear one thing only . . . not making it out of the safe house to carry out the attack.

Classifying Terrorist Operatives by Skills Level

The traditional method of categorizing terrorist groups and operatives has been to classify them by their philosophy or region of operations. This is an excellent method for academics, but for anyone involved in detecting, responding to, or analyzing terrorism, there is a more exact method: classifying terrorist groups by their relative level of experience and skillfulness in terrorist activities. The reason that terrorist skills levels matter, now more than ever, is their ability to project these skills past the combined resources of the world's intelligence and homeland defense agencies. The officer on the street, the soldier on patrol, and the intelligence analyst need to know not just whom they are dealing with but *how skillful these people are.* Some groups are going to be naturally more adept than others in certain fields, but there is a very clear hierarchy of skills. Government-trained terrorist organizations are better funded, staffed, and trained than guerrilla or radical revolutionary groups that spontaneously start terrorist attacks. In the same vein, the amateur who is unsupported by anyone may be able to perform a major attack but still lacks professional skills when compared to guerrillas or revolutionaries. We have classified terrorist groups from Class I—the best supported and most skillful—to Class V, the least skillful.

The Terrorist Recognition Guide **defines terrorists in the following manner: Any person or group of people who fail in, reject, or are disenfranchised from political, economic, or personal objectives and deliberately choose to use acts of terrorism as a tool of political violence, a method of protest, or effecting change.**

The need to know terrorists' skills is paramount in stopping them. On the street level, the value of this knowledge exceeds almost every other kind of intelligence except their location and strength. Critical questions must be considered before implementing any antiterrorism measures or counterterrorist operations. Critical information may be found in the answers to these questions: Is the terrorist a combat-experienced guerrilla who learned to fire the AK-47 rifle and RPG-7 rocket launcher from nine years of age? Is he a former American infantry soldier turned antigovernment militiaman who studied *The Anarchist Cookbook* and builds homemade bombs? Is she a member of a foreign intelligence agency with years of special operations skills and weapons training? Is she a logistician with a religious extremist group or a walking bomb? Each answer is going to affect how you deal with these terrorists. You will adjust your tactics according to their skill not yours.

When the Special Operations Forces face a terrorist threat, the first thing they want to know is the relative combat experience and weapons that a group has in its possession. For the intelligence analyst, the general skills level is the key to the structure, including funding lines, potential weapons procurement, and intelligence collection. Law enforcement officers want to know what terrorists will do when stopped for a speeding ticket. SWAT teams want to know if they have the skills level and fire support to conduct an extremely high-risk warrant arrest.

The higher the skills class, the less likely an occurrence of a dangerous individual encounter before they attack. Higher-skills terrorists want to complete their mission and use intelligence tradecraft to blend and slip in and out of foreign societies. Amateurs are usually hotheads who may "hit the steel" at the first sign of law enforcement.

You can see why we need to change the ways we classify terrorist operatives. The following charts are general in scope but will allow you to quickly group threats by relative risk to you and your operations.

Class I Terrorist: The Government-Trained Professional (Including Foreign Intelligence Threats)

U.S. DEPARTMENT OF DEFENSE

Intelligence profile: Government-trained professional terrorists are generally very well trained because of the enormous resources many nations can put into professionalizing a few agents to carry out terrorist acts. Selected from key party personnel, loyal military members, secret police, and intelligence communities, they are trained to carry out missions with maximum secrecy. Class I terrorists may operate with official cover—as diplomats, support staff, or official representatives in embassies or consulate offices. They may also use nonofficial roles (nonofficial cover), including posing as businesspeople, students, merchants, immigrants, or opposition group volunteers. Terrorists trained by the foreign intelligence agencies of Chile, Cuba, Libya, Iraq, Iran, and North Korea have conducted assassinations, mass murders, and abductions, and have supplied other less skillful terrorist groups with weapons, training, and equipment.

Typical Profile of a Class I Terrorist

Age: 22-50.

Sex: Male or female.

Education: University; professional intelligence agency educated.

Upbringing: Middle to upper class; party or political loyalist.

Criminal history: No history prior to recruitment.

Military history: Military special operations soldiers, political party civilians, national intelligence community members.

Most common operations: Assassination, sophisticated explosive bombings, abduction.

CENTRAL INTELLIGENCE AGENCY, REPUBLIC OF KOREA

North Korean Intelligence Officer Kim Chun-Hyee killed 115 people when she placed a bomb on a Korean Air airliner.

Above, North Korean agents tried to use this mini-sub in 1998 to infiltrate South Korea. Upper left and left, Libyan intelligence agents Abdul Basset al-Meghrani and Lamen Khalifa Fhimah were convicted of blowing up Pan Am Flight 103 over Scotland.

Some Organizations That Currently Use Class I Terrorists

Sponsor Organization	Tactical Organization	Area of Operations
North Korean intelligence	Cabinet General Intelligence Bureau	International
Libyan Intelligence Service	External Security Office	Middle East, Africa, Europe
Islamic Revolutionary Guard	Pasdaran-e Inqilab	International

Class II Terrorist: The Religious Extremist Professional

Intelligence profile: Class II terrorists are religious extremists who swear dedication to an extremist cause in their religion and have been channeled into the active cadre of a professional terrorist group. They are civilians who live their lives as professional terrorists. They have no other duty in life but terror. These operatives receive advanced combat skills training, more pay, benefits for their families, and advanced ideological training.

Typical Class II Terrorist Profile

Age: 18-45.

Sex: Male or female (females may act occasionally as suicide bombers but mainly work in logistics cells).

Education: Diverse, but generally university educated.

Upbringing: All classes; generally a devout religious follower.

Criminal history: Often, no criminal background.

Military history: Some have military training and are often trained at local or overseas professional terrorism schools.

Most common operations and experience: Sophisticated and advanced improvised explosive bombings; suicide/martyrdom attacks; explosives and firearms assassination; advanced armed raids/light infantry weapons attacks; kidnappings; skyjackings; maritime attacks; infrastructure attacks; rudimentary weapons of mass destruction; cyberattacks.

Al-Qaeda terrorists may have planned to release hydrogen cyanide under the American Embassy in Rome using this underground tunnel.

Special Characteristics of the Class II Terrorist

Professionally trained: Many are graduates from professional terrorism schools and are often allowed to design and implement low-level operations. Groups associated with al-Qaeda were trained in Afghanistan, Sudan, Lebanon, Iran, Algeria, Yemen, and even the United States. Secret locations may still exist for advanced courses.

Experienced: Senior operatives have gained operational experience through years of avoiding numerous international police and covert intelligence agencies. For example, groups within Israel have managed to avoid an outstanding counterterrorist force that has arrested or killed dozens of terrorist operatives and detained or deported hundreds of supporters. They still manage to carry out waves of suicide bombings in the heart of Israel. Before being allowed to move up the chain, most operatives must participate in supporting other terrorist operations as junior cell members. Professional-level operators are often tested on battlefields around the world.

Martyrdom/suicide candidates: The most devoted ideological candidates are selected by the terrorist leadership for suicide attack missions in groups such as al-Qaeda, Hamas, and Hezbollah. These "martyrdom" operatives and their families are given great stature and respect as the best of the organization and the religion.

Secretive: These are highly secretive and familylike operatives, emphasizing internal security by personally knowing whom they are dealing with and why.

Learn from mistakes: These operatives learn counterterrorist survival lessons from the experiences of teams that have failed or been arrested. When compatriots are arrested, the organization quickly communicates the threat and adapts.

Organizations That Currently Use Class II Terrorists

Sponsor Organization	Tactical Organization	Area of Operations
Usama bin Laden Org. (UBL)	Al-Qaeda	International
Hezbollah	Islamic Jihad Organization	Middle East, North and South America
Hezbollah	Hamas	Middle East (Israel/Palestine)
Hezbollah	Palestinian Islamic Jihad Organization	Middle East (Israel/Palestine)
FATAH	al-Aqsa Martyrs Brigade	Middle East (Israel/Palestine)
UBL	Armed Islamic Group	International
UBL	Egyptian Islamic Jihad	International
None	Special Purpose Islamic Regiment	Russia, Central Asia
Iran	Islamic Change Organization	Middle East

"Extra-special" operations: For missions within the United States or near extremely sensitive locations, terrorist organizations generally use clean operatives who have been specially selected. Often they will have real or cover families, use legal documentation, and may live as "sleepers" for extended periods.

The al-Qaeda Class II Terrorist Operative

The September 11 attack on America has created in our minds an image of terrorists synonymous with al-Qaeda. However, it must be understood that al-Qaeda (AQ) is not one group but a collective of organizations that cooperate and receive funds and orders from Usama bin Laden.

Al-Qaeda is the hub of a network of many groups and individuals who are of a like mind. It is an inspirational global organization that motivates individuals to join the proclaimed jihad and become comrades in arms.

Above, Hamas suicide bomber Izz al-Din al Masri. Below, known al-Qaeda organization members, Ahmed Hannan, Karim Koubriti, and Farouk Ali-Halmoud.

Operatives come from almost every country in the world with a Muslim population. It is believed that members hail from more than fifty countries and operate in over ninety. Captured members have been natives or residents of countries including Algeria, Argentina, Bolivia, Bosnia-Herzegovina, Burma, Egypt, England, France, Germany, Indonesia, Italy, Kuwait, Libya, Malaysia, Morocco, Pakistan, Paraguay, the Philippines, Russia, Saudi Arabia, Somalia, Sudan, Tajikistan, United Arab Emirates, the United States, and Uzbekistan—to name a few. Although al-Qaeda was originally comprised of mostly Arabs, its members come from almost every race.

Al-Qaeda may have approximately two hundred to three hundred active leadership and terrorist operatives worldwide. It should always be presumed that there are at least a few dozen AQ operatives and supporters in the United States at any given time. The numbers of active supporters worldwide are conservatively estimated in the thousands.

Their attacks include the 1993 World Trade Center bombing in New York City; the 1998 bombings of American embassies in Nairobi, Kenya,

FEDERAL BUREAU OF INVESTIGATION

Saif al Adil

FEDERAL BUREAU OF INVESTIGATION

Umar Mohammed Ali Rezaq

FEDERAL BUREAU OF INVESTIGATION

Fazul Abdullah Mohammen

FEDERAL BUREAU OF INVESTIGATION

Mustafa Mohammed Fadhil

FEDERAL BUREAU OF INVESTIGATION

Abdulmajid Dahoumane

FEDERAL BUREAU OF INVESTIGATION

Anas al Liby

and Dar es Salaam, Tanzania; the 2000 bombing of the USS *Cole* in Aden, Yemen; and the September 11 attacks on the World Trade Center and the Pentagon.

After the attack by U.S. forces on its base in Afghanistan, AQ immediately began to reconstitute into a broader, less centralized follow-on organization. Its operatives and inspired activists will continue their jihad, possibly in greater numbers than before. They are a formidable enemy but not unbeatable; compared with other terrorist groups such as the Irish Republican Army (IRA) and Hezbollah, AQ thinks big. Spectacular simultaneous attacks are its modus operandi. However, al-Qaeda has always relied on simple tactics in executing its attacks.

For the investigative team, it may be a little reassuring to know that al-Qaeda has always left a massive trail of tips and hints despite its emphasis on operations security. Many of the TAPIs prior to the 9/11 attack were clear and unambiguous to a trained intelligence analyst. It is up to intelligence and law enforcement to find, analyze, and act aggressively on intelligence discovered through investigation.

Class III Terrorist: The Radical Revolutionary or Quasi-Religious Extremist

Intelligence profile:

- **Radical revolutionaries** fit the traditional model of the European and Latin radical revolutionary terrorist of the 1960s and 1970s and popularized by Hollywood. This class of terrorists is generally harder to find. These operatives are usually trained inside the group, with some advanced professional training in foreign countries—although such training is becoming increasingly harder to obtain. Such operatives have gained operational experience through years of avoiding police and planning operations. They generally

Propaganda for radical revolutionary terrorist groups 17 November (left) and the Tamil Tigers.

HELLENIC NATIONAL POLICE, GREECE

Organizations That Currently Use Class III Terrorists

Sponsor Organization	Tactical Organization	Area of Operations
Sinn Fein	Provisional Irish Republican Army (PIRA)	UK/N. Ireland
None	Real IRA (RIRA)	UK/N. Ireland
None	Euzkadi Ta Askatasuna (ETA)	Spain/Europe
None	Red Army Faction (RAF)*	Germany
None	Red Brigade (BR)*	Italy
Libya, Iraq	Abu Nidal Organization (ANO)**	Middle East
PLO	Popular Front for the Liberation of Palestine (PFLP)	Middle East
PLO	Tanzim	Middle East
None	Japanese Red Army (JRA)**	Asia, Middle East
None	Aum Shinrikyo (AUM)*	Asia, Russia
LTTE	Black Tigers	Sri Lanka
PKK	Various	Middle East, Europe
None	November-17*	Greece
Cuba	Andres Castro United Front (FUAC)*	Nicaragua

*Believed to be defunct, but recently seen active (circa 2003).

**Believed to be defunct.

Red Army Faction terrorist Andrea Klump (above) was arrested in Austria in 1999. Her partner, Horst-Ludwig Meyer (below), was killed during an arrest by an Austrian SWAT team.

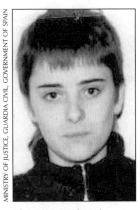

Class III terrorist Leirre Echevarria Simarro of the Basque Separatist and Homeland Movement (ETA).

learn survival lessons when compatriots are arrested, and operational and personal security is a critical concern. Many active groups are radical nationalists.

- **Quasi-religious extremists:** Unlike the religious extremist professional (Class II) model, these terrorists have far less skill and capability. They may live a secular life but secretly fight for a religious-based political cause. Irish Republican Army members, for example, are Catholics seeking political reunion with the Catholic south of Ireland against the Protestant loyalists.

Typical Class III Terrorist Profile

Age: 20-50.

Sex: Male or female.

Education: From no education to university educated.

Upbringing: Average to upper-middle-class family background.

Criminal history: None or minor criminal involvement prior to recruitment.

Military history: Some possible former military.

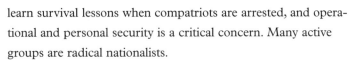

Japanese Red Army terrorist wanted poster.

Most common operations and experience: Improvised bombs; arson; pistol/sniper assassination; small raids and robberies; kidnappings; tactical operations; rudimentary chemical attacks.

Class IV Terrorist: Guerrilla/ Mercenary Soldier

Intelligence profile: Class IV terrorists are generally the most predictable of terrorists, because they fall back on basic military training and equipment used in military or paramilitary experience. Basic infantry weapons such as the AK-47 and M-16 are preferred weapons in their armed forces and provide the most reliable firepower for their terrorist operations.

- **Guerrilla terrorists** are proficient at general military operations for their country of origin. They occasionally have some urban terrorism experience, but this is limited to bombings, simple assassinations, ambushes, and light infantry weapons assaults. Some countries use very young children as soldiers to conduct surveillance or act as gunmen.

- **Mercenaries:** Since the 1960s and even more recently in Yugoslavia and Africa, Western mercenaries have conducted terrorist acts. French mercenary Colonel Robert Denard conducted several coups d'etat in the Reunion Islands after 1975, for instance, as well as numerous acts of terrorism including summary execution of the former leaders, until the French military intervened and arrested him. South African, British, and American mercenaries have been arrested worldwide while attempting to carry out military operations. In 1981, the well-known mercenary "Mad Mike" Hoare tried to topple the government of the Seychelles. Foreign mercenary groups, like guerrilla soldiers, usually have excellent combat proficiency in general military operations.

Mercenary Bob Denard

Organizations That Currently Use Class IV Terrorists

Sponsor Organization	Tactical Organization	Area of Operations
Hutu Guerrillas	Interahamwe	Africa (DR Congo, Rwanda, Uganda, Burundi)
RUF	Various	Africa (Sierra Leone)
FARC	Various	South America (Colombia, Ecuador, Panama)
Cuba	National Liberation Army (ELN)	South America (Colombia)
MILF	Abu Sayyaf Group	Asia (Philippines)
Various	Unita	Africa (Angola)
None	Movement for Social Justice	Africa (Chad)

Typical Class IV Terrorist Profile

Age: 10-50.

Sex: Male or female.

Education: Little to none.

Upbringing: Urban or rural poverty, raised in combat culture; some middle class; upper-class leadership.

Criminal history: Minor criminal or none.

Military history: Guerrilla army training, some urban terrorist internal training.

Most common operations: Improvised explosives and military explosives bombings; weapons and explosives ambushes; weapons and explosives assassinations; armed raids; kidnappings; occasional suicide bombings; hostage barricade.

Class V Terrorist: Amateur (Civilian, Untrained Criminal, or Militia-Vigilante)

Intelligence profile: These groups may have large numbers of people, but they have rudimentary terrorist experience. Many paramilitaries may subcontract themselves to terrorist groups with higher capability and carry out easy tasks such as abductions and assassinations for money. Often these financial arrangements may use ethnic or territorial rhetoric as a "political" mask for money-making goals.

American militia groups are a low-level variant on paramilitaries. Rarely do they carry out large-scale attacks, such as the bombing of the Murrah Federal Building in Oklahoma City; for the most part, their acts have been small in scale and limited by law enforcement. This does not mean they could not become a significant threat. Often they will carry out sympathetic, follow-up harassment attacks after major external attacks on America. In the counterterrorism community, there is a saying: "The second attack is almost always an American."

Timothy McVeigh (above) and Eric Robert Rudolph (below).

Typical Class V Terrorist Profile

Age: 10-65.

Sex: Male or female.

Education: Little to none.

Upbringing: Urban or rural poverty, raised in criminal and/or combat culture; some middle-class or upper-class leadership.

Criminal history: Minor criminal or none.

Military history: Guerrilla army training, some urban terrorist internal training.

Most common operations: Simple, improvised explosives bombings; kidnappings; suicide bombings; improvised bombs; arson; pistol or sniper assassinations; physical intimidation and maiming; drive-by shootings; small raids and cash robberies; easy kidnappings.

The instigator of the 2001 anthrax attack on the U.S. Senate may have been a Class V terrorist with access to Class I terrorist weapons. This incident remains under investigation.

Organizations That Currently Use Class V Terrorists

Sponsor Organization	Tactical Organization	Area of Operations
None	AUC	South America (Colombia)
None	Covenant, Sword, Arm of the Lord (CSA)	North America (USA)
None	Earth Liberation Front (ELF)	North America, Europe
None	Army of God	North America (USA)
None	Aryan Nation	North America (USA)
CPM—Nepal	People's War	Indian subcontinent (Nepal)
None	Free Aceh Movement	Asia (Indonesia)
None	Corsican Army (AC)	Europe (France)

3

INTELLIGENCE PROFILING A SUSPECTED TERRORIST

Rule Number One: Consider Everyone a Potential Terrorist

- Terrorist recognition and identification can be effectively performed only through intelligence profiling of suspected terrorists.
- Racial profiling alone blinds the observer to other terrorist groups on the attack.
- Adopt intelligence profiling: Learn to recognize the behaviors necessary to plan, prepare, and carry out a terrorist act.

Terrorist groups should be tracked by collecting the best intelligence possible. This basic information collection must then be matched against the profile of the members known to be in that group. The difficulty of profiling terrorists is that many characteristics and beliefs about terrorist operators are based on investigators' personal stereotypes, not intelligence. Virtually all of those stereotypes are based on unevaluated information, movies and television, or the personal bias of the observer.

Basic Questions to Be Considered When Intelligence Profiling

Let us assume you have a terrorist suspect under surveillance or in custody. Ask yourself or intelligence staff the following questions.

1. Does the suspected operative come from a known terrorist group?

It's good to determine whether the suspect acted alone or as part of a group. If not alone, which group is suspected or believed to be responsible for the incident? Was the group working in cooperation with other terrorist groups? If so, the profile may branch out to include those supporting groups' operatives.

2. What is the suspect's nationality?

Where is the suspect from? Is he local, foreign resident, or immigrant? If a group, from which nation does the suspected group recruit its members? If the answer is more than one country, the intelligence profile may change from operative to operative. One stereotype is that U.S. domestic terrorists are not really terrorists but a criminal nuisance. As the 1993 Oklahoma City bombing and the July 4, 2002, Los Angeles Airport shooting at the El

Al ticket counter showed, however, being a U.S. citizen or long-term U.S. resident does not rule a person out as a potential terrorist.

3. What are the suspect's race and culture?

Race alone is a poor individual identifier of a terrorist operative. Groups may adapt to security that targets suspect races by using operatives who are, or seem to be, of a different race. If security forces specifically seek and screen non-Caucasian men, for example, then a good group could shift to using Caucasian females to support the operation. Here are some questions you should ask yourself when evaluating a terrorist operative's race:

- Have operatives from a specific race been positively identified as belonging to a suspected group? If so, from which race?
- Can people from this specific race be confused with another race?
- Are the group's known operatives of a distinct ethnic minority or majority of a particular nation?
- Have people of different races been used by this group for attack, penetration, logistical support, or finances?
- Will focusing on one race blind me to other operatives from other cooperating groups?

4. What is the suspect's age?

Like race, age alone is a poor identifier of a person on a terrorist mission. Terrorists can be of almost any age. Young children are usually not operatives but can be tasked as couriers, lookouts, and future recruits. Many groups have youth organizations that use children as operatives.

5. What is the suspect's sex?

Terrorism is an equal-opportunity employer. It is clear that both men and women are capable of performing virtually all of the operations on a terrorist menu. Unless there is specific intelligence on the sex of the operative, intelligence profiling should be gender neutral. If a group almost always uses male operatives, the observer should expect the eventual use of females to foil security and to facilitate penetration.

6. What is the clothing worn by the suspect?

Clothing can identify certain types of operations due to a need to conceal weapons, explosives, and equipment. Bulky jackets worn in summer or long knee-length coats on a clear day can conceal bombs and machine guns. The clothes that a terrorist operative wears are not a good indicator of intent, however. Stereotypical images of terrorists wearing black masks, Arab-style kaffiyehs, or black uniforms like SWAT teams are rarely borne out in reality. Competent terrorist operatives will dress to suit the environment they wish to operate in.

- **Did the suspect try to conceal a weapon?** The following weapons can be concealed by certain clothing using the following matrix:

Coat Length	Assault Rifle	Submachine Gun	Shotgun	Pistol	Bomb	Grenade
Ankle	Yes	Yes	Yes	Yes	Yes	Yes
Knee	Yes (folding stock)	Yes	Yes (FS)	Yes	Yes	Yes
Midthigh	No	Yes	Yes (sawed)	Yes	Yes	Yes
Hip	No	Yes (mini)	Yes (sawed)	Yes	Yes	Yes
Baggy shirt	No	Yes (mini)	Yes (sawed)	Yes	Yes	Yes
Tight shirt	No	No	No	Yes	No	Yes

7. What is the suspect's physical condition?

The physical condition of the operative may reflect the mission. The September 11 hijackers needed physical force to overpower passengers and crews. Al-Qaeda emphasized weight and martial-arts training for the 9/11 skyjackers. The more professional terrorist will stay in good physical condition. Criminal enterprises operating in a terrorist capacity also tend to use former military types, among whom muscle and endurance are valued. Amateurs, paramilitaries, and militias reflect the culture they come from physically as well as operationally. A lean Colombian right-wing paramilitary member may differ greatly in physique from an overweight American militiaman.

8. What is the suspect's native language?

The language that operatives speak can be an initial indicator of their nation of origin when other identification is not possible. Some operatives are multilingual, but one language may dominate their conversation. On the other hand, an accent is a general indicator of foreign nationality—but care must be taken to precisely identify the language. For example, a person who speaks English well but with a noticeable French accent may be from Louisiana, Michigan, Indiana, Canada, France, the Caribbean, North Africa, the Pacific islands, or Central Africa. Note that first-generation legal immigrants may speak with a foreign accent as well as a foreign language, whereas second-generation immigrants may have absolutely no identifiable foreign accent.

9. Does the suspect possess incriminating documents?

- **Passport identification:** False or multiple passports are a good reason to begin suspecting a person as a terrorist operative. Still, some nations have flexible passport laws or allowances for legal, multiple passports. Remember, an operative may be traveling on entirely legal documents from friendly nations.

- **Pocket litter:** Small items such as scrap paper, Post-it notes, bank statements, and other materials are good evidence sources.

- **Concealment:** Where the documents are concealed is also a good indicator of a terrorist operative (or for that matter a drug smuggler, diamond trader, or other nonterrorist). Are the documents sewn into clothing? Hidden in shoes, baggage, or other concealed conveyance?

- **Clearly suspicious books/documents/sensitive intelligence:** The person suspected may be carrying materials that directly support terrorist violence. Books such as group tactical manuals, philosophy, and bomb-building cookbooks are just one indicator. However, direct intelligence—such as clearly written ransom notes or bombing claim letters and plans—should arouse a much greater level of suspicion. A terrorist involved in the 1993 World Trade Center plot was arrested at the airport carrying bomb-making manuals.

- **Clean operative:** On the other hand, is the operative completely clean? An absolute lack of anything except cash and one piece of suspect identification may be indicative of an operative en route to a mission or joining a cell.

10. Does the suspect possess weapons?

Is the suspect carrying a legal or illegal firearm? If the suspect is carrying a firearm, is it a common weapon in the United States, or is it exotic here but fairly common globally, such as the Russian Tokarov or Makarov pistol? Such weapons could indicate overseas training;

people like to use weapons they are familiar with. Other indicators may include:

- **Flashy weapons:** Is the suspect carrying a stainless-steel or gold-plated weapon as opposed to a normal blued (dark) weapon? Such conspicuous weapons are preferred by those with greater concern for looks than for mission-specific functionality, such as criminals or Class IV or Class V terrorists. A flashy weapon may indicate a terrorist with a commercial supply source. Invariably, people who want flashy weapons also want full-sized, large-caliber weapons (the larger the caliber, the better).

- **Technology-heavy weapons:** Does the operative use very sophisticated technology in weaponry, to gain precision fire? These enhancements indicate a trained profession-al—or an amateur who likes the look of the enhancements. Only the precision of the fire will tell you for certain. Westerners are more likely to use such enhancements than are foreign terrorists. Technological enhance-ments might include high-intensity tactical weapons lights, laser aim-ing modules (with or without night observation devices), reflex shooting sights with luminous aiming reticles (such as Trijicon ACOG, Reflex, or Leopold tactical sights), or high-powered sniper optics on assault rifles.

> **When is racial profiling alone appropriate? When you have specific intelligence on a specific person! Always "intelligence profile" a suspected terrorist.**

11. Did the suspect use concealment tradecraft?

Tradecraft is any method or technique developed for intelligence officers or terrorist operatives to carry out their mission. *Concealment tradecraft* refers to techniques of concealing and infiltrating any weapons, explo-sives, or other components that might tip off authorities to the mission. An example of group tradecraft might be concealing detonation cord in a guitar string package, or attempting to smuggle plastic explosives in one member's shoes.

12. Does the suspect carry large quantities of money?

Many drug mules, smugglers, unscrupulous businessmen, and other people attempt to move money illegally across borders. Terrorists are no exception. Large quantities of cash, possibly found in multiple con-cealed locations, may indicate a terrorist operative when combined with other evidence. In July 2002, for example, a man suspected of being an al-Qaeda terrorist was arrested entering the United States with twelve million dollars in false cashier's checks.

13. Does the suspect use political or religious rhetorical statements?

Does the suspect immediately spout off rhetoric or verbal threats? When combined with other TAPI or evidence, this could be a red flag.

14. Have I considered the "X Factor"?

This is a personal bias check. Ask yourself, "Could I be absolutely wrong about this person?" Weigh your answer against the accumulated evidence.

TERRORIST TRAINING

errorists can be identified by the type of training they have received. Terrorists may be trained as individuals or as a group. Below are some methods of training that terrorists seek out and acquire:

- **Self-education:** Lone members learn skills from individual reading, videos, or other materials.
- **Commercial school training:** Members may attend commercial shooting, knife-fighting, surveillance, or other courses providing skills that could contribute to an overall mission.
- **Safe-house training:** Members train together typically in cells of three or five members, at a covert location within the area of operations.
- **Professional terrorist school training:** Members train at a dedicated terrorist training center or course in a remote part of their country or overseas in a sympathetic foreign country.

Terrorist Training Schools and Camps

In the 1960s and 1970s, many schools for terrorists were run directly by certain state governments. The Soviet Union, for instance, conducted courses through the KGB's Executive Action Department (Directorate S, Department V). They were responsible for training designated terrorist groups in murder and lethal attacks (*mokrie dela* or "wet affairs") that involved terrorist assault, personnel assassination, abduction, and other terrorist skills. This training was expanded to include sabotage against critical infrastructure such as nuclear power plants, rails, and energy production.

Though many of these formally trained terrorists have retired from active operations, many others are now members of the senior leadership of active terrorist groups. Their experiences, lessons learned, tradecraft, and battle concepts are still valid. It should be assumed that such wisdom has been passed down to new operatives through courses and manuals.

Other nations and even terrorist groups have formed professional terrorism schools. Libya, Palestine, Syria, Iraq, Iran, Pakistan, Lebanon, and India have hosted official and unofficial terrorist training centers. Legal training in firearms or attack skills that can be applied to terrorist acts are offered in many countries, including the United States.

Countries with Known Terrorism Schools (2003)

- Cuba.
- North Korea.
- Iran.
- Pakistan.
- Syria.
- Lebanon.
- Palestine.
- Sudan.

Terrorist Combat Training

Terrorists must learn how to use weapons and explosives as a basic part of their paramilitary duties. Training comes in three levels: basic, intermediate and advanced.

Basic Training

- Weapons parts familiarization.
- Basic rifle firing.
- Throwing hand grenades.
- Laying and fusing landmines.
- Firing rocket-propelled grenades.
- Suppressing fire and firing on the move.
- Cover and concealment.
- Basic camouflage.

Intermediate Training

- Mortars and rockets.
- Advanced rifle and grenade use.
- Rifle-mounted grenade launchers.
- Battle tactics.
- Leadership.
- Terrorist tradecraft in foreign countries.
- Basic improvised explosive devices and booby traps.

Advanced Training

- Urban battle tactics.
- Advanced battle tactics.
  - Close-quarters combat (CQC).
  - Sniper and long-rifle skills.
  - VIP close protection.
- Advanced improvised explosive devices.
- Advanced bomb building.
- Commercial books or "how-to" military manuals.
  - Bomb-making manuals: *Poor Man's James Bond, Anarchist Cookbook.*
  - Weapons components and repair manuals.
  - Improvised weapons and silencer construction.
  - Chemical explosives formulas.

TERRORIST TRAINING CASE STUDY

Wisconsin Terrorist Training Camp

In 1989 members of the Palestinian terrorist group Hamas are alleged to have run a weekend terrorist training facility outside of Wisconsin. Federal officers learned of the camp by a confession given to Israeli authorities from a Palestinian man, Sharif Alwan, who was arrested in Israel in 1995. Israel claims Sharif was recruited by Hamas before arriving in the U.S. and received cell-level training near Milwaukee. Alwan was under investigation for money laundering and fundraising for a terrorist organization when U.S. authorities learned of his training, and allegedly detailed how he was trained in using M-16 and AK-47 assault rifles, explosive devices, and techniques on how to booby-trap cars. He was also alleged to have gone to Syria and Lebanon for additional terrorist skills training, including the use of hand grenades, rocket propelled grenade launchers, and covert communications. Mr. Alwan asserts that he was tortured into his confession about terrorist training by the Israeli police.

Pre-Incident Indicators of Terrorist Training or Practice

- **Partially built live weapons and devices.**
- **Dummy weapons made of rubber or wood.**
- **Terrorist textbooks and manuals.**
  - *Mini-Manual for the Urban Guerrilla* (general).
  - *IRA Volunteers Manual* (IRA).
  - *Encyclopedia of the Jihad* (al-Qaeda).
  - *FATAH Manual of Operations* (PFLP).

- **Open-source professional tactical manuals:**
  - U.S. Army Ranger handbook.
  - U.S. Army common tasks handbook.
  - U.S. Navy SEAL Tactical Training manual.
  - U.S. Special Forces weapons CD-ROM.
  - U.S. Army FM-21-76 Survival Manual.

- **Videos on military subjects**—combined with other intelligence—could indicate terrorist usage:
  - Sniping and marksmanship.
  - Radioactivity effects.
  - Famous terrorist attacks.
  - Bomb effects.

- **Audiocassettes/CD-ROMs/Web sites on:**
  - Extremist philosophy.
  - Antigovernment propaganda.

Survival and Tradecraft Training

Foreign-born terrorists who are not U.S. residents need more training to prevent attracting undue attention to themselves while preparing for missions. The best way to stay under the radar is to use U.S. citizens as operatives. Otherwise, foreign operatives need to attain legal documents, assume new identities, or further the identities they were assigned. These operatives need to learn tradecraft.

Examples of Operative Survival and Tradecraft

Foreign culture survival: This training may involve operatives learning the local language, getting jobs that legitimize their cover story, learning to use local telephone systems, studying local and national laws in an effort to exploit them, acquiring the same documents that other legal or illegal immigrants have, and using of immigrant support agencies and welfare systems to appear normal.

Identity assumption/cover: Operatives are usually given a cover story and necessary supporting documents to keep the story alive until legal documents are acquired by living in a foreign country. This "cover story" is usually studied until the operative knows it by heart. However, terrorists may inadvertently use real names in correspondence and telephone calls, which they usually cover up by using a "code name" in place of their cover name. *Abu Jihad* and *Abu Nidal* are famous cover names; others such as *The Engineer, the Amir,* and *Commandante Marcos* are also good examples. A nickname like *Carlos the Jackal* is not a good example because it uses the actual name of the terrorist (Carlos Illyich Ramirez Sanchez).

Contact procedures are a verbal or nonverbal signal tradecraft developed by the group or used by a foreign intelligence agency, designed to inform other terrorist group members or leadership of danger or a special situation.

- **A contact signal** may be any kind of nonverbal signal that requests communication or informs the operative that a message is pending. This could be as simple as a half-open window or chalk marks on walls. The only way to detect such a code is through careful intelligence analysis when seemingly routine actions of a suspect (drawing down a certain window shade) repeatedly corresponds to observed events (the suspect meets at a café with a second operative).

- **An emergency contact signal** may be a hasty, onetime signal sending the message that an emergency exists and the operative must take action, such as aborting a rendezvous, canceling an attack, or departing the country.

Interrogation resistance: Operatives are trained to resist physical and environmental punishment, in case of capture. Many terrorist groups train their members by "capturing" them and conducting harsh, simulated interrogation to discover how much they can endure before they will break. Government agencies and the armed forces also emphasize training for the event of being captured by terrorists. Resistance training may include:

- **Physical punishment:** The operative is conditioned to take a beating or given tips on how to endure crude tortures, such as electric shock or mutilations.
- **Psychological preparation:** The operative is trained to focus on noncritical information and to use this as a tool to defeat an interrogator. Sayings from the Bible or Koran, party propaganda, or simple words and phrases may give the operative the fortitude to resist psychological pressures.
- **Escape and evasion (E&E):** Depending on their area of origin, terrorists may have extensive field training and may be skilled in picking locks, breaking bonds, and escaping captivity. Specialized courses or classes and materials in lock picking or escaping handcuffs indicate E&E skills training.

Use of False Documents

Purchase: Hezbollah once purchased one hundred legitimate French national identity cards and fifty valid passports for cash from a corrupt French embassy official in Africa.

Identity theft: Operatives may use the passports or histories of innocent people through identity theft.

Fabrication of documents: Virtually every terrorist organization uses criminally acquired or altered false documents to mask the identity of its members. Many of these documents are produced by professional forgers.

Examples of Terrorist Use of Forged or False Documentation

- **Hezbollah in Latin America:** In 1998, a Lebanese citizen was arrested in Cuidad del Este, Paraguay, forging passports and U.S. residence and work visas (green cards) for Hezbollah operatives entering the United States.

- **Al-Qaeda in Italy:** False Italian national identity cards were found on logistics cell members believed to have been preparing for a cyanide attack on the U.S. embassy in Rome in 2002.

- **Cuban intelligence in the U.S.:** Cuban intelligence supplied an Argentine passport for a Puerto Rican Macheteros terrorist who carried out a $7.1 million armored car heist in Connecticut.

- **Irish terrorists in Colombia:** IRA members captured in Colombia in 2001 used false British passports and identity cards to travel in Latin America to train FARC terrorists (see the photo).

COLOMBIAN NATIONAL POLICE

Irish Republican Army terrorists were arrested in Colombia with these false passports. They were believed to be instructing members of the Revolutionary Armed Forces of Colombia (FARC) in terrorist training camps.

Suicide/Martyrdom Preparation

For definitions and discussion of the suicide/martyrdom attack, see page 264.

Operatives who choose or are ordered to commit suicide or religious martyrdom to carry out their mission would have made final preparations or conducted last rites prior to the attack. If discovered beforehand, following the TAPIs may reveal the intent and, possibly, the location of the impending attack:

Revealing Pre-Incident Indicators: the following TAPIs may indicate a suspect's intent to commit or participate in a suicide/martyrdom attack. This list is in no way complete: If necessary, you should seek advanced training in the recognition of suicide bomber indicators and intelligence.

Safe House Indicators

- Discovery of purpose built suicide bomb kits: waist belts, vests and jackets with explosive devices inserted.
- Finding "mission success" videos or press releases to be distributed after the attack.
- Religious altars in safe houses praising past martyrs. These are often found in propaganda, Web sites, and press releases.
- Finding written or videotaped confessions or suicide notes.
- Discovering "last photos," "martyrdom" banners and posters, or videos of operatives who have yet to carry out attacks.
- Finding highlighted or underlined text in holy books or political manifestos indicating martyrdom.
- Elaborate attack or infiltration plans with no escape route.

Suicide/Martyrdom Bomber Pre-Incident Behavioral Indicators

- Intelligence on suspects who have clearly stated their intent to commit suicide/martyrdom acts.
- Suspect gives away all personal possessions.
- Suspect shows disregard for clear evidence left behind in safe house, during transportation, or at the target.

Palestinian martyrdom bomber Ahmed al-Khatib of Hamas.

Suicide/Martyrdom Bomber Indicators: While Enroute to Mission

The following indicators are published by the Israeli National Police in a pamphlet for citizens called "Only Together Will We Stop Terror."

- **Suspect wears unseasonable clothing:** To conceal the explosive device the bomber may wear clothing that is inappropriate for the weather. Heavy leather jackets in summer may be a crude attempt to conceal a bomb assembly. A coat itself may be the explosive device.
- **Suspect wears bulky clothes:** Clothing that is bulky and visibly over bulges around the chest or waist may be an indicator of a large bomb being worn under a coat or shirt.
- **Obvious or awkward attempts to "blend in" to a crowd:** Often bombers may loiter to find the best target available, such as large

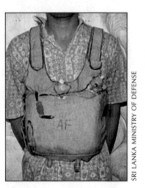

Sri Lankan suicide bomber kit.

crowds, even if they have a pre-set detonation spot. This may require them to loiter. While loitering they may move awkwardly as most people know where they are going. In trying to "blend-in" terrorists may display an unusual or staggered pace of walking or loitering near the walls.

SRI LANKA MINISTRY OF DEFENSE

This suicide bomb vest is a purpose-built garment designed to wrap the bomber in the largest quantity of explosives. This vest is designed for the LTTE "Black Tiger" suicide bombers.

- **Suspect Wearing an Obvious Disguise:** Suicide bombers in Sri Lanka, Chechnya, and Israel often attempted to wear clothing or uniforms which would allow them to blend in. Know and look for incongruous uniform parts on people attempting to gain access to crowded places. Police, soldiers, and ambulance crews are popular ruses.

- **Suspect repeatedly and nervously handles parts of clothing:** The bomber has a specific area where the detonation switch is located. A nervous handling of the clothing near a specific spot where a pull or push switch is located may be an indicator of a bomber rehearsing his action or who is uncomfortable and reassuring himself by touching the concealed location.

- **Suspect is walking at a slow pace while focusing on sides:** Bomber may constantly glance left and right to check for security or law enforcement approaching. Moving slowly allows the bomber to watch the flow of people approaching him and observe for people moving rapidly in his direction.

- **Suspect attempts to stay away from security personnel:** Bomber may angle off or change direction when security personnel are seen. This action may be exaggerated.

- **Suspect is sweating profusely, hesitant and/or nervously muttering:** Uncharacteristic nervousness may be a key indicator when coupled with other indicators. Some extremely disturbed persons reveal the same indicators and this should be used in conjunction with other indicators of a bomber.

- **Perfumed, recently shaved:** In some cultures the bombers may believe that they are enroute to a higher spiritual plane. In this belief they perform detailed pre-mission hygiene including dressing nicely, shaving clean and perfuming themselves before blowing up.

Confronting the Suicide/Martyrdom Bomber

If a suspected bomber is identified you enter a critical and deadly period. The responses must be as discreet as possible in an effort to stop the bomber before detonation. The general law enforcement guidelines for a possible suicide bomber are as follows:

Make a Deliberate Discreet Response

- **Respond Silently and Do Not Alert the Terrorist:** Do not alert the terrorist bomber with sirens as he may detonate pre-maturely.
- **Deploy Observers:** Discreet observation is critical to confronting a bomber that has not yet been tipped off. Observers on the roofs above the suspect, along with snipers if possible should give good observation and an option to stop him.
- **Cover With Snipers:** A suspected suicide bomber may need to be neutralized immediately before reaching a detonating device. The best platform for that is a designated marksman or a trained sniper with a weapon that can assure a shot to the head and central nervous system disruption.
- **Do Not Close on the Terrorist:** STAY AWAY FROM THE SUSPECT! The whole purpose of a suicide bomber is to blow up with maximum number of potential victims. An explosives-rigged suspect who appears compliant may be attempting to lure people or law enforcement in closer so that they may become victims. The BATF recommends a minimum separation distance of 900 feet (300) meters from the bomber.
- **Do Not Attempt Traditional Negotiation:** Hostage negotiators' tactics and techniques may have to be modified if it appears a suicide bomber wishes to negotiate. Committed groups such as al-Qaeda, Hamas, the LTTE and others do not enter into negotiation but simply detonate at the target or when discovered. This should be foremost in the mind of any negotiator.
- **Do Not Shoot for Center of Mass:** Shooting the suspect in the chest or waist may pre-maturely detonate the explosives on a terrorist's body. Shots to the head may be the only sure way of ensuring the terrorist does not explode.

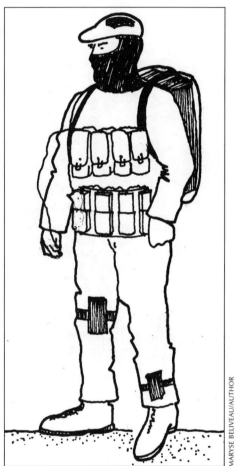

MARYSE BELIVEAU/AUTHOR

Suicide bomber carrying and concealment locations.

In Extremis Response

Suicide/Martyrdom bombers can be stopped at the last moment. The following immediate responses to suicide bombers have been successful in Israel, Sri Lanka, and India. If a serious suicide/martyrdom bombing threat emerges, law enforcement will have to understand *in extremis* techniques to stop the bomber as listed below.

- **Shoot the suspect:** In March 2002 Israeli security guard Eli Federman, 36, stopped a suicide bomber in a car bomb outside of a Tel Aviv disco. After suspecting him of being a bomber he drew his service weapon and shot the bomber. The bomber detonated his belt before dying but only injured four bystanders. Remember that shooting the bomber in the torso or waist may also detonate the device so shots should be oriented to the head.

  Note that U.S. law enforcement rules of engagement may preclude shooting on the basis of suspicion only. It is possible that Extremely Disturbed Persons (EDPs) may behave in such a way or make verbal threats to be a suicide bomber in an effort to induce "suicide by cop." Each agency and officer will have to draw on existing statutes and standards of behavior but you also have to consider the grave risk of a real bomber's results if mistaken.

- **Grab the suspect's hands:** Suspected bombers should not be given the option to blow up. Commanding a suspect to "show me your hands," even with your weapon drawn, may cause the bomber to detonate a hidden device. Knocking the suspect down with a flying tackle and gaining control of the hands may be the only way to prevent a detonation. Several incidents in Israel were thwarted when a security guard grabbed the wrists of the bomber before they could pull down the actuating triggers.

- **Cuff the suspect:** Most bomb belts require the terrorist to pull or push a detonator. Once cuffed, this threat decreases and explosive ordinance disposal teams can operate.

- **Evacuate yourself and the area immediately:** Some groups use remotely detonated back-up systems ("fail safe" devices) to ensure the device explodes even if the bomber is disabled or killed. Cell phones, radio-command devices, or other techniques could cause the device to explode. Immediately evacuate yourself and others from the area and allow an explosive ordinance disposal team to complete the safe handling and removal of the device.

WHY THE TERRORIST CHOOSES THIS PATH: TERRORISM 101

What Is Terrorism?

Exactly what is *terrorism*? For Americans, since September 11, the term has become especially loaded, and is sometimes used to describe acts that are, by widely accepted definition, *not* terrorism. Even worldwide, the term has come to have such heavy rhetorical value that politicians and other leaders have been known to label the actions of their opponents as "terrorist acts." Some actions do qualify as terrorism, and some don't. Often terrorism is seen as dissident bands of unknown individuals striking innocent targets. Other times it is defined as the psychological intimidation inherent in a threat or an act of violence. Clearly, the word is difficult to pin down—but a basic definition can encompass the components that all societies find agreement on.

Definitions of *Terrorism*

There are several variations on the definition of *terrorism;* the following quotes are provided to show those differences.

U.S. Federal Bureau of Investigation

"The unlawful use of force or violence against persons or property to intimidate or coerce a government, the civilian population, or any segment thereof, in furtherance of political or social objectives."

U.S. Department of State

"Premeditated, politically motivated violence perpetrated against noncombatant targets by sub-national groups or clandestine agents, usually intended to influence an audience."

U.S. Department of Defense (DoD)

"The calculated use of violence or threat of violence to inculcate fear, intended to coerce or to intimidate governments or societies in the pursuit of goals that are generally political, religious or ideological."

U.S. DoD Directive 2000.12H

"The calculated use of violence or threat of violence to attain goals—political, religious or ideological in nature—by instilling fear or using intimidation or coercion. Terrorism involves a criminal act, often symbolic in nature, intended to influence an audience beyond the immediate victims."

U.S. Code

"Premeditated, politically motivated violence perpetrated against non-combatant targets by sub-national groups or clandestine agents."

United Nations

"Terrorism is a unique form of crime. Terrorist acts often contain elements of warfare, politics and propaganda. For security reasons and due to lack of popular support, terrorist organizations are usually small, making detection and infiltration difficult. Although the goals of terrorists are sometimes shared by wider constituencies, their methods are generally abhorred."

British Government

"Terrorism is the use of serious violence against persons or property, or the threat to use such violence, to intimidate or coerce a government, the public, or any section of the public for political, religious or ideological ends. The term *serious violence* would need to be defined so that it included serious disruption, for instance resulting from attacks on computer installations or public utilities."

Russian Federation Law 130 FZ to Fight Terrorism

"Terrorism is violence or the threat of violence against individuals or organizations, and also the destruction (damaging) of or threat to destroy (damage) property and other material objects, such as threaten to cause loss of life, significant damage to property, or other socially dangerous consequences and are implemented with a view to violating public security, intimidating the population, or influencing the adoption of decisions advantageous to terrorists by organs of power, or satisfying their unlawful material and (or) other interests; attempts on the lives of statesmen or public figures perpetrated with a view to ending their state or other political activity or out of revenge for such activity; attacks on representatives of foreign states or staffers of international organizations enjoying international protection, and also on the official premises or vehicles of persons enjoying international protection if these actions are committed with a view to provoking war or complicating international relations."

The Terrorism Recognition Handbook*'s Definition*

The definition used in this book offers a more precise description of what constitutes terrorism.

Terrorism is the calculated use of criminal violence or threat of violence by a covert or overt individual, group, entity, special-interest organization, or government agency specifically designed to target people, commerce, and/or infrastructures.

Terrorism is not political activism or "freedom fighting." It is a conscious choice to deliberately select deadly tactics as a criminally symbolic act to spread fear, intimidation, and horror, to popularize or gain support for a cause. It includes intention to extort funds and/or influence an audience beyond the immediate victims. Terrorism is an illegitimate expression of dissent, demand for conflict resolution, or form of psychological warfare that is unjustified at any time.

Terrorism is the calculated use of covert criminal violence or threat of violence: The act must break laws or conspire to break laws that are common to most societies. Though terrorism usually involves violent acts such as murder, battery, and destruction of property, it could also mean nonviolent disruptive acts that are broad threats to safety and result in the mass spread of fear. Terrorist acts are calculated acts; they are not carried out randomly. Many terrorist attacks may seem arbitrary in their execution, but each event has been deliberately planned to create a specific effect.

Terrorism is deliberately selected as a tactic to effect change: The group must make a conscious decision to reject or abandon peaceful political change and further its agenda through the use of terrorist acts and tactics.

Terrorism is the targeting of innocent people, including military personnel: At the heart of an act of terrorism are terrorists who specifically focus their acts of violence on killing, injuring, and/or generating fear in innocent victims. The victim may be the immediate target, especially in assassination and physical intimidation attacks, but terrorists care far more about the psychological impact of the attack on society at large. The purpose of carrying out the act is not only to meet tactical objectives but also to terrorize a population. As explained in the next section, military personnel may never be targeted legitimately by terrorists. Many terrorist groups have tried to arbitrarily designate military personnel and bases as legitimate targets. Even in wartime, however, terrorism remains a criminal attack punishable in criminal courts after the conflict. Terrorists who attack in wartime are considered unlawful combatants under the Geneva Conventions of 1949.

Terrorism is the use of symbolic acts to attract media and reach a large audience: The publicity surrounding an event is critical for terrorists to gain influence and spread fear. The fear effect must extend beyond immediate victims and must symbolize the power of the group; therefore terrorist attacks tend to be spectacular—depending upon the tactics and goals of the organization—and spread fear. No matter how large or small the act, its symbolism is of far greater importance to the perpetrators than its immediate impact on the group's victims.

Terrorism is illegitimate combat, even in war: Terrorism is not a legitimate form of warfare. The rules of warfare were formalized in Convention (IV) Respecting the Laws and Customs of War on Land and Its Annex: Regulations Concerning the Laws and Customs of War on Land (The Hague, October 18, 1907). These rules, which called for armed forces to specifically avoid targeting civilians, were expanded on after World War II. Governments and other groups that target civilians clearly violate these rules.

Terrorism is never justified: The use of terrorism is immoral and unjustified. Terrorists who claim religious conviction for their actions may attempt to use spiritual direction from a higher authority, whether God or a human spiritual leader, as a valid reason for acts of violence. In almost every country, terrorism is a crime. No matter how desperate the situation, choosing to commit an act of terrorism over nonviolent resistance or political activism is not justified.

Are You Capable of Being a Terrorist?

Place yourself in this scenario and consider how you would respond. Consider for a moment that you are a thirty-five-year-old man living in a country that is under military occupation and being settled by people from another culture and religion. The occupation came during a war. From that moment on, you and your family perceive you are being treated as less than human. Curfews from dusk to dawn are commonplace; random killings, sanctioned by the occupying government, of your neighbors by the soldiers are designed to keep you in your home and "peaceful." The army and government hail the settlers for killing civilians and send more armed soldiers after each incident of resistance by your people. The resistance starts by throwing rocks; in response, children are shot with impunity. Your very existence earns you the title of "terrorist." There is no justice system, and the numbers of your friends and family killed or injured reach into the dozens.

One day you come home and find that your wife has been beaten by soldiers while walking your son to school. Her offense? Walking too close to a military convoy. She lies seriously injured in the hospital. A week later while you are driving her home from the hospital with your son, an "instant curfew" is imposed. You have two minutes to get off the road—but your home is thirty minutes away. Soldiers in a tank see you driving down the road during curfew and fire an anti-tank round at your car. This shell designed to kill sixty-ton tanks hits your small car and vaporizes your wife and son. You survive the attack but are despondent. The incident is described to the international media as the army conducting a selective killing against a "terrorist cell." Being a "terrorist," your home is seized while you are in the hospital, and you lose every trace of your family history. The bodies of your wife and son are never returned to you, and you are later arrested.

You are torn with grief and agony and a raging thirst for vengeance. In prison you meet the radical religious branch of your people. They offer you solace and sympathy. They all have similar stories and become your friends. After your release a few months later, you are contacted by a friend of your former cellmates, who suggests a way to resist the enemy. A man meets you and offers you a chance to avenge your family's murder. You will be honored. You will join your family in the afterlife . . . a belief that is already a core part of your religious values. All you have to do is drive a car next to an enemy's convoy, push a button, and blow up along with the enemy soldiers.

Regardless of the rightness or wrongness of the occupation army and the country that sent them, how would you or others in your society react in this situation? Would you be motivated to resist using rocks, firebombs, and grenades if your home were occupied? Would you pick up a gun to fight if your family were killed in the above manner? Would you be capable of detonating a car bomb? Stepping onto a bus full of people and blowing yourself up? When push comes to shove, are you really a person of peace or of action?

This example is not only the scenario being used to attempt to justify suicide terrorism globally. It is becoming a common manifestation of the political, economic, and personal frustration in various cultures. People have become just such terrorists in China, Iraq, Chechnya, Indian Kashmir, Palestine, Afghanistan, and Sri Lanka. Most of us have a point at which we may become capable of acts of political violence. Knowing yours will help you understand the feelings of terrorists. Understand terrorists' feelings, recognize how they use their pain and suffering to justify their deadly acts—then go out and hunt them down!

What Is *Not* Terrorism?

As stated above, many events that create fear or anxiety are quick to be called terrorism, when in fact they *are not*.

For example, criminals—as individuals or in groups—may conduct acts of vandalism including arson, theft, other destruction of property, and even assault or murder. These acts can create an environment of fear and intimidation. However, they do not meet the true definition of *terrorism* if they are not being carried out specifically in order to terrorize a population and affect government policies. Common criminal behavior is not necessarily terrorism unless it supports terrorist groups and terrorist acts.

Extremist political parties often maliciously label opposition groups "terrorists" in an effort to tar their images or justify their elimination. Acts that do *not* constitute terrorism include:

- Common crimes conducted at a local level without intent of exploitation.
- Freedom of speech (even if the source is a hate group).
- Nonviolent civil disobedience.
- Civil disturbances and spontaneous rioting.
- Participation in elective or government processes.
- Protests and assembly to present opposing views and express dissent.
- Conducting acts legal under a nation's laws and international laws.

Security professionals must be careful to preserve society's civil liberties (including those of a terrorism suspect's) unless you have overwhelming reasons, supported by written law and proper authority, to believe that the person represents a clear and immediate danger to society. No matter how distasteful or disagreeable the opinions of others are, no matter how they conflict with your personal political position, the safeguarding of civil liberties is as important as deterring terrorism. The only possible exception would be the imminent use of a weapon of mass destruction based on solid intelligence, which would probably force a nation into a state of emergency or martial law, but only temporarily. If civil rights are permanently stripped away the terrorists have won.

A person with a bomb or a gun en route to a mission is a clear target of the war on terrorism and within your authority to stop; of course, all efforts to disrupt terrorism must be legally sanctioned. Removing, denying, or suspending civil liberties, stifling freedom of speech, or attempting to use the hunt for terrorists as a platform to further personal or political goals against legal opposition hands the terrorists a victory.

Key Points

- **A person who conducts an act of terrorism at any time is a terrorist.**
- **Captured terrorists are not political prisoners; they are criminals. Justice for their acts falls under criminal laws.**
- **Terrorists are not lawful combatants in war. They are unlawful combatants.**
- **Removing or suspending civil liberties, stifling freedom of speech, or using counterterrorism as a political tool gives terrorists an absolute victory.**

It is the conscious decision to use terrorist acts, target innocent victims, operate with criminal intent, and act as a secretive organization that transforms law-abiding citizens into terrorists.

Additional Terms

The following terms are used regularly by the U.S. intelligence, law enforcement, and defense communities responsible for dealing with terrorist threats.

Antiterrorism (AT): *Defensive* and preventive measures taken to reduce vulnerability to terrorist attack. Such measures may include installing physical security systems, providing and analyzing foreign and domestic intelligence, distributing information about threats, and training for response to potential future incidents. Limited response to a potential attack, such as an augmentation of security forces, is also an antiterrorism measure. Making the community and the public aware of potential terrorist threats is one principle of AT; this handbook is intended to be a key antiterrorism tool.

Counterterrorism (CT): *Offensive* measures taken in response to a terrorist attack, after it occurs. Within the context of a U.S. military response, CT includes the overt or clandestine use of forces to locate and neutralize terrorists and their facilities, rescue hostages, and recover intelligence on terrorists.

- CT may include a wide variety of measures, from armed military action (such as the 1998 Tomahawk cruise missile attack on the Zawar Kili terrorist training center in Afghanistan) to clandestine operations (for instance, the DEA/FBI/CIA sting that led to the arrest of Lebanese hijacker Fuwaz Yunez in 1987).
- CT may also include alerting homeland security forces and the National Guard, or deploying first responders such as emergency services, disaster management, fire departments, urban search and rescue, or the Centers for Disease Control. In case of an attack that is believed to be imminent, search and seizure teams such as FBI SWAT and hostage rescue teams, the Department of Energy Nuclear Emergency Search Teams (NEST), and the Federal Emergency Management Agency's Community Emergency Response Teams (CERT) may deploy to the incident site.

Combating terrorism: The U.S. government program against terrorism that includes antiterrorism, counterterrorism, and all other aspects of the tracking, defense, and response to terrorism throughout the threat spectrum.

Force Protection (FP): The U.S. Department of Defense program for the defense of military and government assets from terrorist and unconventional warfare attack. The philosophy of "detect, deter, and defend" is the foundation of military force protection.

WHAT TERRORISTS BELIEVE

The Historical Context of Terrorism

Terrorism is not a new phenomenon; it may be one of the oldest forms of illegitimate political dissent. The use of violence or the threat of violence to "send a message" to political leaders, or society at large, has occurred throughout recorded history. Groups such as the Zealots and Sicari in biblical Palestine, and the Assassins of eleventh-century Persia, are often cited as historical terrorists.

The eighteenth and nineteenth centuries generated forms of terrorism that are still used today. It was the French Revolution leader, Maximilien Robespierre who coined the term *terrorism*. He publicly advocated its use as a political tool and employed public executions by guillotine to seize popular attention and terrify French society.

Modern terrorism has its broadest roots in the mid-nineteenth century. The fathers of modern terrorism originated largely in Russia, where numerous groups, anarchists, and terror-advocating philosophers emerged, such as Sergi Nachayev and Mikhail Bakunin. Terrorism spread throughout Europe, where numerous heads of state were assassinated. It eventually came to the United States with the assassination of President McKinley in September 1901 and the Wall Street bombings of 1920.

After the Russian Revolution of 1917, Russian terrorism further expanded and was encouraged by the communist leadership. Lenin, also known as the "Red Prince," encouraged collective terrorism. After World War I (triggered by the murder of Archduke Ferdinand by a Serbian terrorist), the Irish Republican Army under the leadership of Michael Collins used terrorism to win independence for the southern counties of Ireland. Modern terrorism saw its greatest social and ideological advances after World War II, although its foundation was laid in the mid-1880s.

In the past few decades, terrorism has become increasingly prevalent in our minds as a force of political change. As world politics have shifted, new political and ideological movements have emerged around the globe, some using terrorist violence to further their aims. In addition, international media coverage has given terrorists and their acts more visibility than ever. As our definition of *terrorism* suggests, the more public attention is focused on an attack, the more effective the attack is considered by terrorists.

As the September 11 attacks revealed, the world stage provided by the Internet, by 24/7 news networks, and by other international media, can deliver just the kind of attention terrorist groups rely on. Billions of people can now witness the aftermath of a terrorist act nearly instantaneously.

Historical Events That Influenced Today's Terrorism

Which developments have had the greatest effect on fostering terrorism since the end of World War II? Below is a list of the most influential movements and events.

Revolutionary and Anticolonial Political Opposition

Much of the political upheaval over the last fifty years can be traced to the end of colonialism in Africa and Asia, and the fall of communism throughout much of the world. Revolutionary and other political opposition movements emerged in great numbers during these decades, and many groups have used terrorist tactics in attempts to overturn governments, pursue their own nationalist agendas, or promote other political interests. Some examples include:

- The Stern Gang/Irgun/Lehi (Israel).
- The Mau-Mau (Kenya).
- National Liberation Front, or FLN (Algeria).
- African National Congress (South Africa).
- Manuel Rodriguez Patriotic Front—Autonomous, or FPMR/A (Chile).
- Provisional Irish Republican Army (Northern Ireland).
- Weather Underground (United States).
- Baader-Meinhof Gang—Red Army Faction, or RAF (Germany).
- Action Direct (France).
- Dev Sol (Turkey).

Unchecked Governmental (aka Establishmental) Terrorism

Some state governments have used their own law enforcement or intelligence organizations to act as terrorist groups against their own people or against foreign dissidents. This is called governmental, or establishmental, terrorism. Some historical examples include:

- Libyan intelligence.
- North Korean intelligence.

- Iran's Revolutionary Guards.
- The former Soviet Union's KGB.
- Mao's Red Guards in China.
- Iraq's Fedayeen Saddam.

The Rise of Modern Islamic Extremism

Contrary to many popular images, Islamic fundamentalism is not a category of terrorism; it is simply a religious classification. Terrorists who may be fundamentalist in their beliefs are best referred to as Islamic extremists. However—and unfortunately for the image of Islam—Islamic extremist groups have frequently adopted terrorist tactics in order to gain attention and support for their political and religious platforms. After monarchies, socialist governments, and military administrations assumed political control of many majority Muslim nations (mainly since the end of World War II), some extremist religious groups began resorting to assassinations, bombings, and kidnappings to fight what they perceive as unholy and exploitive regimes. Events that have encouraged Islamic extremism to spread include the following:

Siege of the Grand Mosque in Mecca: In 1979, a multi-national group of armed Sunni Muslim militants seized control of the Grand Mosque in Mecca, Saudi Arabia, to protest the royal family's perceived lack of adherence to Islamic principles and to install a man they believed was the "Mahdi," a prophecized savior. The group allegedly included the brother of Usama bin Laden and infiltrated in bin Laden construction trucks.

Iranian hostage crisis: After the 1979 Islamic Revolution in Iran and with the encouragement of the Ayatollah Khomeini, religious students seized the American embassy in Tehran. The Iranian government eventually took responsibility for the hostage taking and held fifty-five Americans for 444 days in protest of the United States' ongoing support for the exiled Mohammed Reza Pahlavi, the Shah of Iran, who was perceived by many as a corrupt dictator. Iran quickly became a major sponsor of Islamic extremist terrorism worldwide after this event.

Anti-U.S. terrorism in Lebanon: Members of Hezbollah ("Party of God") in Lebanon and its action arm, Islamic Jihad Organization (IJO), carried out suicide bombings against the U.S. Marine barracks and two American embassies in Beirut, killing more than 250 Americans. They also conducted numerous skyjackings and a massive kidnapping campaign designed to force the United States out of Lebanon, seizing more than seventy-five Westerners residing in that country. The United States' secret payments of weapons to Iran as ransom for the release of these hostages later emerged as the Iran-Contra Affair.

Russian invasion of Afghanistan: Russia's invasion of Afghanistan during the 1980s and its eventual defeat helped catalyze the rise of Usama bin Laden's al-Qaeda organization. These former anti-Russian "holy warriors" were drawn from the thousands of Muslim volunteers who had been recruited to fight the Russians with Pakistani, Saudi Arabian, and American support. Known as Afghan-Arabs, postwar terrorists now claim they are fighting to protest U.S. foreign policy in the Middle East and America's military presence in Saudi Arabia, and to promote the liberation of Palestine and the establishment of Islamic states throughout the Muslim world. Al-Qaeda carried out numerous deadly bombings against American targets in the 1990s and killed more than three thousand people. Dozens of sister organizations, started by former Afghan-Arab veterans and inspired or financed by al-Qaeda, have sprung up throughout the Middle East, Africa, Asia, and Central Asia.

The Palestinian Intifada (1987-1993, 1999-present): A spontaneous popular uprising of Palestinians living in the Israeli-occupied West Bank and Gaza Strip against the Israeli army occurred between 1987 and 1993 and again in 1999. This uprising or Intifada (in Arabic) occurred when Palestinians rebelled against the conditions of their occupation and started open combat against the Israeli army. The rebellion inspired many supporters throughout the Middle East to contribute money and political clout in achieving a negotiated settlement for the Palestinian people. This effort culminated with the return of Yasser Arafat to the West Bank and appeared to be on the fast track toward a comprehensive solution. In 2000, however, Palestinian negotiators broke off talks, and a visit by Israeli politician Ariel Sharon to the al-Aqsa mosque in Jerusalem set off the second Intifada. This Intifada quickly turned into a war of personalities between Arafat and Sharon. Its most significant feature has been the Israeli focus on destroying Arafat and the PLO, which allowed the more violent Palestinian extremist movements to fill the void. The extremists took the opportunity to perfect suicide bombing against the Israelis within Israel. In 2000, only one suicide attack occurred in Israel. But in 2001, the extremist Iranian-backed Hamas and Palestinian Islamic Jihad Organizations, as well as the new FATAH splinter group the al-Aqsa

Martyr's Brigade, started a suicide bombing campaign that saw eighty-eight attacks. In 2002, as Israeli military action in Palestine increased, so did the suicide attacks with almost one hundred fifty occurring mainly inside of Israel. The Palestinian cause has become the food of rhetoric for many Islamic terrorist groups and Arab governments.

The U.S. invasion of Iraq (2003): This invasion toppled dictator Saddam Hussein but inflamed many nations in the Muslim world. It may be a new chapter in the rise of Islamic extremist terrorism.

Incorporation of Narco-Conglomerates and International Criminal Organizations

Over the past two decades, drug-trafficking groups around the world have grown into multinational criminal corporations. Worth billions of dollars, they use terrorist methods to influence governments and protect their assets. For example, criminal organizations and drug traffickers in Colombia and Chechnya have pioneered the mass subcontracting of amateur terrorists to conduct abductions and other acts of terrorism that can earn a given group millions of dollars in ransoms and protection rackets, and fund other terrorist acts.

Availability of Weapons of Mass Destruction

Weapons of mass destruction (WMD), largely the domain of governments until recent years, have become attractive to terrorists for their ability to create large-scale fear and panic.

Biological weapons: The 2001 anthrax attack on the U.S. Senate proved more frightening than destructive. The media coverage surrounding the contamination of the Senate office buildings and the unfortunate deaths of several victims created a perfect storm of rumor and panic.

However, a truly fearful prospect would be the release of highly fatal viruses such as smallpox. The smallpox virus can be released and spread among millions of people before it is detected, since its incubation period is approximately two weeks. A U.S. government exercise that simulated a terrorist release of smallpox showed that more than three million people could die within thirty to sixty days of the appearance of the first incidence. The usage of a human-deployed biological weapons system (HUMANBIOWEP; see chapter 12)—a suicide operative deliberately infected with diseases such as smallpox—is the most viable terrorist weapon and far more attainable than a nuclear weapon.

Chemical weapons: The first large-scale modern-day terrorist use of chemical WMDs was carried out in 1993 by Aum Shinrikyo, a religious-cult-turned-terrorist-group in Japan. The group manufactured Sarin nerve gas and distributed it on several occasions. These weapons give terrorist groups the capability to create large numbers of casualties with generally unsophisticated technology.

Nuclear and radioactive weapons: Much attention has been focused on the possibility of a nuclear bomb being sought after by terrorists. Neither nuclear nor explosively dispersed radiological devices (called dirty bombs) have been used in a major terrorist attack to date, but dozens of attempts to acquire radioactive material have been documented worldwide since the 1970s.

Ideologies Terrorists Espouse

When it comes to justifying terrorist violence with a certain ideology, the human imagination knows no boundaries. An *ideology* is a set of values or principles—a belief system—that may motivate people to act. Most political and religious ideologies are, at their core, based on noble ideas, but as we see far too often, they can become twisted to serve the ambitions of a few and take on violent tendencies. Other ideologies, such as white supremacy, are based on hate and fear, and actually espouse, at their core, the use of violence as the desired means to an end.

People who carry out acts of terrorism invariably claim they are acting in the name of a religious, political, philosophical, or other type of cause. It is important to understand the particular ideology claimed by a terrorist group, in order to better predict its targets and methodologies.

Following is a partial list of political, religious, and other ideologies that have been used by terrorist organizations to justify their violent actions.

Political and Policy-Based Ideologies

Marxist-Leninist communism: The main objective of this political model is worker ownership of the means of production, resulting from the overthrow (violent, if necessary) of the bourgeois class. Theoretically, such a revolution would produce a classless society. Historical enemies of communists are the property-owning class and the state systems that keep the "owners" in power, including politicians, military, and police. Some current terrorist groups with communist roots include the Tupac Amaru Revolutionary Movement (MRTA, or Shining Path) of Peru, which has attempted to replace Peru's government with a revolutionary Marxist regime, and the Red Brigade of Italy, which attacked the Italian government and businesses in an attempt to remove Italy from the Western Alliance and punish Italian participation in NATO. Thought to be defunct after 1991, the Red Brigade (with new, younger adherents) is believed to have resumed operations in Italy in 2002.

Stalinist communism: The key feature of Stalin's attempts at furthering a socialist revolution was the creation of a one-party state (and the consequently brutal suppression of opposition). The underlying result of Stalinism was the lack of workers' rights; dictatorial rule through a cult of personality; and the distortion of history. Whereas Marx stressed the idea of a proletariat revolution from below, Stalinism emphasized strict implementation of socialism from the top down. In the Soviet Union, this ideology resulted in a classic example of state-run terror campaigns. Some mafia and old-guard Russian groups, who have used terrorism as a localized tool, still believe Stalinism is the best system for Russia today.

Peruvian Communist Party poster.

Maoist communism: Maoism is a Chinese variant on Marxism. It stresses cultural characteristics (such as strong family ties), unceasing class struggle, and constant party oversight. Mao Tse-tung also advocated the use of terrorist campaigns against counterrevolutionaries. Ideologically, Mao adapted Marxism to apply to the peasant masses, rather than the working classes of Europe; and today, many peasant revolutionary terrorist groups throughout Asia and Latin America stem from Maoist-type philosophies rather than those of Marxism, since their origins are more rural than urban.

Castro and Guevarist communism: The communism of Fidel Castro (and his deputy Che Guevara) has been based since the 1950s on the Marxist-Leninist model. Its major characteristics include elections to a general assembly, the cult of personality centered on Fidel Castro, and Cuba's explicit efforts to export its brand of communism to other Latin American countries. Groups that have adopted this philosophy include the Colombian Army of National Liberation (ELN), the Revolutionary

Armed Forces of Colombia (FARC), and the defunct Farabundo Marti National Movement (FMLN) of El Salvador.

Fascism/neo-fascism: A state philosophy based on glorification of that state and its supreme leadership, paired with total individual subordination for the greater good of the state. The state is thus justified in all actions that promote its own survival, such as imperialism, unilateralism in foreign policy, and ethnocentrism. The philosophy since the end of World War II has been referred to as neo-fascism. Nazi Germany and Italy under Benito Mussolini are classic examples of fascism; modern examples would include Chile under Augusto Pinochet and Francisco Franco's Spain. All used their national intelligence agencies (such as the Nazi Gestapo and Chile's DINA) as terrorist organizations.

European neo-Nazism: A contraction of the German word *Nationalsozialismus*, Nazi ideology in the 1930s and 1940s stressed support for ethnic-based nationalism, anti-Semitism, and anticommunism. Today, neo-Nazi groups in Europe, often youth based, have mainly nominal and iconographic ties to true Nazism and are generally focused only on racist agendas. They often espouse violence against immigrants and tend to deny Nazi atrocities. European neo-Nazi groups and their cells in Germany have conducted, and been convicted of, firebombings and murders of Turkish and Arab immigrants.

American neo-Nazism: Characterized by xenophobia and idolization of Adolf Hitler and the Nazi Party, American neo-Nazis are fewer in number and less politically active than their European counterparts. American neo-Nazis, by virtue of the diverse makeup of U.S. society, expanded Hitler's concept of a master race to include non-Aryan ethnicities, including Greeks, Slavs, and Hispanics. They also differ from European neo-Nazis in their use of Christianity to justify racist beliefs and thus gain broader support. Numerous neo-Nazi groups operate quietly within the United States under the umbrella of, and in complete cooperation with, the Christian Identity white supremacy movement. Emerging American groups such as World Church of the Creator and the RAcial HOly WAr movement (RAHOWA) have conducted murder, small-scale arson, and financial robbery in an effort to create a terrorist capability.

Anarchist/nihilist: These two ideologies stress the need for immediate, violent destruction of established order and were popular in Eastern Europe and Russia/the Soviet Union in the late nineteenth and early twentieth centuries. Nihilists see Western values as baseless and maintain no loyalties or fundamental beliefs in an existence they view as purpose-less. To nihilists, social justice can be achieved by reason alone. Anarchists, emphasizing individual freedom of action, similarly seek to bring about a stateless world system and to eliminate all hierarchical structure for the good of humanity. Combined, these two concepts make for an extremist, disorganized belief system bent solely on violent over-throw of the current world order. Modern-day anarchists have been con-necting in a global movement of civil disobedience and street action and have yet to reach the horrible levels of assassinations seen a century ago.

Ethnic and national independence movements: Perhaps the broad-est political category of all—and one encompassing myriad political philosophies—is that of ethnic groups seeking to establish independent nations for their people. In many parts of the world, centuries-old "nations" of people were split apart or subsumed by the modern nation-states created in the nineteenth and twentieth centuries; during the past few decades, many have sought to reclaim their historical iden-tities and homelands. Faced with colonial political repression, many nationalist movements have resorted to terrorist acts to achieve their goal of independence—and many have succeeded. Countries such as South Africa, Israel, and Nicaragua have all gained independence using acts of terrorism to pressure existing governments. Active groups, including the Tamil Tigers (LTTE) of Sri Lanka, the Kurdish Communist Party (PKK) in Turkey, and Palestinian groups in Israel such as the PFLP, PLO, and DFLP, have not yet succeeded in their efforts to gain independent states, but have continued using terrorist tactics up through recent years.

Environmentalism: Environmentalists are advocates for the state and quality of the earth, its inhabitants, and its resources. Some groups choose to act in violent ways that constitute terrorism. For example, the Earth Liberation Front (ELF) operates in decentralized cells acting in the interest of environmental preservation. ELF seeks to hurt businesses responsible for environmental destruction, drawing attention to its cause through the destruction of property. Its socialist-leaning ideology claims to be based on nonviolence against either humans or animals, but it car-ries out and advocates performing violent acts that may kill and injure innocent people.

Antiglobalization: These groups seek to slow, halt, or reverse the forces of globalization—the (some believe) uncontrolled and rapid eco-nomic, cultural, and technological interaction among diverse parts of the world. Many view globalization—specifically the increase in international trade and the Westernization of business culture—as a threat to local practices and customs, and they fear the eventual loss of these societal qualities to a new, Western-dominated global order. Others simply oppose negative by-products of economic globalization such as accelerated environmental destruction and labor exploitation.

Animal rights: Animal rights advocates preach the ethical and humane treatment of animals. Generally an extremely peaceful movement, it encompasses some smaller groups that have adopted terrorist tactics as a method of protest. For example, the Animal Liberation Front (ALF) resorts to criminal actions—most often the malicious destruction of property—in an ongoing fight to end animal cruelty and the exploitation of the earth for profit. The ALF is classified as a potential terrorist group due to its advocacy of arson and bombings, and the message it sends despite its claims to be opposed to harming human life.

Religious Extremist Ideologies

Islamic extremism is the belief that traditional Islamic values must be universally adopted to defeat the encroachment of Western influence and return to the purest form of Islam. Radical Islamists perceive that Western cultural and economic influences, the sponsorship of pro-Western Muslim governments, the creation of the state of Israel, and the dilution of traditional Islamic law (Sharia) are all violations of the Koranic scriptures by illegitimate Muslims who have abdicated their responsibility to maintain the values of the faith and the people.

Christian extremism is the belief that the teachings of Christianity, with Jesus Christ as the source of spiritual salvation, should be the basis of all political decisions and teachings.

- **Ecumenical Marxism (liberation theology)** is based on the belief that Christianity and its Gospels stipulate preferential treatment of the world's poor; it is therefore every Christian's duty to ensure the fair treatment of all others. Liberation theology, with its Marxist implications, developed in the late 1960s and is often blamed for encouraging violent revolution in defense of social justice and equitable wealth distribution.
- **The Christian Identity Movement** is a conservative, racist extension of "Anglo-Israelism." It promotes the belief that members of the Anglo-Saxon, Celtic, Germanic, and/or Scandinavian cultures are racial descendants of the ten ancient lost tribes of Israel.

Christian Identity, in its various forms, asserts that the people of these cultures are "God's chosen people," while Jews are direct descendants of Satan and Eve. These groups categorize nonwhite races as soulless "mud people" on par with animals. Identity followers emphasize that Christian teachings justify not only racist doctrine, but extremist violence as well. To them, Armageddon will be manifested in an inevitable race war, necessary for the establishment of Christ's kingdom on earth. The largest representation of this movement has been the Ku Klux Klan, whose adherents often engage in paramilitary survivalist training. The Klan operated in the United States as a domestic terrorist organization with near impunity for a century and remains a threat today.

Anti-abortion/right to life: This political/social movement—predominant in the United States—promotes the belief that human life begins at fertilization; therefore abortion, at any stage of pregnancy, is murder. Extremist proponents of this philosophy believe direct action is necessary to prevent abortions from being performed, including bombing abortion clinics and assassinating abortion providers. The Army of God is one such violence-condoning group; members believe that they are carrying out God's will as part of a Christian holy war. Hundreds of acts such as sniper assassinations, bombings, biological agent (anthrax) threats, and acts of physical intimidation have been perpetrated by anti-abortion terrorists. The 1996 Olympic Park bombing in Atlanta, Georgia, is believed to have been perpetrated by suspected anti-abortionist terrorist Eric Robert Rudolph.

Militant Zionism stems from the Jewish movement that arose in the late nineteenth century and was advocated by leading intellectuals such as Theodore Herzl, in response to growing anti-Semitism in Europe. Zionism called for the reestablishment of the Jewish homeland in Palestine as a solution to the Jewish Diaspora. Modern Zionism is concerned with the support, development, and continuation of the state of Israel. Extremist believers such as the Kach Group and Kahane Chai support the perpetuation of a sovereign, all-Jewish homeland in Israel—at almost any cost.

Hindu extremism is a henotheistic religion recognizing one God, as well as that God's manifestation in other deities. The principal religion of India, Hinduism centers on the principle of the Brahman (one God), positing that all of reality is unified. Hindu scriptures do not support most forms of violence, yet they make allowances for its use in self-defense against the evils of the world. Extremist Hindus support the perpetuation of the Hindu religious majority in India over the minority Muslims and Sikhs. This largely ethnic conflict has led to the formation of many indigenous terrorist groups and corresponding countergroups (such as Sikh extremists—see below).

Sikh extremism: The Sikh religion is an offshoot of Hinduism, promoting a love of God and humankind. Believing that all people should be treated equally, Sikhs make no distinctions along lines of race, caste, or creed. Sikh men are identifiable by their turbans and uncut hair and beards, and Sikhism's adherents believe in transmigration of the soul as a result of a person's deeds. In modern-day India, a Sikh minority actively seeks to create an independent state of Khalistan in northern India and has carried out numerous attacks, including the assassination of Indian prime minister Indira Gandhi and the destruction of an Air India 747 airliner over the Atlantic Ocean, which killed 244 passengers.

Messianic salvation/apocalyptic cultism is an extremist belief in Jesus Christ's expected return to Earth for the purpose of delivering salvation to the worthy followers of a particular ideology, such as that of a self-designated prophet who creates a cult around his beliefs. Such cults foresee an inevitable and relatively immediate apocalyptic end of the world and thus seek to prepare themselves for the upcoming battle between good and absolute evil. Cultist groups, such as the American Concerned Christians, were expelled from Israel around the millennium celebrations, after the discovery of plots to conduct massacres in an effort to bring on the second coming of Christ and end of the world. In addition, the American Movement for the Establishment of the Temple has threatened to "liberate" the Temple Mount in Jerusalem through force, and then blow up the Dome of the Rock Mosque (Islam's third holiest site) and build the Third Temple of Israel on it.

Occultism: The word *occult* derives from a Latin word meaning "concealed." Occultists believe that their secret practices allow them to tap into the paranormal world and thus gain insight into the mysteries of life. Basic beliefs include the ability to contact the dead and work beyond established laws of physics. Occultists are often attracted by promises of power and the appeal of inheriting esoteric knowledge, of which the general public is believed to be ignorant.

Paganism/animism: These belief systems include the ancient view that souls give life to all beings, including apparently inanimate objects, and that these souls are separate beings before birth and after death.

Holy men, trances, and idols are common facets of animistic societies, and earth-centered polytheism is characteristic of pagan societies. In the 1960s, paganism gained popularity as an environmentally friendly ideology emphasizing nature worship and the immanency of multiple deities. The Mau-Mau of Kenya (active in the 1960s) carried out massacres of civilians and acts of terrorism. They combined many pagan and animistic beliefs with political action aimed at expelling Europeans, who were seen as political oppressors.

"Cold Hard Cash" Ideology: Continuing Criminal Enterprises (CCEs)

A politically active CCE is an organization that operates within a nation and uses its illegal financing to gain political leverage. It may resort to terrorism to drive home its level of power.

Non-politically active CCEs are collective racketeering organizations that are solely interested in safeguarding or advancing criminal operations. These groups do not involve themselves within the political structure of a nation but will use terrorism to warn or challenge governments or rivals. Mafia organizations worldwide, particularly the violent ones in Eastern Europe, are good examples.

Drug-trafficking CCEs or "narco-corporations" use the power of their finances and resources to effect change by corrupting societies and governments. They use terrorism to protect their resources, punish investigators, or intimidate members of the population at large. Colombian drug lord Pablo Escobar ordered a civil airliner destroyed in order to kill five witnesses; along with those five, more than a hundred other innocent people died. The M-19 terrorist group conducted a full-scale, thirty-five-man suicide attack on the Colombian Palace of Justice that killed more than a hundred people and all of the country's Supreme Court justices to destroy the Cali Cantel's extradition papers.

Mercenaries are guns for hire, working for payment and/or the "romance of combat."

- **Ideological mercenaries** are those who conduct military operations for political, religious, or social beliefs as well as payments in cash. French mercenary Bob Denard conducted acts of terrorism and military operations numerous times in nations he had a political affinity for.
- **Nonideological mercenaries** are the classic mercenaries who carry out operations, including terrorist acts, for cash payment.

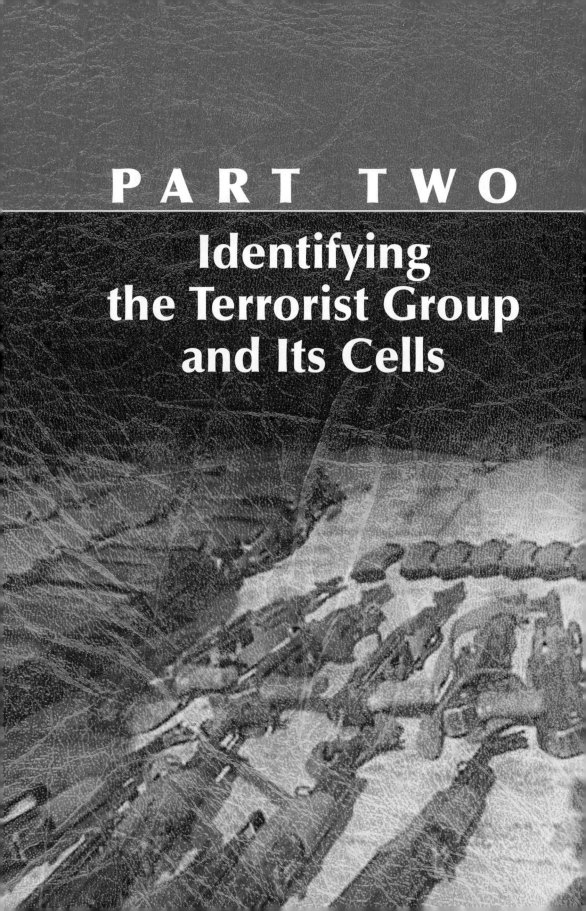

PART TWO

Identifying the Terrorist Group and Its Cells

TERRORIST GROUP ORGANIZATION

Common Characteristics of Terrorist Groups

Terrorists use violence: Terrorist operations entail violence or the threat of violence. Some groups that use violent means may also carry out terror operations that do not use violence in the traditional sense, such as cyberterrorism or bomb threats, but may result in disruption that heightens the sense of fear and terror.

Terrorists operate in all environments: Many terrorist groups, formerly localized, have begun to operate with increasing ease throughout the world. Most organizations can move easily from urban to rural environments, so the myth that terrorists are mainly urban is no longer applicable. Many terrorists seek the anonymity and privacy rural areas offer.

Terrorists operate covertly: Terrorist operations are, not surprisingly, usually synonymous with secrecy. A few groups have been known to issue warnings before carrying out an attack, generally with a goal of creating shock value and then benefiting from the media attention the attack generates.

Terrorists are often well organized: Some terrorist groups are well organized; others are largely amateurs. The number of members has little effect on effectiveness or efficiency of an organization. Large, effective organizations such as the PKK, IRA, Hezbol-lah, al-Qaeda, and the FARC operate within their home countries or worldwide. An individual terrorist acting alone (American domestic terrorists refer to them as "lone wolves") have also been extremely effective, such as the American "Unabomber" Ted Kaczynski and the suspected 1996 Olympic bomber Eric Robert Rudolph.

> **Terrorist groups organize for just three reasons: preparing for attacks, planning for attacks, and conducting attacks.**

Terrorists act deliberately: Terrorism never occurs randomly. The desired effect is to make it seem random, but each act is deliberate—even if the exact moment of the attack is unknown to the public or to every member of the terrorist cell.

Terrorists employ high mobility: Terrorist operations are high risk in nature and require the ability to move rapidly to and from operations areas. Terrorists require the mobility inherent in cars, motorcycles, and subways. They usually don't move to the target on foot, except perhaps at a critical point of an operation that requires it, such as an assassination. International groups need access to secure air or rail transportation routes. Local groups may use buses as an effective way to blend into a mass of people.

Terrorists use short-duration firepower or effects: No matter what weapon terrorists choose, it is selected to provide the appropriate level of firepower or force to accomplish the mission. If the mission requires engaging armed personnel, the terrorists' firepower will ideally exceed the maximum amount of defensive fire they will face; otherwise a group will use short-duration, overwhelming fire to effect shock and surprise. The level of firepower will vary according to mission. Low-level firepower, such as a .22 caliber pistol, might be chosen for its small size and minimal detectability against an unarmed victim. If the mission is a bombing, the bomb will be sized for intent. For example, mass destruction requires a large, powerful, well-positioned bomb; gaining media attention requires a moderately sized bomb in a public place; assassination requires a small but precise bomb.

Terrorists are media dependent: Terrorism generally thrives on media attention. The purpose of terrorist operations is to transmit fear and publicize a cause. No matter how destructive an attack, and no matter whether anyone claims it, the event will succeed in generating publicity—and terror.

ETA terrorists conducting a press conference.

Terrorist Areas of Operation

From where do terrorist groups generally operate? The following phrases are commonly used by the antiterrorism community to describe organizations based on area of operations. A group may change its area of operations at any time.

- **Local terrorists:** Individuals and groups that operate only within a small locality.
- **Regional terrorists:** Individuals and groups that operate within a defined geographic region within a nation's borders.

- **National (domestic) terrorists**: Individuals and groups that operate within a nation's borders. The FBI refers to events that occur in the United States and conducted by American citizens as domestic terrorism.
- **Transnational terrorists:** Individuals and groups that cross one or more borders to conduct operations. For example, Pakistani-backed Islamic terrorists cross the border between Pakistan and India's Kashmir.
- **International terrorists:** Individuals and groups that operate in multiple countries around the world.

Classifying Terrorist Sources of Support

Governmental (establishmental) terrorism: The use of law enforcement, internal security, intelligence, or other official agencies to conduct terrorist acts against foreign nations, the nation's own people, or foreign dissidents.

State-directed (aka state-sponsored) terrorism: Terrorism ordered and controlled by a nation that uses a terrorist group as a tool in carrying out government policy. The term *state sponsored* is often used in place of the more accurate *state directed*. Examples include Harakat ul-Ansar (Pakistan) and the Mujahideen al-Khalq (Iraq).

State-supported terrorism: Terrorist groups that operate independently but receive financial, material, intelligence, or operational support from one or more foreign nations. These groups enjoy the approval and support of nations but are not told what or where to strike. Since governments only marginally control them, they are harder to deter. Examples include the IRA, Hamas, and the Palestinian Islamic Jihad (PIJ).

Independent (non-state-supported) terrorism: Terrorist groups that are completely independent of support of a foreign government. These terrorist groups are potentially the most dangerous, because they are not subject to political pressures. Al-Qaeda is an independent terrorist group.

Terrorist Group Structures and Membership: Who Orders Terrorist Acts?

The leadership of a terrorist group is often publicly known and is its most identifiable part. Charismatic personalities such as Usama bin Laden (al-Qaeda), Renato Curcio (Red Brigades), Abdullah Ocalan

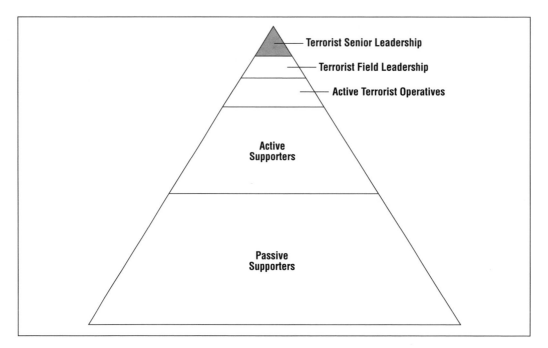

Terrorist Organizational Support Pyramid

(PKK), Velupillai Prabhakaran (LTTE), or Yasser Arafat (PLO) are well known and provide a face for the grievances of the group. *The terrorist leadership orders and is responsible for terrorist acts* even though some decisions may be left up to the field leadership or the individual operative.

Terrorist groups are generally composed of five subgroups that make operations possible;[1] the senior leadership, field leadership, active operatives, active supporters, and passive supporters. The operational makeup of terrorist organizations is based on a pyramidal support structure.[2] An analysis of terrorist groups since 1990 reveals that a new level of leadership between the active cadre and senior leadership is making more and more operational decisions to insulate the group's leaders—the field leadership. Decisions to select targets and to carry out operations are increasingly being made at the field leadership level. The modified pyramid includes the following levels of support:

- **Senior leadership:** These are the hard-core supporters who believe in the cause of the group without question. They include ideologues, theologians, and others who attempt to justify the acts of terrorism. The leadership creates strategic plans and decides whom to strike, what to strike, and where to strike, unlike terrorism

1. Terrorist groups typically do not refer to their leadership using these terms. TRH uses NATO-style military chain-of-command terminology to standardize the levels of involvement by terrorists.
2. This structure was developed for the U.S. Army's combating terrorism program. The traditional model is composed of four structures: active leadership, active cadre, active supporters, and passive supporters.

of the 1960s and 1970s, leaders usually do not participate in tactical operations.

- **Field leadership:** These are the select terrorist operatives who control large geographic areas and command the active terrorists. The field leadership often designs terrorist attacks and gets them approved by senior leadership. The field leadership participates in operations in a supervisory role.
- **Active operatives:** These are the primary covert members of the terrorist organization who collect intelligence and supply and conduct the actual attacks.
- **Active supporters:** These are civilians who truly believe in the cause of the terrorist group and offer unquestioned support, sometimes acting as couriers, providing emergency safe houses, and acquiring materials.
- **Passive supporters:** Civilians who unknowingly support the terrorists' political or religious organization.

Terrorist Command and Control Structures

The type of organization a group uses depends on its level of sophistication and what works best geographically. The Defence Intelligence Agency classifies terrorist groups into two command and control structures: centralized authority structure and decentralized authority structure.

1. A centralized authority structure

Provides the terrorist cells and manpower with all support, intelligence, and supplies from one source either in depots or caches belonging to the organization. The benefits are unified and controlled action as well as making large quantities of resources available for missions. The difficulty of this structure is that it creates a large group that can be infiltrated. Well-known traditional communist and guerrilla terrorists such as the German Red Army Faction and the Italian Red Brigade used this structure.

2. A decentralized authority structure

Allows groups at the individual or cell level to provide for themselves with minimal direction or support from the group's leadership. The benefits are that they can make decisions based on detailed local intelligence, have better awareness of the security environment, and use few group resources. This structure is also more prone to fractionalizing or groups acting in rogue operations, however. International groups like al-Qaeda or groups that operate in difficult security environments such as Hamas and the Palestinian Islamic Jihad prefer this structure.

Organizational Models

The purpose of a terrorist organization is simply to ensure that the absolute most effective and secure terrorist activities are carried out successfully. Each group may select the best model based on its area of operations, security, and resources. These models are provided to show that terrorist groups generally have simple communications and command structures. Terrorist groups are structured in one of the three general organizational models: functional, operational, and independent.

1. Functional structure:

This is a centralized structure. The group (see page [x-ref]) is commanded by the senior leadership, which passes orders down directly to a command and control cell or to cells that operate strictly in their specialty area (intelligence, tactical operations, logistics). This is one of the oldest and most secure of organizational structures, because the terrorist group's unique cell functions are kept highly compartmentalized. Each cell may be completely unaware of the other cells' existence; often, cells do not communicate directly with each other. If one cell is stopped or arrested, the other cells remain in place, and the mission may even continue if a replacement cell arrives in time. Communications within this form of structure take place between the terrorist senior leadership and each cell with secure methods.

2. Operational structure:

This is a decentralized structure. The group is commanded by its senior leadership, which passes orders down to a series of "combined cells." These combined cells run their own intelligence, supply, and attack operations with the same group of people. This is a highly risky structure for operatives, because the arrest of one cell member can stop all operations. Al-Qaeda uses this structure.

3. Independent cell structure:

This is a centralized structure that is similar to the operational structure described above, except that there is no independent senior leadership. The group operates as one body and performs all the cell functions necessary to carry out an attack. Cell members may perform several different roles.

Religious Terrorist Organization Structure

- **Spiritual leader:** Typically, this is a charismatic person who sets the spiritual and political agenda for the group. The leader has

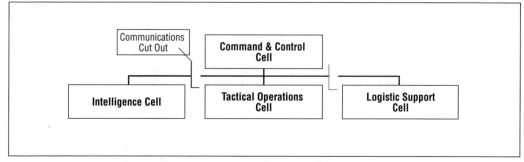

Terrorist organizational structure: "Functional" organization structure.

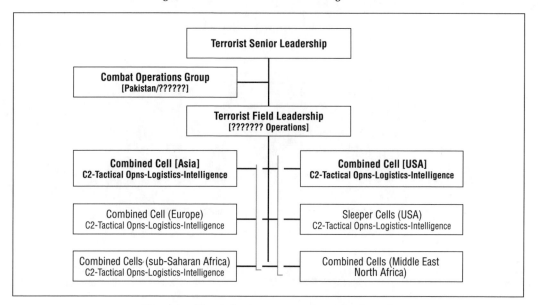

"Operational" organization structure. Example: al-Qaeda.

direct communications with the group's "public" (such as a political party or social services organization) wing, but maintains secret
communication paths with the operational (terrorist) division.

- **Council or other body of religious leaders:** A cohesive group
  that supports and advises the spiritual leader on the use of terrorism and its religious or political suitability.
- **Laypeople and supporters:** Active supporters who support the
  decisions and teachings of the spiritual leader, even if they involve
  terrorist acts.
- **Political wing:** Active supporters who provide political power,
  influence, and money.
- **Covert terrorist wing:** Militants who use violence to advance the
  spiritual goals of the spiritual leader.

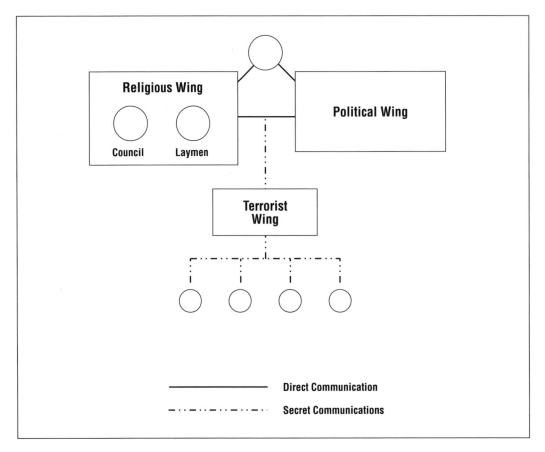

Religious terrorist organization structure.

Political Terrorist Organization Structure

- Political leader: This is generally a charismatic figure who sets the overall political goals of the group.
  - Political deputy/operations officer executes and/or distributes orders from the leader.
  - Operational liaison officer passes on the secret orders of the leadership to the operatives who will carry out terrorist acts.

Combined Cell Organization Structure

A self-contained covert unit, the combined cell can be used by terrorists of any ideological leaning. This group may be one person (lone wolf) or a small group of people operating together (combined cell).

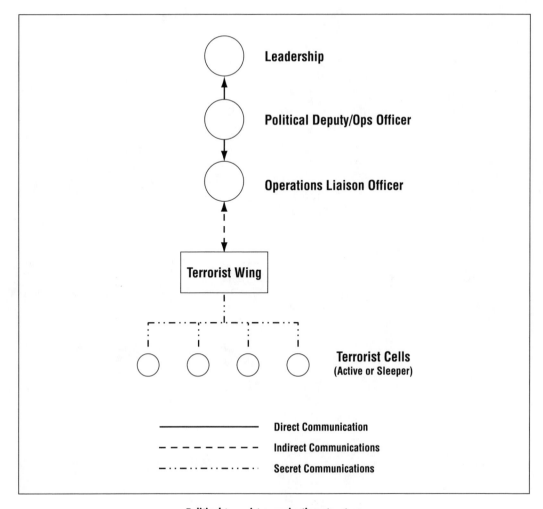

Leadership

Political Deputy/Ops Officer

Operations Liaison Officer

Terrorist Wing

Terrorist Cells
(Active or Sleeper)

———————— Direct Communication

— — — — — — — Indirect Communications

— · · — · · — · · — Secret Communications

Political terrorist organization structure.

This system is highly advocated by white supremacist and neo-Nazi groups within the United States. Technically, the Usama bin Laden Organization seeks out and supports independent combined cells within Muslim countries and provides guidance and finances to their operations, but has little direct control over their structure or targets. These groups are marked by members who conduct all the necessary support, intelligence, and attack operations with the same group of people.

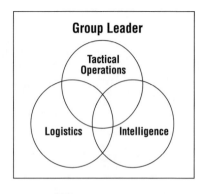

Group Leader

Tactical
Operations

Logistics

Intelligence

Combined cell organization.

8

THE TERRORIST CELL

Terrorist cells are secret, small teams of terrorists who operate as a group either on orders of a commander or independently. The cell is the fundamental unit of a terrorist group. Cell operations and their members are the least understood part of terrorism. Their operations are always secret and never seen, until they attack.

Cells are often referred to by other names in a terrorist organization's communications and statements. Depending on the group and its national origin, cells may be referred to as fronts, commandos, *groupos,* or wings. The Irish Republican Army called cells active service units; in Sri Lanka, the Tamil Tigers call their cells cadres. Many terrorist groups will name their cells after slain members; an example was a cell of Germany's Red Army Faction was known as the Gudrun Essenlin Commando.

Types of Terrorist Cells

The Terrorist Recognition Handbook uses NATO-style military chain-of-command terms to standardize the terminology of terrorist cells. Terrorist groups don't refer to themselves with the following terms but use terms that better suit their ideology and culture.

- **A command and control cell (C2)** is comprised of external or internal supervisors who make final decisions and supervise execution of attack. They may be leaders of or participants in any of the following cells.
- **Tactical operations cell (TACO-PS):** The person or team that actually carries out the act of terrorism. Also known as combat cells, attack cells, action teams, or operational cells.
- **An intelligence cell (INTELL)** collects data, makes recommendations, selects targets, and provides information to hit the target.
- **Logistics cell (LOG):** People who are organized to provide supplies or support to the other cells. These may include bomb makers, black marketeers, doctors, lawyers, bankers, couriers, and others needed in an emergency. Also referred to as the auxiliary cell, support cell, or assistance cell.
- **A combined cell (Combined)** is a team of terrorists so small it must perform all the functions of the four cells named above. The al-Qaeda organization often uses combined cells to maximize its manpower.

- **A sleeper cell** is any one of the above types of cells that infiltrates a geographic region and lies dormant until activated for a mission. Sleeper cells are distinguished by their ability to blend into their surroundings until given orders to carry out their mission. Once activated, of course, the cell is no longer a sleeper.

Keep in mind that cells may operate independently or in coordination with each other, depending upon their mission.

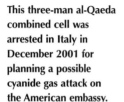
This three-man al-Qaeda combined cell was arrested in Italy in December 2001 for planning a possible cyanide gas attack on the American embassy.

CARABINIERE, MINISTRY OF JUSTICE, ITALY

Operative Membership Pools

Terrorist groups must draw operatives from a body of manpower known as a pool. Pools of manpower come in two forms: open and closed.

Closed pools of operatives are professional or dedicated terrorists who are consistently used by the leadership. These members are active cadres and supporters chosen for skills and reliability. They are generally a known number of personnel and may be the heart of the terrorist group. Smaller groups have used this system successfully and were only degraded through arrest or death of the operatives. The German terrorist group Red Army Faction lost its last two closed-pool operatives in 1999 with the arrest of Andreas Klumpf and the death of Horst-Ludwig Meyer in a SWAT raid. The group is now considered defunct.

Open pools of operatives rely on active cadre and field leadership to recruit lower-level operatives and train them to support their missions. These core personnel do not have to risk themselves completely and can form new cells as necessary. Al-Qaeda uses this system.

Terrorist Cell Size

The number of cells, the number of operatives per cell, and the group's overall structure depend upon several factors:

- **Group skills:** Better groups use small cells of three to five people. Unskilled groups use larger numbers of people. Al-Qaeda, a professional group, prefers to use large cells of four to 20 members—but they are independent enough to create their own cells. Blood-connected groups such as criminally bent families also

Terrorist Cell Participants by Mission

An SRSI Corp. study of more than fifteen hundred terrorist attacks has yielded the following average numbers of terrorist cell members participating in tactical operations between 1968 and 2002.

Terrorist Act	# Operatives	Roles of Operatives
Explosives bombing—dropped	1-2	1 bomber, 1 security/driver
Explosives bombing—thrown	1	1 bomber
Explosives bombing—suicide	2	1 bomber, 1 security/driver
Explosives vehicle bomb—suicide	1	1 Bomber
Firearms assassination	1-2	1 Shooter, 1 backup shooter
Firearms ambush	3+	3 Shooters
Explosives ambush	2	1 Shooter, 1 lookout/backup
Skyjacking	3-5	1 Commander, 2-4 guards
In-flight bomb—dropped	1	1 bomber
In-flight bomb—suicide/martyrdom	1	1 bomber
Arson	1-2	1 arsonist, 1 lookout
Armed raid	5-10+	1 commander, 4-9 shooters
Light infantry weapons attack	3+	1 commander, 2-4 shooters
Surface-to-air missile attack	2	1 lookout, 1 missile launcher
Abduction	3+	1 driver, 2 gunmen/guards

tend to use larger cells. The larger the group, the greater the chance of compromise.

- **Mission risk:** If the mission is high risk, smaller numbers of operatives may be more effective. The more permissive the environment—that is, the easier it is for operatives to move around and carry out their tasks—the more people may be involved without jeopardizing an operation.

- **Manpower:** Some groups make deliberate decisions to limit the cell size for reasons mentioned above; others simply don't have enough manpower and are forced to work with the few people they have.

- **Money:** Limited resources may also limit the number of operatives carrying out a mission. Well-funded groups such as al-Qaeda, the IRA, and Hezbollah may be able to finance dozens of terrorists simultaneously.

How Cells and Leadership Communicate

Cells communicate with leadership and/or with each other via two methods: direct and indirect.

Direct communications offer surety that the message is received, and mistakes are minimized. They are also less secure, however, and can be compromised through arrest or infiltration by agents. The methods of direct communications are:

- **Face-to-face meetings with known people:** A dangerous but often necessary method of communications. Newer groups that are just beginning to establish communications, or groups whose loyalties can be assured by members, use face-to-face meetings as a way of definitively confirming a person's identity and the authenticity of the communications. If a police or government infiltrator is discovered, the group can hold, interrogate, and even eliminate the person. Groups without blood ties or extremely strong ideological ties are more susceptible to infiltration, defection, and arrest of members, which could compromise the entire organization.

- **Face-to-face meetings using anonymous names:** This method of communications involves face-to-face meetings between strangers, identified to each other only by code names or *noms de guerre*. Some groups, including al-Qaeda and the now defunct Abu Nidal Organization (ANO), use this system in training schools and during operations. Their members are identified only by code names such as *Abu Jihad* or *Abu Saif*, not their real names.

Indirect communications offer maximum security and protection from interception, but also increased opportunity for errors. Messages can be lost, misinterpreted, or broken if a member or system is destroyed or lost. The indirect method requires an elaborate "lost communications" procedure and follow-up security checks.

- **Cutout communications:** Use of cutouts is an age-old indirect communications and security technique that allows the leadership to deliver orders to an operative, securely. A cutout can be any break in the direct line of communications; such as a courier or trusted agent who assists communications between two people who may not know each other. New cell members receive orders from an unknown commander appointed above them. These orders are delivered to the operatives via various indirect methods. Often, messages are in code and may be concealed by embedding in books, newspapers, and other written documents. This system generally goes undetected, but terrorist operatives must follow orders from people whose legitimacy they cannot confirm. The main strength of a cutout system is the inability of operatives, if they are arrested, to identify senior group members. This minimizes the damage caused to the organization by the compromise of an individual or cell.

- **Cutout through electronic systems:** The same indirect communications principle described above is used, but electronic media serve as the channels of communications—such as secure Internet chat rooms, three-way telephone conversations, or the use of forwarded e-mail messages that are encrypted and relayed by hand on disk.

- **Mail drop:** Here the postal system or electronic mail delivery is used to send and receive communications. Regular post or delivery services can be used to deliver written mail, floppy disks, memory chips, or SIM cards, all of which may or may not be encrypted in order to send or receive orders. Authentication may be done by code words or passwords that are sent via separate secret communications.

- **Dead drop:** Information is left at a prearranged location known only to the group members. Terrorists using dead drops reflect a measure of training by an intelligence-trained agent. Agencies suspecting usage of dead drops should contact the appropriate FBI office to ensure that trained counterintelligence officers conduct countersurveillance.

Terrorist Command and Control Cells

Some groups may use a supervisory team of professional terrorists that operates and commands subordinate cells. Other groups go so far as to dispatch field leadership officers to check up on the status of the operation and provide the other cell leaders with mission support. Both are called command and control (C2) cells. The C2 cell generally contains two to three terrorists in the following roles:

- **The operative in charge (OIC)** serves as the overall mission commander as well as the tactical operations cell leader. May be near the target during the attack, or observe from a distance.
- **The assistant operative in charge (AOIC)** is a deputy helping the OIC execute the mission.
- **A driver/messenger** supports the OIC and AOIC in movement and communications with leaders and other cells.

Terrorist Intelligence Cells

The intelligence cell is the eyes and ears of the terrorist organization. It is extremely important because its members conduct target selection—they guide the decision as to who or what will be attacked, when an attack will be carried out, and the most effective means for doing so. Typically, INTEL cell members are the most experienced members of the organization. Once surveillance has been conducted and tactical decisions made, the cell creates a briefing package for both the senior and field terrorist leadership. When the decision to strike is made, it is then passed on to the tactical operations cell. The package describes the plans and feasibility of the attack to terrorist leadership and is usually delivered via courier.

The intelligence cell rarely participates in an attack because its members would risk being identified—especially if countersurveillance efforts picked up their repeated presence at a given location. Occasionally, they do participate; al-Qaeda used a combined cell in the bombing of the American embassy in Nairobi, Kenya, in which an intelligence cell member helped carry out the attack. His involvement later helped to identify the supporting terrorists and break up the rest of the cell. Intelligence cells generally employ the following participants:

Cell Leader

- An experienced terrorist.
- Highly trusted; "leads from the front."

- Actively participates in collecting information.
- Responsible for the security of the cell.
- Reports only to a designated superior or directly to the organization's leadership.

Surveillance Team

The surveillance team observes and reports on targets being considered for attack. Skilled groups use dedicated, highly trained people for this task.

- Combined groups may use logistics cell personnel or nonterrorist supporters for surveillance.
- May be a single individual.
- Unlikely to use handheld radios to communicate with other members when actively conducting surveillance. More likely to use cell phones or report verbally after surveillance is completed.
- Identifiable by position and behavior (see chapter 13: Terrorist Surveillance Techniques for details).
- Look for the "four sames": same type of people, in the same place, at the same time of day, doing the same activity.
- Look for behaviors that, at first glance, might appear normal, but may be out of context. For example, a couple picnicking near a lake next to a nuclear power plant may appear normal, but picnicking every day for a week or an absence of food makes this activity suspicious.

Photography Team

- Usually one or two people, male or female.
- Identifiable by behavior: people using still or video cameras, overtly or discreetly.
- Films subjects not typically photographed by tourists: embassies, building entrances and exits, security personnel, and so on.

Penetration Team

- This may be an intelligence cell or tactical operations cell member who has received the proper penetration information. For this reason, all penetration attempts need to be evaluated as the start of a real attack.
- Enters target area for surveillance purposes.
- Usually one or two people, male or female.
- No radio communications until the mission is complete (cell phone, hand signals, or other nonverbal methods may be used).

- May walk the attack pattern they intend to use (called a pre-attack walk-down).
- Will attempt to enter a facility using ruses, false IDs, or false stories.
- May try to use unusual entrances or exits; may be seen pacing or undertaking close observation of a facility.
- Will dress to look like facility staff, tourists, fishermen, hunters, runners, or the like.

Security/Driver

- Usually one person, male or female.
- Stands off to the side to watch the team's flank.

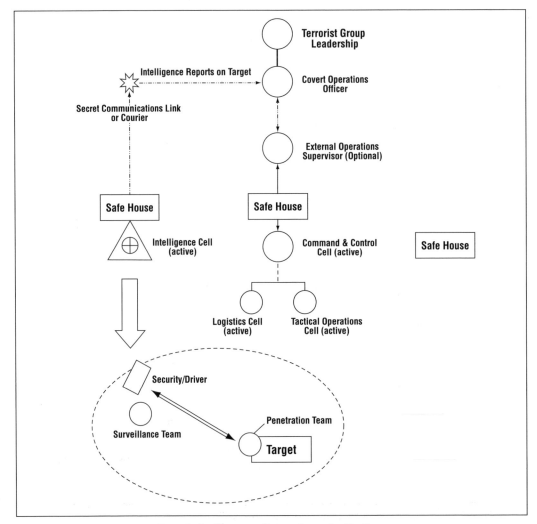

Terrorist intelligence cell reporting and collection.

- May double as an escape driver.
- May use predetermined signals for the team to break off surveillance.
- Identifiable by behavior: a single person sitting in a running vehicle; a vehicle that circles the area repeatedly; horn honking that brings other people back to a vehicle; a loitering person one block away from the objective.

Terrorist Tactical Operations Cells

- **Cell leader:** This person is usually the overall mission commander, as well as the head of the attack arm. The tactical operations cell leader personally leads attack operations.

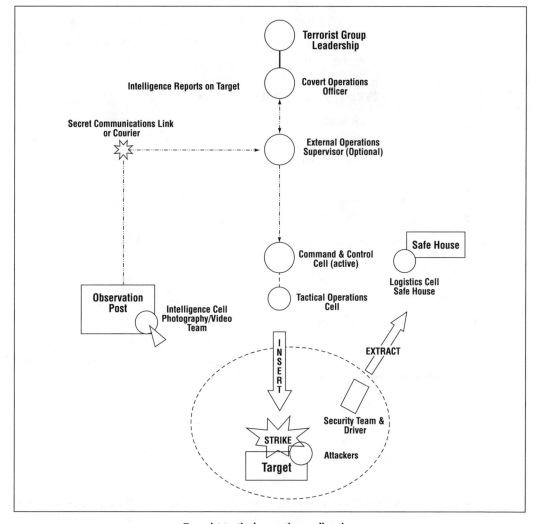

Terrorist tactical operations cell action.

- **Tactical operatives:** The number of operatives depends largely upon the mission at stake. The operatives' job is to carry out the actual attack according to plan. This might involve assassinating a target, dropping (leaving behind) bombs, carrying out a suicide mission, or any other type of attack.
- **Rear/flank security:** The cell may require a final security check of the target before the attack, covering routes of approach that police or security forces may use when they arrive. This team member may be armed, or just act as a lookout.
- **Insertion/extraction driver:** This may be the same driver from the logistics cell or a specially designated person with evasive driving skills. Teams that arrive by vehicle and expect to depart in the same vehicle designate an insertion/extraction driver. This driver may stand off from the operations area and act as a lookout; he or she may also be on the ready to provide more firepower or drop off weapons and supplies.

Terrorist Logistics Cells

- **Cell leader:** Supervises all cell members' duties and is responsible for acquiring the supplies necessary for an attack. May fulfill the duties of another cell member as well.
- **Supply officer:** Obtains needed weapons, equipment, and supplies through either legal or criminal methods.

> **Detecting a terrorist cell is an unambiguous sign that a decision has been made to prepare for or execute an attack.**

- **Driver:** Provides transportation for tactical operations and intelligence cells and moves the group's supplies and personnel.
- **Bomb master:** Conducts all phases of assembling bombs, with the exception of delivery. Rarely takes part in the attack unless the arming procedure is complex or the device is a "special" weapon such as a dirty radioactive bomb or nuclear fission bomb. However, lone wolf terrorists such as the Unabomber used couriers for delivery.
- **Arms handler:** Expert in acquiring and preparing weapons and explosives components.
- **Courier:** Receives and delivers written communications, passes voice messages, makes and receives money transfers; may also

locate supporters outside the organization when necessary for funding and additional assistance.

- **Emergency support teams:** These are not de facto members, but active supporters of the organization. They may include emergency medical support comprised of doctors, nurses, surgeons, and specialists who will provide services and treatment to injured terrorists. Another component may be emergency legal support, such as lawyers and other legal professionals who will represent members of the group if arrested and work toward their release from jail. Perhaps the most important group would be those who provide emergency financial support, or those who provide money and supplies in an emergency, with no questions asked.

9

TERRORIST STRATEGIES AND TARGET SELECTION

Terrorism is not random. Like any good military force or covert agency, terrorist groups require the use of strategy. The advantage of strategy is that terrorists have the ability of striking in a seemingly random manner. The terrorists almost always take the initiative. Law enforcement and security forces tend to respond to the terrorists' strategy. If you know the strategies, however, you can better predict terrorists' actions and take the initiative away from them.

Terrorist Strategies

Terrorists Prefer Simple Strategies

- Contrary to most beliefs, terrorists are successful because they stick to simple strategies. The September 11 attacks on the World Trade Center and Pentagon may appear to have been sophisticated, but in fact they were quite simple in planning and execution.
- Because terrorism is dramatic and widely publicized by the news media, simple acts are given greater scope and meaning than even the terrorist intends. The news media, psychologists, and law enforcement often make the mistake of seeking deeper goals in an operation than the group sets for itself. This makes the group appear very powerful—almost untouchable.
- The beauty of terrorism—as the terrorist sees it—is the apparent lack of logic. Fear arises when people wonder what could make a rational human being do such horrible things against innocent people. This is a form of psychological torture that enhances the terror in terrorism. The media sense this and amplify the fear exponentially.

> **The terrorist needs to get lucky just once. Antiterrorist forces must be lucky all the time.**

- Terrorist operations, because they are scripted, can be boiled down to a simple template. Most terrorists have a goal they feel that will be reached with enough attacks. Therefore the attacks, once started, usually won't stop until a particular goal is reached, the terrorists are destroyed by counterterrorism forces, or prosperity and social change make the terrorist group seem irrelevant.

Strategic Objectives

Strategic objectives are specific goals or stepping-stones in the organization's long-term mission. There are nine strategic goals for terrorist attacks. Note that many terrorist acts have multiple strategic objectives that may or may not all be fulfilled although the mission itself is successful. These objectives are:

1. Intimidation: Attacks are designed to transmit fear to the victims so they will bend to the will of the terrorist group in the future.

2. Destruction: Attacks are intended to destroy the social or political order and enemies through the actual destruction of commerce, property, or infrastructure.

3. Acquisition: Attacks designed to gain new recruits, money, or weapons could be accomplished through robbery, raids on armories, or impressing a sponsor with the boldness of the attack.

4. Extortion or demand: Attacks require the victim to make some concession, such as parting with money, or force another choice the victim does not wish to make.

5. Influence: Attacks are designed to gain power or set in motion acts that might change or influence policies and/or political decisions.

6. Overreaction: Attacks are designed to ensure that a government overreacts and oppresses its own people. Such overreaction may be projected through curtailment of certain basic freedoms of individuals, through the limiting of basic human rights, or through actions that may be seen as more horrific than those of the terrorist. The 2003 U.S. invasion of Iraq is considered by many experts an overreaction to the 9/11 attacks.

7. Revenge and reciprocity: Attacks are carried out to exact revenge upon an enemy for the death of a group member or damage to the group's integrity.

8. Satisfaction: The book *Who Becomes a Terrorist and Why* asserts that some terrorist leaders attack just for the satisfaction of harming their "enemy," and this is borne out by the fact that such groups (including al-Qaeda) never claim responsibility.

9. Survival: Attacks demonstrate that the terrorist group is still active. This strategy is often used in conjunction with acquisition, when sponsors need to be assured that the group is viable.

Tactical Objectives

The tactical objectives of the terrorist organization are the *street-level goals* of the actual terrorists conducting the attack. See chapter 15 for more details on the phases of a terrorist attack. Tactical goals fall into four general categories:

1. Action: Attacks show that the terrorists are capable of carrying out the operation as planned. Terrorists at the street level simply want to successfully execute a violent operation, propagate the news of the operation, and make demands for concessions or influence. Successful or unsuccessful, any attack that gets out the door of the safe house meets this goal.

2. Demonstration: The objective is to attract the attention of the victim and society through the news media or word of mouth and demonstrate the power of the terrorists. The group must publicize the event in such a way that the strategic goals are eventually met. Unfortunately, this goal is often met through the execution of hostages, indiscriminate bombings in crowded areas, or dramatic acts such as skyjackings. News media coverage is critical to this goal.

3. Demands: Often the terrorist group will make demands whether a terrorist act is successful or not.

4. Escape: Getting away alive is becoming less of an option for many terrorists as we witness the increased usage of suicide/martyrdom attacks. This is a tactical objective (the terrorists themselves may want to escape), not a strategic one, because the leadership may be concerned only with the terrorist act and not the life of the terrorist.

Misdirection and Deception Strategies

- **Misdirection** is the feint strategy of leading authorities to believe that the terrorist attack will occur in one spot, and then striking in another. For example, a terrorist group could explode a small bomb in one place while the actual attack will occur elsewhere after law enforcement has responded to the first explosion. Once security has been lessened in one place, the attack occurs in a weak sector. The German Red Army Faction did this once by placing a series of hoax bombing calls to the police so they could conduct an abduction in another area devoid of police. The 1994 al-Qaeda-planned Project Bojinka included an elaborate misdirection by planning the assassination of the pope as twelve U.S. airliners were blown up over the Pacific Ocean.

- **Deception** is the strategy of masking the true intent of the approach or execution of an attack. The Trojan Horse is a good example of a deception strategy. The M-19 guerrillas of Colombia seized a diplomatic reception and all of the attendees in February, 1980, by posing as a soccer team in a field across the street prior to the attack. Two terrorists infiltrated the party as guests. In 1996, Tupac Amaru of Peru used deception in a surprisingly similar operation by infiltrating a catering company and working as the wait staff for a high-level diplomatic reception. Members took and held more than four hundred hostages for three months.

- **False Flag** is a strategic misdirection technique. It is usually used by Class-I terrorist groups (government intelligence agencies) but can be used by any organization. These operations come in two types: false flag attacks or false flag organizations.

- A *False Flag Attack* is intended to make the law enforcement or intelligence agencies of one nation believe that a different terrorist group or country has conducted an attack. In law enforcement this may be called framing a suspect. These strategies deliberately "frame" an unsuspecting group by planting unambiguous evidence of terrorist activity. Evidence is usually in the form of plans, explosive devices, weapons, intelligence, literature, insignia, uniforms, and even dead bodies of actual terrorists who were captured and killed for just this purpose. For example, the "Lavon Affair" in 1954 was an Israeli intelligence false flag operation that bombed American and British cultural targets throughout Egypt in an effort to discredit President Gamal Abdul Nasser.

- A *False Flag Organization* is a terrorist group or intelligence agency that may recruit and/or handle real terrorist operatives under false pretexts in an effort to make them believe they are working for a particular terrorist group or agency (in other words, under a *false flag*).

Wave Strategies

Wave attacks employ large numbers of identical incidents stretched throughout a period of time. The most effective wave attacks over a wide area are calculated to project a random appearance while spreading law enforcement thin. Wave strategies, apart from bombing and hoax waves, require a relatively good support organization, freedom of movement, and financing.

- **Bombing waves** generally target heavily crowded spots. Sometimes bombing waves use secondary bombs designed to explode in the immediate aftermath, while the first explosion is being investigated. This makes law enforcement seem powerless and public areas seem fraught with unimaginable danger. Bombs can be of any type, including packages, suicide bombers, and car bombs. The Unabomber used a long-term variant of this strategy, with precisely targeted mail bombs sent over the course of years.

- **Abduction waves** generally target wealthy people in areas with poor and/or corruptible police protection by terrorists who have a well-organized infrastructure. Colombian, Brazilian, and Mexican terrorists and criminal organizations continue to conduct most terrorist abductions, though Asian and Middle Eastern groups are also skilled in this activity.

- **Skyjacking waves:** The September 11, 2001, attack was the first major skyjacking wave since the early 1970s. Rarely does a group have the capability to conduct multiple skyjackings. When a skyjacking occurs, it must be assumed that it is the first in a wave until evidence proves otherwise. September 11 has shown that appropriate defensive action needs to be taken to prepare for multiple attempts.

- **Crime waves:** Terrorists need finances. If they are domestic terrorists or if they operate from a foreign nation, they may resort to waves of crime to fund their planned operations. This is a dangerous strategy because it brings terrorists into close contact with law enforcement.

- **Hoax waves:** This is a common terrorist tactic. After a succesful attack on a target, the terrorist may send a wave of hoaxes to spread fear and make law enforcement react in multiple places. Hoaxes degrade response and disperse counterterror resources. After the September 2001 anthrax attack, several hundred hoaxes were performed by a wanted American anti-abortion terrorist against abortion and family planning clinics.

Strategy Execution Time Lines

Terrorists often plan attacks according to the time they have to develop and execute a plan. These time lines can be categorized as:

- **Hasty attack:** An attack developed and executed over a few hours or days is called a hasty attack. A hasty time line is not going to result in a large-scale, well-executed attack unless the target is so soft or the defenses so unreliable that any type of attack is possible at leisure. Supplies and surveillance may be rushed to the scene, making the attack highly detectable. Small-scale attacks such as arson, pistol assassination, firearms assaults, or hand grenade bombings fall into this category.

- **Normal attack:** An attack that is developed and executed over a period of weeks is a normal attack. This is generally the most common time line, because it allows adequate time for surveillance, for collection of supplies, or for bringing in specific teams to conduct the attack. Most conventional attacks by organized groups will be spaced out over a few weeks.

- **Deliberate attack:** An attack developed and executed over months or years is a deliberate attack. This time line is used for extremely secure targets or highly complex missions. Virtually any type of attack can be planned and slowly executed for the highest possibility of success.

Target Selection (T2—Terrorist Targeteering)

It is critical to understand the terrorists' target selection process. Being a process, it is observable and predictable. The target selection process depends upon the desires of the terrorist senior leadership, the feasibility of the entire operational plan as evaluated by the field leadership, and the street-level data collection and recommendations of the terrorist intelligence cell.

- The selection of a target based on strategic importance and physical characteristics is known in military parlance as targeteering. The people who evaluate and select the target are called targeteers. When used in relation to a terrorist group, it is referred to as Tee-Two (T2) or terrorist targeteering.

- It is the terrorist field leadership and intelligence cell that generally select the specific target, but anyone in the group can be designated a targeteer. The responsibility of T2 is generally given to an experienced tactical operations officer who handles intelligence cell functions.

- The senior leader will issue an attack ("go") order when a plan meets strategic goals of the group or if a specific target must be struck for symbolic or political purposes. The terrorist senior leadership could also demand that a target be struck but leave it to the field leadership and intelligence cell to figure out a way to make it happen regardless of results.

Terrorist acts are never really random. They are *seemingly* random. The role of the targeteer is to decide on a specific target based on diverse values to achieve maximum dramatic impact by using the *three basics of tactical action* (or the *Laws of Ambush*):

- **Speed:** The target must be struck quickly to enhance effect of fear.
- **Surprise:** The victim must be taken completely unawares. Nothing should transmit the impending operation except for only the vaguest of threats.
- **Violence of action:** The incident should strike terror and fear into the hearts of its victims through its absolute horrific violence.

The M.O.M. Target Selection Principle

The people engaged in mission specific planning will use the same simple criteria that most military targeteers use:

- **Motive:** Does the group have a reason for selecting this target? Al-Qaeda selected the Pentagon for its symbolism of revenge for the 1998 cruise missile attacks on the Zawar Kili terrorist training center and for being the heart of American military planning.
- **Opportunity:** Does the group have the opportunity to effect a strike against its enemies that is both meaningful and effective? The targeteer will make it a priority to create or wait for the appropriate time, circumstances, and environment to strike.
- **Means:** Does the group have the materials, manpower, secrecy, and support to carry out the mission? The T2 will discuss this with field leadership and logistics leaders to determine the level of support the mission will have.

General Target Categories

Terrorist targeteers generally divide potential target sets into two basic types: hard targets and soft targets.

Hard Targets

Hard targets are people, structures, or locations that are security conscious and difficult to attack successfully. These targets usually have:

- Heavy physical security.
- Active countersurveillance or security cameras.

Simplified M.O.M. Targeteering

1. Can we do it?

2. Do we have the opportunity to do it?

3. Do we have the personnel and equipment to do it?

4. "Go" decision: strike the target.

- Random routines and patterns of operations.
- Air cover.

Examples might include the White House, national military command centers, nuclear reactors, and military bases on high security alert.

Soft Targets

People, structures, or locations that usually have less security or are open to the public are considered soft targets. They generally have:

- No or poor physical security.
- Physical security that's made to look hard—but on inspection is actually weak.
- No or little countersurveillance or cameras.
- Set routines and patterns of operation.
- No ability to respond or counterassault.

Examples include individuals with poor security posture, masses of people, unguarded facilities, and difficult-to-guard structures and facilities.

Specific Target Categories

Specific target categories have their origins in the defense intelligence community but have been modified to fit into the terrorism intelligence system. The targets that terrorists choose—depending on the strategy they use—fall into some of the categories we use here.

Strategic value targets (STRAT-VT) are those that would have an impact on the long-term ability of a victim society to function in a crisis, or that represent mass infrastructure value:

- Executive leadership (presidents, cabinet members).
- Strategic reserves (fuel depots, fuel refineries, nuclear storage).
- National command centers and national security locations.
- Entire cities.

High-payoff targets (HPT) will, if damaged or destroyed, immediately contribute to ongoing strategic plans of the terrorist group or its economic allies:

- Critical energy targets.
- Stock exchanges and economic trading hubs.

High-value targets (HVT) will, if damaged or destroyed, contribute to the degradation of the victim society's ability to respond militarily or sustain itself economically:

- Military and federal law enforcement headquarters, or emergency command centers.
- Federal government offices and judicial centers.
- Critical commerce personalities.

Low-value targets (LVT) will, if damaged or destroyed, contribute to localized fear and temporary harassment of the victim society:

- Noncritical public or commercial infrastructure.
- Localized transportation.

Tactical-value targets (TAC-VT) will, if damaged or destroyed, degrade local law enforcement's ability to respond to threats in the immediate area of the attack:

- Individual or small numbers of military or police forces.
- Low-level military or civilian leadership.
- Low-level law enforcement supervisors.
- Police or military dispatch centers.
- Military bases or equipment.

Symbolic-value targets (SYM-TGT) will, if damaged or destroyed, heighten public fear of the terrorist group:

- Innocent people.
- National treasures or landmarks.
- Prominent public structures.
- National representatives or diplomats.

Ecological-value targets (ECO-TGT) will, if damaged or destroyed, damage the natural resources of a victim society:

- Large bodies of natural resources.
- Wide areas of agricultural resources and industries.

Remember

Final terrorist target selection will depend on:

- **Mission:** The *ultimate goals* the senior leadership wants to meet.

- **Opportunity:** The *feasibility* and possibility of a successful operation as reported by the field leadership.

- **Means:** The *capability* to covertly deploy the cells necessary to carry out the act.

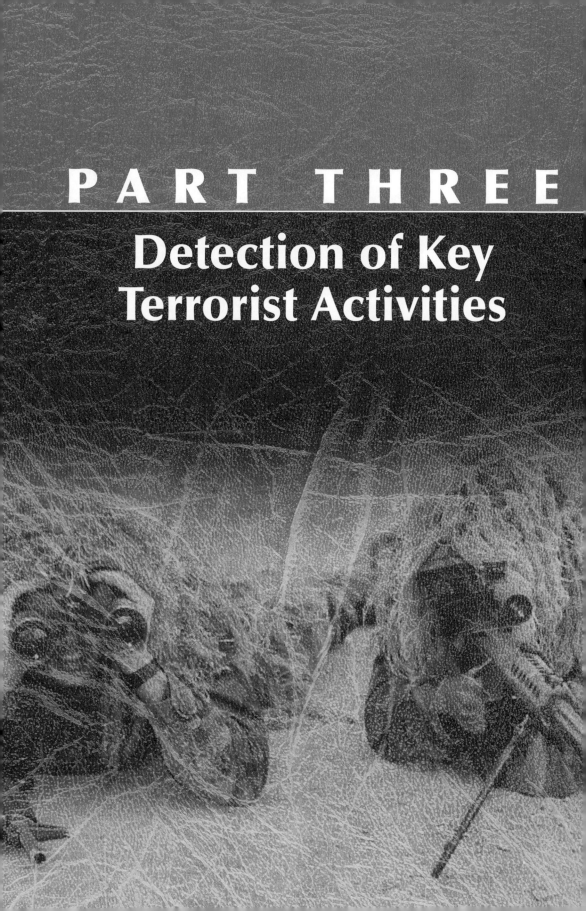

PART THREE

Detection of Key Terrorist Activities

10

TERRORIST PREPARATIONS FOR ATTACK: SAFE HOUSES, FINANCES, AND MOBILITY

T he safe house is one of the key nodes of terrorist operations. A detected and seized safe house may compromise cells, plans, and materials to be used in an attack. A safe house may be detected by informants, by suspicious neighbors, or through activities of surveillance teams. Virtually every terrorist group has a series of safe houses used as bomb factories, supply centers, or weapons armories. The location of a safe house gives an indication as to the kind of mission it is connected with.

Identifying Safe Houses

A safe house is a secure location where a terrorist can prepare for or recover from operations. A safe house could be used as a:

- Logistics center or armory.
- Planning center.
- Rest stop and rearming location.
- Bomb production factory.
- Indoctrination center.

Terrorist Operations Planning Center

A safe house may be used as a command and control center, a planning room, and a briefing room as well. If a safe house is a planning center, it may include the following:

- Intelligence cell planning board.
- Surveillance board with photos of targets.
- Watch assignment board.
- Map wall.
- Mock-up tabletop or sand models.
- Videotape for propaganda and rehearsal.

In 2000, for example, the New Zealand authorities arrested five Afghan refugees for planning a terrorist attack on Sydney's Lucas Heights nuclear power plant. Their safe house in Auckland, New Zealand, was a full command center with conference room, marked-up mapboards, planning materials, and a photo board of entries and exits at the nuclear plant.

In another case, a joint Pakistan ISI/CIA raid in February 2003, netted Khalid Sheik Mohammed, a senior al-Qaeda leader. His safe house included computers, plans, and address books of al-Qaeda associates.

Armory

A major use of the terrorist safe house is as a weapons armory. Armory raids could yield exact plans of attack and deprive the tactical operations cell's equipment for the mission. The type of attack can generally be determined through the weapons and equipment found in the safe house. For example, the German government carried out a series of counterterror raids in 1988 called Operation Autumn Leaves, discovering a terrorist supply center in Frankfurt full of Yugoslavian AK-47 rifles, grenades, fourteen blocks of dynamite, six sticks of TNT, and twelve pounds of Semtex plastic explosives. This raid also unearthed intelligence that led to further raids on other safe houses and a car, in which a Toshiba model 453 radio was found that turned out to be an altimeter-equipped bomb identical to the one that blew up Pan Am Flight 103 over Scotland.

In January 2002, Italian authorities nabbed al-Qaeda supply master Sami Ben Khemais "The Saber" and three others with firearms, explosives, chemicals for explosives, and cyanide. On April 5, 2002, in an Italian carabinieri predawn raid on Ben Khemais's apartment in Milan, Italian police found thirty cell phone cards, most of them cloned from stolen Italian cards, and almost forty training and propaganda videocassettes from Afghanistan and Chechnya. These items are typical of terrorist safe houses. This cell also attempted to transport hydrogen cyanide crystals in containers made to look like tomato cans.

Bomb Factory

ISRAELI DEFENSE FORCES

Palestinian Hamas terrorist detonators found in raid of safe house in Nablus.

The terrorist bomb factory, at first sight, is not an obvious facility unless you know what to look for. The major components of a bomb generally need to be handled separately. The bomb maker (aka the bomb master) may work in a clean space with lots of table room. The electronics or electrical activators, the chemical or explosive detonators/fuses, and the explosive materials must all be assembled in some order to create a proper explosive chain. Explosive ordnance disposal (EOD) bomb technicians can quickly distinguish an electronic repairman's or handyman's bench from a bomb master's working table.

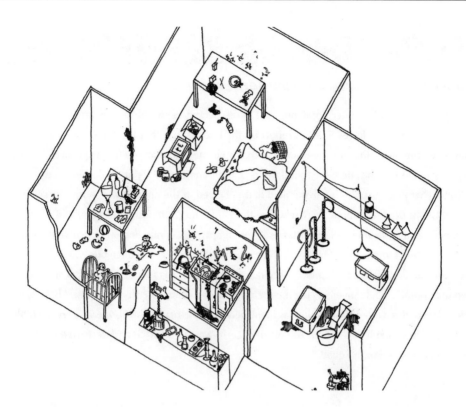

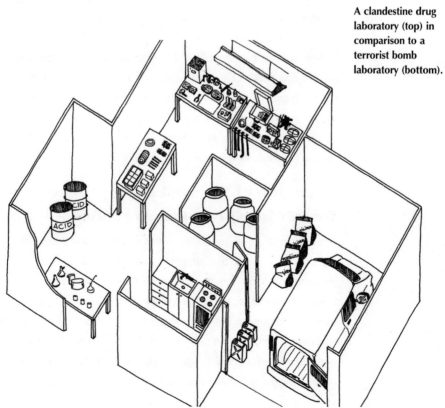

A clandestine drug laboratory (top) in comparison to a terrorist bomb laboratory (bottom).

CASE STUDY

Al-Quaeda Safe House In New Jersey

After the 1993 World Trade Center bombing, the FBI discovered the bomb factory on Pamrappo Avenue in Jersey City, New Jersey. The FBI report on the house states that the "house was full of acids and other chemicals that had been used at that apartment to manufacture explosives. Traces of nitro-glycerin and urea nitrate were found on the carpet and embedded in the ceiling. It appeared that a chemical reaction involving acid had occurred in the apartment." A nearby self-storage facility was used as a supply center where the FBI found "300 pounds of urea, 250 pounds of sulfuric acid, numerous one-gallon containers, both empty and containing nitric acid and sodium cyanide, two 50-foot lengths of hobby fuse, a blue plastic trash can, and a bilge pump. While examining the trash can and bilge pump, a white crystalline substance was found. A chemical analysis identified urea nitrate. While inventorying the materials in the storage center, six 2-quart bottles of brown liquid were discovered. The liquid was identified as home-made nitro-glycerin, very unstable in the condition in which it was found. The nitro-glycerin was transported and destroyed by the New Jersey State Police Bomb Squad."

However, bomb factories—like methamphetamine drug labs—are dangerous places to work in. On March 6, 1970, a Weather Underground bomb factory blew up in New York City's Greenwich Village. The explosion killed three people, including the female bomb maker. She was so close to the device that they could only identify her by the fingerprint on what remained of her fingertip. Two men also died in the explosion. It was later discovered via other documents in the house that they were building dynamite and nail bombs for an attack on Grand Central Station.

Detection of Terrorist Supply Chains
Terrorist Supply Is an Indicator of Future Activity

No matter what operation terrorists select, they will always need supplies. Detection of the supply chain can lead directly to cells and planned missions. Small amateur terrorist groups and individuals can buy commercial chemicals to make homemade explosives, or buy commercial weapons such as hunting rifles, pistols, or shotguns and make firebombs, propane tank mortars, and improvised chemical gases from pool supplies. Residences and lodges can be used as temporary laboratories, storage facilities, and safe houses.

Captured Safe-House Caches as Indicators of Mission			
	November-17 (Athens 2002)	PFLP-GC (Frankfurt 1988)	al-Qaeda (Rome 2001)
Pistols	10	1	X
Assault Rifles	1 (G-3)	6 (AK-47)	-
MP-5 SMG	3	-	-
PM-12 SMG	1	-	-
Uzi SMG	1	-	-
Shotguns	1	-	-
Silencers	3	-	-
Rifle grenades	-	8	-
Hand grenades	4	10	-
Mortar rounds	-	6	-
RPG-7 rounds	-	1	-
3.5" bazooka rounds	12	-	-
Ready-made Bombs	-	2	-
Detonators/caps	NA	81/11	-
Explosives (in lbs.)	-	32	-
Chemicals (in lbs.)	-	-	10 hydrogen cyanide
Propaganda/videos	Yes	Yes	Yes
Associated Tactic	Assassination & bombing	LIWA* & bombing	WMD**

*Light infantry weapons attack.

**Weapons of mass destruction.

As terrorist groups grow in sophistication, they require more extensive logistics support, financing, and administration. Some groups, such as the IRA, the PLO's al-Fatah, or the Kurdish Communist Workers Party, have an entire supply bureaucracy supporting them. No matter the size of operation, tracking suspicious legal and illegal supplies and supply sources can lead you directly to terrorist cells.

Terrorist organizations that have made a decision to strike a target or start the process of finding targets must supply the operatives tasked with the mission with finances and supplies. No matter the level of operation, or the number of people involved, terrorists will have various needs.

Safe Houses

- Rent.
- Food.
- Electricity.
- Cable television (for intelligence collection).
- Storage.

To activate and sustain this type of support, terrorists need an identity and banking services. You may be able to detect this type of support by finding discrepancies between who pays the rent or utilities and who actually lives in the safe house.

Intelligence Cells

- Binoculars.
- Night-vision equipment.
- Cameras.
- Video cameras.
- Vehicles for drop-off and pickup.
- Payment for informers or insiders.
- Computers.
- Darkroom with photo-processing chemicals.
- Digital systems printer for photo enhancement.

Tactical Operations Cells

- Rifles, pistols, and machine guns.
- Explosives and grenades.
- Chemicals.
- Weapons of mass destruction components.
- False identity documents.
- Vehicles.

Methods of Acquiring Supplies

Legally: Terrorists use themselves or supporters to acquire materials and supplies legally on the open market.

Illegally: Terrorists steal the equipment they need themselves or purchase it on the black market.

- **Amateur crime:** Terrorists may use low-level criminal methods such as robbery or theft as a way to acquire equipment, systems, and weapons or their components.
- **Professional crime:** Terrorists may use highly involved and developed criminal pathways, pipelines, and institutions to covertly acquire material. This includes international gun smuggling, illicit commercial transactions, and false bank transfers.

Detecting Terrorist Logistics Cells

Logistics cells have a higher probability of being detected because they often deal with low-level criminal underground and open-market purchasing. These cells involve more people in supply because they cannot afford to bring with them all resources needed for an operation. Smaller groups may task everyone available to work as one large logistics group instead of in a separate cell.

Detecting Terrorist Logistics Cell Activities

Terrorist logistics at a local level are generally legal, but underworld criminals are extensively used, too. It is this contact with the underworld and the strange pattern it creates of legal and criminal activity that make terrorist logistics cells detectable.

MINISTRY OF JUSTICE, GUARDIA CIVIL, GOVERNMENT OF SPAIN

Spanish police forces captured large quantities of materials and equipment from an al-Qaeda safe house.

Canvass criminal and public informants. Seek out informants and check for tips and reports that will yield terrorist attack pre-incident indicators such as:

Unusual illegal weapons purchases without any paperwork (or bribes given to forge paperwork) and by casual hands:

- Illegally converted machine guns or assault rifles (M-16, AK-47, FAL, Uzi, MP-5, and so forth).
- Semiautomatic assault rifles, shotguns, or pistols.
- High-capacity pistol magazines (fifteen to nineteen rounds).
- High-quality sniper rifles and scopes (Barrett .50 caliber, Leopold tactical scopes, and others).

- High-capacity rifle/MG magazines (Beta Mag and RPK 100 Round Drum, or the like).
- Automatic weapons conversion kits (sear pins/triggers).
- Unusually large quantities of military-grade ammunition (say, 7.62 x 39mm armor piercing).
- Unusual quantities or requests for specialty ammunition—armor piercing, incendiary tracer, beehive rounds, or frangible—by an overly enthusiastic person who seems unaware of what it is for, one who seems to know too much for the stated purpose, or any other person who just evokes suspicion.
- Unusual modifications to high-caliber sniper ammunitions, including questions concerning exploding tips and toxin-filled rounds (mercury, cyanide, other toxins).
- Specific U.S. or foreign military-grade explosives (C-4, RDX, Semtex, Comp-B, or the like).
- Quantities of commercial explosives (dynamite, TNT, nitroglycerine, et cetera).
- Rockets, grenades, or unusual foreign weapons (AKSU Krinkov SMG, PM-12 SMG, 40mm grenade launchers).
- High-volume-fire military weapons (GAU-7 mini gun, M-60E2 machine gun, M-249 squad automatic weapon).

Unusual purchase of legal products: There could be multiple purchases of these explosives precursors.

- Ammonium nitrate fertilizer (bomb component).
- High-octane racing fuel or bulk fuel oil for no apparent purpose.

Unusual payments: The suspect purchases guns, supplies, or components with:

- Large quantities of cash.
- Electronic purchase systems such as PayPal or Yahoo wallet.
- Electronic funds transfers from new checking accounts.
- Money orders.
- Multiple Western Union transfers (instead of one single transfer).
- Fake credit cards.
- Real credit cards that do not match the buyer.
- Trade in explosives or firearms.

C A S E   S T U D Y

Open Purchase of Materials

In 1995, Timothy McVeigh was the largest cash purchaser in the state of Kansas when he purchased fertilizer for his bomb at a feed store and refused to fill out the forms that would have given him discounts and saved him sales tax on a two-thousand-dollar purchase. The feed store owner thought it was unusual but didn't report it.

- Renting vehicles for cash, with minimal identification, a lack of concern about deposits or damage clauses, and seeming indifference to vehicle return dates. All of these may occasionally be just an indifferent person or a criminal attempt to steal a vehicle, but possible terrorist usage should be weighed with all other available information.

Buying firearms through newspaper classified personal sale ads or ammunition from private reloaders. Look for those who:

- Make smaller purchases over time to evade detection, or multiple purchases of identical merchandise from multiple sources to spread out the suspicion. Suspicious activity might include buying one hundred rounds of AK munitions from ten separate dealers over the course of a few days, for instance, or buying a hundred rounds from one or more dealers over the course of months until ten thousand rounds are accumulated.
- Set up a machine shop to mill out AKs and grenades.
- Buy detailed how-to books and military equipment at gun shows relating to chemical bomb formulas. A terrorist detained in 1993 had books such as these in his checked baggage when he was detained in New York City trying to enter the United States.

Firearms dealers need to watch out for and report under-the-table or unusual legal weapons purchasers whom they suspect to be terrorist armorers. One of the terrorists convicted in the 1993 World Trade Center bombing had a federal firearms license to buy guns as a dealer and supplied AK-47 rifles for mujahideen to train with in New Jersey. Additionally, there are chemicals—gases and large-volume medicines— that could, when combined or processed could have a terrorist purpose (see chapter 12).

Storage of Supplies

Supplies require storage. Storing supplies in a safe house may be obvious and hazardous. A secure location is needed to accommodate the many different ways terrorists hide and store their supplies. Many of the hiding methods used by criminals and intelligence agents are also used by terrorists in storing supplies.

Short-Term Storage

- **Concealment devices (CDs)** are deliberate modification of normal household items such as mattresses, desks, tables, or children's toys, to conceal money, documents, passports, or weapons.
- **Lockers:** Storage lockers, rental spaces, closets.
- **Barrels:** Plastic fifty-five-gallon drums and trash cans are commonly used for chemical and explosives storage.
- **Creating hidden storage space** via holes cut into walls, false ceilings, and other hidden empty spaces for hasty concealment of materials and weapons.

Long-Term Storage

- **Bunkers:** Secure terrorist safe houses may burrow into the ground and create a large weapons storage bunker. In May 1993, a terrorist weapons bunker exploded in a suburb of Managua, Nicaragua. It turned out to be a way station for many different terrorist groups supported by the Sandinista Liberation Front. Tons of explosives and hundreds of assault rifles, machine guns, RPG-7 rockets, and launchers were found. It also included hundreds of "real name" and false passports. Surprisingly, two of the valid identification documents were of Canadian citizens Christine Lamont and David Spencer, who were captured in Brazil in 1989 for the terrorist abduction of supermarket millionaire Albilio Diniz.
- **Underground caches:** Pits or holes dug into the ground designed to hold barrels, cases, or wrapped boxes of ammunitions and weapons. They are usually buried, and the location is marked in some way for later retrieval.

CASE STUDY

The Booby-Trapped Safe House of a Suspected Religious Extremist Terrorist

On the morning of August 23, 2002, an American doctor was arrested for plotting to attack and kill Muslim worshipers at St. Petersburg, Florida, mosques. Dr. Robert J. Goldstein, age thirty-seven, was arrested for possession of destructive devices and plans to attack civilian targets. The FBI later confirmed that Goldstein was planning a terrorist attack. He documented his plan to attack about fifty Islamic mosques throughout Florida and to destroy a Tampa Bay Islamic education center. "He had a list of what he wanted to target and the directions on how to get there," according to Pinellas County Sheriff's Detective Cal Dennie. Police were called to Goldstein's home before dawn Friday after his mother asked that they make a safety check. His wife, Kristi, also called police, saying her husband was acting unstable and was threatening to kill her.

Police negotiated for thirty minutes before he surrendered. Once they searched his home, sheriffs found a large cache of weapons: forty licensed semiautomatic and automatic assault rifles, sniper rifles, and thirty bombs, rockets, mines, and grenades. Included in the cache was at least one Barrett .50-caliber sniper rifle, two M-72 light anti-armor weapon (LAAW) rockets, two Claymore antipersonnel landmines, hand grenades, and a five-gallon gasoline bomb with a timer and a wire attached. The home was rigged with trip wires and surveillance cameras.

When authorities found the bombs, they evacuated residents in Goldstein's two-hundred-home complex. "If one of those bombs were to have gone off, that town house would have been destroyed," said Agent Carlos Baixauli with the Bureau of Alcohol, Tobacco and Firearms. "If the others exploded, we would have lost most of that townhouse complex."

Police also found detailed operational plans for the attacks, including documents. Goldstein had drafted an eleven-point "mission template" for attacking the St. Petersburg Islamic education center. He included details that covered everything from what uniform he would wear to techniques for getting rid of his fingerprints and preparing for hand-to-hand combat if necessary. For example, his bomb delivery plan included statements such as "Set timers for approximately 15-20 minutes to allow for enough time to get out of area, but to confirm explosions has [sic] been successful." The template reads, "OBJECTIVE: Kill all 'rags' at this Islamic Education Center—ZERO residual presence—maximum effect. . . . The amount of explosives should be ample to take down the building(s)."

Terrorist Transportation and Mobility

Transportation is a critical need of a terrorist group, offering speed to get to the target, insertion and extraction, or a firing platform. Terrorists, like criminals, prefer to use untraceable vehicles for their missions. Some may opt to rent vehicles. Vehicles are not limited to cars or trucks. Many groups are adept at using aircraft, boats, and movement on foot to carry out or support their operations.

Getaway cars: These vehicles are selected for the following factors, depending on the missions:

- **Size:** A small car may be desired for urban areas or car bombs. Large SUVs may be needed for off-road work.
- **Horsepower:** Terrorists will pick cars with the maximum available horsepower and may modify the engine to gain more than the car is rated.
- **Seating capacity:** A vehicle with substantial seating capacity may be needed for armed raids or missions that require more than four terrorists. In Latin America and Africa, terrorists use pickups as improvised personnel carriers during raids.
- **Intended purpose:** The mission will dictate the type of vehicle needed. An SUV may be needed as a large bomb. The PIRA uses vans as mobile sniper platforms for its large Barrett .50-caliber sniper rifles or as mortar carriers for its scuba tank mortar shells.
- **Availability:** How easily could a specific vehicle be stolen or hijacked? Can the vehicle be rented without being traced? These are the questions each group asks and plans for.
- **Armor:** Do terrorist leaders need to equip themselves to survive an ambush? For instance, the mission may entail having to go through a hailstorm of fire. In that case, terrorists may buy or steal a purpose-built bank armored car. Many Colombian and Mexican narco-traffickers and their terrorist groups use armored Land Rovers and Mercedes vehicles similar to those used by government officials.

Motorcycles: Terrorists may use motorcycles to conduct reconnaissance or as highly flexible assassination platforms. The FARC of Colombia and the Greek group November-17 use two-person motorcycle attack teams to assassinate victims.

- Colombians prefer high-speed drive-by attacks with a small submachine gun such as an Uzi.

- The Greek November-17 group used two riders with a .45-caliber pistol.
- The key to a motorcycle assassination profile may be that both riders wear full-face helmets. One victim in Greece saw the riders in his car's rearview mirror and knew what it was . . . in his experience, no other person in Greece rode a motorcycle with a helmet!

Recreational vehicles (RVs): Special attention should be paid to these vehicles. The RV is a self-contained operations platform. Many police agencies use them for command centers, laboratories, and negotiation centers. Terrorists could also use RVs for a number of purposes, including:

A Ryder van similar to that used by the first World Trade Center bombers in 1993.

- Mobile safe house.
- Mobile attack coordination and command center.
- Mobile armory and chemical-biological laboratory.
- Mobile hostage jail.

Vans, buses, and trucks: Special attention should be paid to these vehicles. The larger the vehicle the terrorist has, the greater the range of uses it could be put to. Panel vans, roll-back trucks, converted passenger buses, and commercial tractor-trailer trucks are perfect platforms for:

U.S. DEPARTMENT OF JUSTICE, FEDERAL BUREAU OF INVESTIGATION

Pay special attention to vans, RVs, and trucks.

- Large-scale explosive devices.
- Chemical weapons.
- Long-range mobile sniper platforms.
- Mortar carriers.
- Personnel carriers.

Identifying Indications of Terrorist Truck Bombs
Interagency OPSEC Support Staff Information Bulletin 02-002

28 March 2002

The Federal Bureau of Investigation recently conducted an analysis of truck bombings to determine whether any unique characteristics exist that might help identify, in advance, potential terrorist activity. The FBI's analysis determined that terrorist attempts might be pre-empted by remaining alert for a number of "indicators," which are outlined below. While the presence of an indicator does not in and of itself suggest terrorism as a motive, the FBI's analysis reflects that further examination of the particular circumstances of each case might be in order when one or more of the following indicators is present:

- Theft or purchase of chemicals, blasting caps, and/or fuses for explosives;

- Theft or purchase of respirators and chemical mixing devices;

- Rental of storage space for chemicals, hydrogen bottles, etc;

- Delivery of chemicals to storage facilities;

- Theft or purchase of trucks or vans with a minimum 2,000-pound capacity;

- Trucks or vans that have been modified to handle heavier loads;

- Chemical fires, toxic odors, or brightly colored stains in apartments, hotel rooms, or self-storage units;

- Small test explosions in rural or wooded areas;

- Hospital reports of missing hands or fingers or of chemical burns on hands or arms;

- Chemical burns or severed hands or fingers that have gone untreated;

- Physical surveillance of potential targets (surveillance may include videotaping, particularly focusing on access points);

- "Dry runs" of routes to identify any speed traps, road hazards, or bridges and overpasses with clearance levels too low to accommodate the truck;

- Purchase of, or illicit access to, facility blueprints.

Aviation and Flight Support

Some terrorist groups such as the PLO, FARC, and al-Qaeda have access to excellent air support, including small airplanes, executive jets, charter airplanes, and helicopters.

- **Private/personal aircraft:** Al-Qaeda had a T-39 Saberliner passenger jet to transport weapons and leadership from Pakistan to Sudan and Kenya. Furthermore, Bin Laden is alleged to have used executive jets supplied by private citizens of Saudi Arabia or the United Arab Emirates.
- **Specialized aircraft:** Crop dusters and helicopters are believed to have been sought by members of al-Qaeda for chemical or biological warfare dispersal systems. North Korean intelligence agencies use specialized small aircraft such as the An-2 Colt and Hughes MD-500 "Little Bird" helicopters to smuggle agents in and out of South Korea or for commandos to seize airfields.
- **Friendly airlines:** Terrorists often fly on airlines that are friendly to the philosophies of their leadership or accept their cash. Afghanistan's Ariana (before the Taliban was defeated), Iran Air, Libyan Arab Airlines, Syrian Airlines, and financially strapped sub-Saharan African airlines that are open to bribes can fly operatives to countries where it may be possible to transfer to a regular airline without suspicion being aroused.
- **Mercenary/corporate flight logistics:** Many contract airlines may actually be mercenary flight services. Russian, Yugoslavian, and Ukrainian flight companies will fly anyone almost anywhere for a price.

Maritime Transportation

In many parts of the world, terrorists use the ocean as an excellent mode of infiltration and supply. Support vessels include:

- **Motor vessels:** Commercial merchant vessels have been used by terrorist groups worldwide to transport weapons and operatives and for suicide attacks. Members of the LTTE routinely lure patrol boats alongside only to blow both ships up. Some merchant vessels act as mother ships to carry smuggled supplies to small boats on enemy shores. This is actually quite an effective way of moving heavy materials and manpower.
- **Small craft/skiffs/Zodiac raiding craft:** Inflatable rubber boats or high-speed boats can be used to shuttle supplies and people to and

Terrorists may use a variety of small craft to smuggle weapons and insert personnel. This boat was intercepted off of Lebanon carrying weapons and terrorist operatives.

Israeli naval forces intercept an illegal Iranian terrorist weapons shipment off Palestine aboard the merchant ship *Karine A.*

from planned missions. The PLO, FARC, and Abu Sayyaf Group use small boats for resupply, and for piracy or abduction.

- **Commercial maritime logistics:** Many legal transportation methods exist, including the lease or purchase of containers, sea-land cargo boxes, and even taking legal jobs on ships.

Computers, Communication, and Intelligence (C2I)

Modern terrorists are more than ever using computers, high-technology communications equipment, and various levels of communications security. With the sophistication of today's technology, a secure communications pathway can be set up virtually anywhere, even on a mobile handheld wireless device such as a BlackBerry. Terrorists employ computers to create target databases using information technology. Highway abductions increasingly involve terrorists who go online to check the database and determine the most lucrative abduction they could stage. The FARC group of Colombia actually has a victim database that includes earnings information on all millionaires in the country, so if they are encountered at an illegal roadblock, they can be immediately abducted. Other groups use computers to store target data, photos, and reports.

The computer is also a perfect communications device. Many groups such as the al-Qaeda–backed Islamic Army of Aden-Abiyan use computers as a primary communications system via e-mail and chat rooms. Al-Qaeda also has a policy of using floppy disks to deliver reports by hand for follow-on transmission from insecure locations, such as Internet cafés and friends' homes.

Secret Communications

Terrorists need secure communications systems. Ciphers and codes have been used for centuries to secure messages and letters. To paraphrase cryptographer Simon Singh in *The Code Book,* lives hang on the strength of ciphers.

Terrorists assume that their manual electronic communications are often intercepted. For them, the communications pathway only needs to be open as long as the operation isn't detected before the mission is completed. They need a buffer of time in which secret encoded communications should be undetected, and thus need codes strong enough to hold off being broken until the last possible moment. The techniques that terrorists have used to communicate secretly include:

Laptop computers and modems belonging to the Islamic Army of Aden Abiyan terrorist cells made up of Moslem British citizens.

Written codes and ciphers: Older groups that have been trained in tradecraft by the Soviet Union or a foreign intelligence agency may still use written or document-based code and cipher systems.

Internet encryption: Commercial programs that encode e-mail messages offer a highly sophisticated way to ensure the security of their communications using software programs such as Pretty Good Privacy (PGP) or weaving messages inside digital photos using Steganography.

Secure voice communications: This is a way of securing voice communications made on handheld radios, satellite telephones, and regular telephones. Digital encryption and other voice-masking security modules that attach to communications equipment can be purchased in the open market. Though not secure against agencies with the right tools, they can render some intercepts incomprehensible for the short term. See the next paragraph for handheld communications that may use these systems.

Voice Communications Systems

Telephones may be a moderately secure way for terrorists to communicate. The nationwide boom in telephone and proprietary cellular systems such as Nextel, T-Mobile, Verizon, and Sprint makes random efforts to collect information difficult. U. S. law enforcement wiretaps involve many legal hurdles, though that changed with the 2001 USA Patriot Act. Throwaway global phone cards are found everywhere.

AUTHOR PHOTO

This photo of a diplomatic protective officer trainee was sent via the Internet with a message encoded in it using Steganography. The al-Qaeda organization is believed to have used this method to send secure messages and reports.

Timothy McVeigh—the man who bombed the Oklahoma City federal building, killing 168 people—communicated with his fellow conspirator Terry McNichols via public phone. After his arrest, the FBI conducted an impressive tracking study of each call placed publicly through McVeigh's phone card, which was purchased under a false name.

Satellite telephones give terrorists direct access to quick communications links with people on the other side of the world. Terrorists can easily purchase into systems such as INMARSAT, GlobalStar, and Iridium using Thrane & Thrane or Nera phone terminals, Motorola, Kyocera, or subscribe to the new Thuraya satellite mobile phone system (dedicated to the Middle East and Africa) for instant global communications.

VHF/UHF tactical handheld radio: Terrorists on the rampage may use secure radio systems, similar to police radios, to coordinate their attacks and movements. The terrorists involved in the takeover and hostage barricade at the Japanese embassy residence in Lima, Peru, openly wore handheld VHF/UHF radios. Commercial radios made by Yaesu, Motorola, and Marconi have been seen in terrorist hands.

Identification of Terrorist Financing

Terrorists use diverse methods to procure the capital necessary to finance their organizations and activities.

Cultural or ethnic support organizations: Legitimate organizations that support cultural or ethnic causes or goals of their people may, in some cases, provide financial support to other groups, pursuing the same goals, that are involved in terrorist activities. The IRA was supported financially by the Irish Northern Aid Organization (NORAID), based in the United States. NORAID has branches all over the country and is a main collections source of supporters' contributions. Until 1991, the U.S. government allowed funds to be collected by Arab groups to fund the Office of Jihad Services or Maktab al-Khadimat (MAK), in order to recruit fighters against Russia but many eventually joined al-Qaeda.

Legal investments can fund terrorist organizations and operations. In the early 1970s, the PLO started buying partnerships in airlines, as well as purchasing duty-free shops in airports, with financial backing from Libya and other Arab countries.

Protection rackets involve the collection of fees for security and protection services provided by a legitimate company with known ties to a terrorist organization. In Northern Ireland, both the Irish Republican Army and Ulster Defense Regiment (UDR) have created a number of apparently legitimate private security companies throughout the areas they control. These "security companies" offer legitimate services to all businesses in their area for a regular legitimate fee. They will exhibit the brutal nature of terrorism only when a potential client refuses the services offered.

Legal businesses may be used by terrorists. These are legally operated and owned firms whose income is used to fund terrorist organizations and activities. Usama bin Laden, for example, is using a network of retail shops selling honey, owned by him and other members of the al-Qaeda organization, to generate funds for terror missions. These stores are found throughout the Middle East, Pakistan, and especially Yemen. They provide a legitimate source of income for Bin Laden's terrorist network.

State support involves the intentional and direct financial support of terrorist organizations and activities by an established and recognized state government. For example, Colonel Muammar al-Qadaffi, dictator of Libya, is known to support extremist and terrorist organizations. He has used the government's wealth from the oil industry in Libya to support the IRA, PLO, PFLP, DFLP, and PFLP-GC to the tune of approximately a hundred million dollars a year.

Charitable organizations: Nongovernmental organizations can be established to funnel legitimate donations from supporters to fund terrorist organizations and activities without the explicit knowledge of the donors. The Afghan Support Committee (ASC) is a nongovernmental organization established by Usama bin Laden. The ASC claims that donations to the organization are given to widows and orphans, and then uses the donated money to fund al-Qaeda operations.

Collection of tributes: Payments made knowingly to a terrorist organization for protection, secrecy, or false service of some kind.

Kidnapping for ransom: Collection of money for the assured safe release of hostages. The FARC of Colombia is believed to have made over two hundred million dollars in ransom from the release of abducted Colombian citizens.

Extortion or blackmail involves the collection of money for the assurance of nondisclosure of some damaging information or material. This includes, for instance, the extortion of Sri Lankan expatriates by the LTTE in the U.S., Canada, and Britain for funds to "protect" loved ones back home.

Smuggling: Surreptitious transportation or smuggling of goods to sell for cash often supplies terrorists. To generate income for Hezbollah, cigarettes were smuggled from North Carolina into Michigan for resale at a higher price without Michigan's higher cigarette taxes being paid. The profits were sent to Lebanon and financed attacks on Israel.

Illegal banking activities: The direct involvement and assistance, by a financial institution, in the financial operations of a known terrorist organization. In 1985, the CIA and British Intelligence (MI6) linked the Bank of Credit and Commerce International (BCCI) to the funding of terrorism. Usama bin Laden had accounts with BCCI when it was shut down in 1991.

Fraud: A scheme that involves the deceptive collection of some kind of benefit, such as money. Manufacturers' coupons generate eight billion dollars annually—inserts from recyclers, newspaper distributors, and small newsstands are purchased in bulk to collect the unused coupons. The coupons are then clipped, sorted, and shipped for reimbursement. Funds are then smuggled out of the United States and used to fund terrorist activities.

Drug trafficking: The illegal production and transportation of drugs for profit which are channeled into terrorist operations.

Narco-trafficking protection: The collection of money, usually a set percentage of profits, for the assured security and protection of cultivators and smugglers of drugs. FARC provides security and protection for the coca farmers in Colombia for a fee of 10 percent of the profits. In 1986, this alone provided the FARC with almost $3.38 million each month.

Illegal taxation: The collection of a percentage of citizens' incomes in areas under the control of a terrorist organization.

Government subsidy fraud: The fraudulent collection of government-funded cash subsidies for the purposes of procuring money for the funding of terrorist organizations and activities. In Ireland, for example, Thomas "Slab" Murphy generated more than three million dollars each year for the IRA by using various forms of subsidy fraud. Murphy collected subsidies by exporting goods, mostly pigs, cattle, and grain, from southern Ireland into Northern Ireland. A subsidy was offered to exporters to counteract the discrepancy in taxes. The goods were then smuggled back across the border into southern Ireland, where they could once again be exported north. Using a "straw buyer" in the process, it was continued over and over again with the same goods. The money was channeled into terrorist activities.

Private donations: The contribution of money to a known terrorist leader or organization with the full knowledge that the money will be used to fund the terrorist organization and its activities. Usama bin Laden is thought to have used a great portion of his own personal fortune to directly fund al-Qaeda's terrorist activities.

Document forgery: The creation of fraudulent documents with intent of selling them for a profit such as false identification papers and Social Security cards. This is a classic method of raising funds.

Counterfeiting: The creation of false currency with the intention of recirculation. It is believed the Iranian-backed Lebanese terrorist group Hezbollah produced and distributed hundreds of millions of high-quality U.S. hundred-dollar bills and used them for black-market purchases. The quality of these forgeries prompted an entire change of U.S. paper currency.

TERRORIST TOOLS: CONVENTIONAL WEAPONS IDENTIFICATION

Terrorist Weapons Sources

Terrorists acquire weapons in a variety of ways. Attention should be paid to how terrorist suspects get their weapons and equipment—this is a precise indicator of their missions and present and future supply sources.

Manufactured weapons are purpose-built weapons by gun manufacturers and could be acquired in three ways:

- **Open market:** The weapons are purchased legally at gun stores, gun shows, through gun dealers, through newspaper advertisements, or on the Internet.
- **Black market:** The weapons are purchased illegally through disreputable gun dealers or people with access to the weapons. For example, on June 17, 2000, the FBI set up and arrested twenty-four foreign-born men in Florida who attempted to purchase two hundred FIM-92A Stinger missiles, night-vision observation

AK-47 rifles and explosives line the deck of the terrorist logistics ship *Karine A* destined for Palestinian terrorists.

devices, Beretta machine pistols, M-203 grenade launchers, M-72 LAAW anti-tank rockets, and anti-tank guided missiles. They also tried to launder $2.2 million acquired from illicit sales. The purchasers appeared to represent a foreign government, but it could easily have been a terrorist group. To show how serious they were in their task, the subsequently arrested suspects were willing to pay up to $150,000 per Stinger missile.

- **Theft:** Armed raids on government, military, National Guard, or police armories. Weapons may also be lifted off dead bodies of policemen and solders killed in raids or at remote police posts. This technique is the mainstay of terrorist guerrilla (Class IV) groups in countries with civil wars such as Colombia, Nepal, and Peru.

- **Homemade or improvised weapons:** Amateur terrorists, criminals, paramilitaries, and guerrillas in some parts of the world become adept at fashioning homemade weapons that are effective until they can acquire factory-made weapons. The most common weapons are bombs and shotguns.

Manual Weapons: Knives, Clubs, and Garrotes

Some amateur terrorist groups in the remote third world still use bladed weapons to attack their enemies. Guerrilla terrorists from countries such

Al-Qaeda explosives cache.

as Indonesia, the Philippines, Burundi, Rwanda, and the Democratic Republic of Congo routinely use machetes and improvised knives to carry out assassinations and hostage executions. In 1970, for example, the ultra-radical Japanese Red Army performed its first act of terrorism by hijacking an airliner to North Korea, having first stormed the airport with samurai swords. In 2001, al-Qaeda hijacked four airliners with razor-bladed box cutters and knives less than three inches long. In March 1977, the African American Hanafi Muslim group laid siege to the Washington, D.C., B'nai B'rith society building with members brandishing samurai swords, threatening to behead the hostages they took. In 1996, the Free Papuan Movement had time to kill two Western hostages with a machete before elite Indonesian commandos rescued the remainder.

Law enforcement officers should be aware that knives, machetes, or any sharp-edged instrument in the hands of a skilled third-world terrorist or an American, especially former felons (handcuffed knifings are routinely taught and practiced by inmates), is a deadly situation to contend with. The advantages of these weapons are that they are compact, deadly, freely available, and easy to manufacture.

Explosives and Bomb Components

Explosives are the single most common weapon in a terrorist arsenal. Bombings generally account for more than 75 percent of terrorist acts. Explosives that are factory produced include hand grenades, C-4 plastic explosives, and landmines; they can also be homemade through chemical formulas or improvised household products. Bombs come in various shapes and sizes. The entire subject of bombing is too extensive to document in this book, but the following is a representative summary of bomb types and tactics.

Factory-Produced Bombs

Explosive blocks are purpose-built blocks of plastic explosives or self-contained explosive material used in military or commercial applications.

Mortar bombs are plastic or metal-cased bombs aimed in the direction of a target and ballistically lofted through the air to explode upon contact. They require a catapult or tube launcher, which can be made or purchased (see page 135).

Aerial bombs: In some countries, military aerial bombs are found in war zones, or they could be stolen from an armory. These can be modified to be used as a land explosive, such as by a roadside or in a building, or emptied of their explosive filler to create smaller bombs.

Terrorist bombs usually contain metal fillers designed to kill or injure innocent people. This shrapnel came from the victims of a suicide bombing in Israel.

Hand grenades are small hand-tossed bombs that send small particles of shrapnel out over a small distance to kill or maim.

Landmines are bombs that are laid on or in the ground, and are generally stepped on or detonated when a victim comes by. Military land mines can also be taken apart as explosive filler for improvised bombs or mines.

Homemade or Improvised Bombs

Improvised bombs are referred to as IEDs or improvised explosive devices. They can be made with explosive fillers and simple containers, which can be concealed in many ways.

ISRAELI DEFENSE FORCES

U.S. M-67 grenade.

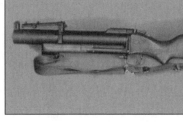

M-79 40 mm grenade launcher
(ASG, IJO, FARC, ELN).

Iranian grenade.

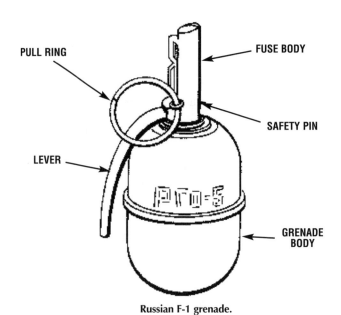

Russian F-1 grenade.

M-203 40mm grenade launcher
mounted under M-4 carbine used by
the PLO, Hamas, PIJO, IJO, ASG.

Sample of Known Hand Grenades Used by Terrorists

Weapon	Country	Usage	Known Groups	Region
RGD hand grenade	RU	Common	Various	All regions
F-1 hand grenade	RU	Common	Various	All regions
RGO hand grenade	RU	Common	Various	All regions
RGN hand grenade	RU	Common	Various	All regions
M-67 hand grenade	USA	Common	Various	All regions
L2A2 hand grenade	UK	Common	Various	Europe, Asia

Booby-Trapped Devices

- Telephones/cell phones.
- Radios.
- Banners or posters.
- Flashlights.
- Books.
- Toys (stuffed animals, radio-controlled cars).
- Liquor bottles.
- Fountain pens.
- Canteens or bottles.
- Candy boxes.
- Food cans.
- Bicycles.
- Letters.
- Saddle bags.

Improvised Explosive Devices

- Pipe bomb.
- Nail bomb or grenade.
- Coke bottle bomb.
- Directional (shaped) charges.

CASE STUDIES

In-Flight Bombing

The bomb placed aboard UTA Flight 77 from Brazzaville,
Congo, in 1989, which blew up over the Sahara Desert,
was made of a Samsonite attaché case with a lining filled with
layers of PETN explosive. The explosive weighed 5.3 to 11
ounces. The timer and detonator of the bomb were combined
in a quartz wristwatch set to go off when the boarded flight was
at an altitude of thirty to thirty-three thousand feet. It was
believed to have been placed by a Libyan intelligence operative.

A Libyan terrorist
planted a bomb that
blew up UTA flight 772
while flying over the
Sahara desert from
Brazzaville, Congo, to
Paris. The bomber may
have departed the plane
after a stop in Chad.

Vehicle Bombing

In the 1993 World Trade Center bombing, terrorists packed a Ryder Rental Agency
one-ton Ford F350 Econoline van with twelve to fifteen hundred pounds of homemade
urea nitrate explosive and three containers of compressed hydrogen gas.

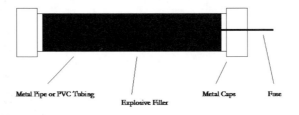

Metal Pipe or PVC Tubing   Explosive Filler   Metal Caps   Fuse

Pipe bomb.

Improvised explosive device,
Sandy Springs professional building.

Improvised explosive device,
1996 Olympic Park bombing.

Handguns: Pistols and Revolvers

High-capacity (up to twenty bullets) semiautomatic pistols and six-shot revolvers are handguns. They are concealable personal weapons designed to kill at point-blank range. Handguns can even be constructed for concealment in innocuous items such as ink pens, lighters, folding knives, or umbrellas. Terrorists use semiautomatic pistols and revolvers for assassinations at ranges from one to five feet. As with all other weapons, terrorists can acquire them through purchase or theft as production-made items. Production weapons are sold worldwide, and very high-quality handguns can end up in very austere regions.

AUTHOR PHOTO

Sample of Known Handguns Used by Terrorists

Weapon	Shots	Country	Usage	Known Groups	Region
Glock 17	17	AU	Occasional	Various, Libyan intel	All regions
Colt M-1911	8	USA	Common	Abu Sayyaf Group, November-17	Asia, Europe, L. America, USA
Browning High Power	13	BEL	Common	Various	Europe, Asia, Middle East, Africa
MAB PA-15	15	FR	Occasional	Dev Sol	Middle East, Europe, Africa
HK-P7	8	GER	Rare	Red Army Faction	Europe

Submachine Guns and Machine Pistols

Next to the AK-47 assault rifle, the terrorist weapon of choice is the submachine gun (SMG), due to its extremely high rate of fire and compactness. Terrorists prefer using this weapon in urban areas, where they

need to conceal a weapon when infiltrating but also need massive firepower on a target. There are many types of high-quality, reliable manufactured SMGs. Most SMGs are chambered in 9mm, though other calibers such as .40 (10mm) and .45 are used widely, too, in the United States and Europe.

M-4 Carbine rifle.

Automatic Assault Rifles (Long Rifles)

The modern automatic assault rifle is the first choice for terrorists. Terrorists use weapons from government and military stockpiles such as the American-made M-16 rifle or its civilian counterpart, the AR-15.

- Terrorists and criminals prefer the assault rifle for its notoriety and volume of fire.
- Guerrillas use them because they are generally the exact weapons they have trained with in the military.
- A professional terrorist selects the assault rifle for the same reasons above but will factor in the good use of range, knockdown power of the bullet, and its ability to penetrate glass, steel, and people.
- Older infantry rifles such as the British Lee Enfield, the American M-1 Garand, and Russian SKS and Mosin/Nagant exist in the stockpiles of smaller, more regional or amateur terrorist groups.

Sniper Rifles

Sniper rifles are high-powered weapons designed to kill individuals at great distance. Often a trained sniper can shoot fifteen hundred yards or more. This rifle is a powerful terrorist tool that allows the shooter to kill with near invisibility. Sniper threats are extremely difficult to detect, because the sniper usually moves after the first shot. Law enforcement takes great pains to provide countersniper teams for defense of high-value targets. Two terrorist groups, the PIRA and al-Qaeda, have long-distance Barrett .50-caliber sniper rifles that can easily kill from more than a mile. In March 2003, Serbian Prime Minister Zoran Djindjic was assassinated by as many as three gunmen with high-powered sniper rifles.

U.S. DEPARTMENT OF DEFENSE

AK-47SU

U.S. DEPARTMENT OF DEFENSE

MP-5N SMG

U.S. DEPARTMENT OF DEFENSE

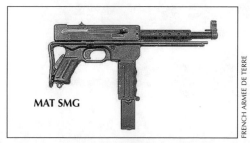

MAT SMG

FRENCH ARMÉE DE TERRE

UZI SMG

ISRAELI DEFENSE FORCES (IDF)

Sample of Known SMGs Used by Terrorists

Weapon	Shots per Clip	Maker	Usage	Known Groups	Region
Uzi	30	IS	Common	Various	All regions
MP-5	30	GE	Occasional	Various	All regions
M-12	30/40	IT	Occasional	Various	Europe, Middle East
Vz-61 Skorpion	20	CZ	Occasional	Various	Europe, Middle East
AKSU74 Krinkov	30	RU	Rare	UBL	Europe, Russia, Middle East
M1928 Thompson	20	USA	Rare	PIRA	Europe, L./N. America
MAC-10	30	USA	Occasional	PIRA	All regions
Colt SMG	32	USA	Occasional	PLO	Middle East, Europe
Carl Gustav 45	36	SW	Occasional	Various	Middle East, Asia, Africa
MAT49	32	FR	Occasional	Various	Middle East, Africa, Asia

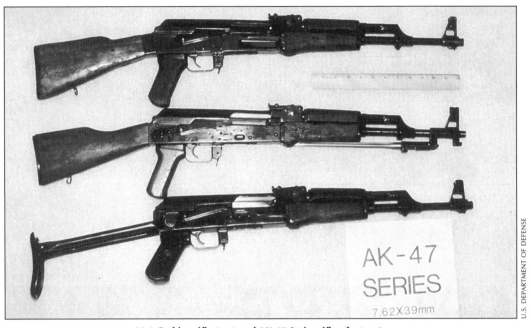

U.S. DEPARTMENT OF DEFENSE

M-4 Carbine rifle (top) and AK-47 Series rifles (bottom).

Sample of Known Assault Rifles Used by Terrorists

Weapon	Shots	Maker	Usage	Known Groups	Region
AK-47/74	30	RU	Very common	Virtually all	All regions
M-16/AR-15	30	USA	Common	Various	L. America, Middle East, Asia
G-3	20	GE	Common	Various	L. America, Middle East, Europe
Galil	35	IS	Occasional	FARC/ELN/ PLO	L. America, Middle East
SKS	20	RU	Very common	Virtually all	All regions
M-14	20	USA	Occasional	ASG	Philippines
M-4/CAR-15	30	USA	Occasional	PLO	L. America, Middle East
M-1	8	USA	Occasional	PLO/ASG/ FARC	L. America, Middle East, Asia

U.S. DEPARTMENT OF DEFENSE

Sample of Known Sniper Rifles Used by Terrorists

Weapon	Caliber	Maker	Usage	Known Groups	Region
M-82A1 Barrett	.50 caliber	USA	Occasional	PIRA, AQ	Europe, Central Asia
Ruger M-77	7.62mm	USA	Occasional	Various	Europe, L. America, USA
Dragunov	7.62mm	RU/YU	Common	Various	Middle East, Africa
Lee Enfield	7.62mm	UK	Common	Various	South Asia, Africa
Mosin/Nagant	7.62mm	RU	Common	Various	Russia, Asia, Middle East

Accuracy International sniper rifle.

ITALIAN MINISTRY OF THE INTERIOR, CARABINIERI

> ## Terrorist Sniper Attack Case Studies
>
> **Spain:** In July and August 1985, King Juan Carlos of Spain was stalked by an ETA terrorist sniper while on vacation in Mallorca. The sniper claimed to have had the king within shooting range three times but could not fire without being captured.
>
> **Palestine:** In February 2002, a skilled, probably professionally trained sniper from the Palestinian terrorist group Tanzim methodically killed ten soldiers and civilians at a checkpoint in the West Bank. The sniper held the army and police down for more than an hour and then escaped undetected.
>
> **Ireland:** Provisional Irish Republican Army terrorist snipers killed more than 268 British soldiers and civilians in Northern Ireland between 1970 and 1999. One incident used a Barrett M-82A1 .50-caliber sniper rifle that blew through a soldier's body armor, front and back, killing him. IRA snipers generally fire from a van, making it a mobile sniping platform.

U.S. DEPARTMENT OF DEFENSE

Shotguns

Shotguns are area-clearing weapons. They fire multiple (six to twenty or more) bulletlike projectiles and are effective at short distances. If configured to fire "slugs" (solid bolts of metal), they can penetrate heavy materials such as doors, walls, and metal. Shotguns are very common in the third world as hunting weapons, and many terrorists use them if automatic assault rifles are unavailable.

Amateur groups often use homemade or improvised shotguns and pistols. The homemade shotguns (see the photo) in Asia, Latin America, and sub-Saharan Africa are effective and could quickly be manufactured.

Sample of Known Shotguns Used by Terrorists

- SPAS-12.

- Mossburg Model 500 shotguns.
- Remington Model 800 shotguns.
- Russian Saiga shotguns.

Heavy or Light Machine Guns (Crew Served)

When terrorists need fierce and devastating heavy firepower, they select a crew-served machine gun. Both heavy (HMG) and light (LMG) machine guns are called "crew-served" weapons because they usually require two people to operate. Many are operable by one person and provide heavy firepower using relatively large bullets. Many terrorist groups use these weapons for light infantry weapons attacks (LIWA). HMGs are used for anti-aircraft and armored vehicle attacks. Most can belt-feed hundreds of rounds of ammunition. Others use boxes or magazines of ammunition.

M-60A3 light machine gun.

U.S. DEPARTMENT OF DEFENSE

Sample of Known Light Machine Guns Used by Terrorists

Weapon	Maker	Usage	Known Groups	Region
M-60 / M-60E3	USA	Common Rare	ASG PIRA	Philippines N. Ireland
BAR	USA	Rare	ASG/PLO	Philippines, Middle East
M-249	USA	Rare	-	Europe, N. America
PKM	RU	Very common	Various	Middle East, Asia, Africa, Russia, Central Asia
RPK/-74	RU	Very common	Various	Middle East, Asia, Africa, Russia, Central Asia
RPD	RU	Very common	Various	Middle East, Asia, Africa, Russia, Central Asia
BREN	UK	Occasional	Various	Indian subcontinent

M-2 .50 caliber
heavy machine gun.

U.S. DEPARTMENT OF DEFENSE

Russian RPD light machine gun.

U.S. DEPARTMENT OF DEFENSE

Sample of Known Heavy Machine Guns Used by Terrorists

Weapon	Maker	Cartridge	Usage	Known Groups	Region
M-2	USA	12.7mm/ .50 cal	Common Rare	ASG PIRA	Asia, Africa, Europe
DShK	RU	14.5mm	Very common	Various	Middle East, Asia, Africa, Russia, Central Asia

Anti-Tank Rockets and Guns

Rocket launchers, rocket-propelled grenade (RPG) launchers, and recoil-less rifles are used to provide a devastating amount of firepower

U.S. DEPARTMENT OF DEFENSE

for the terrorist. Fired from the shoulder, the single most common terrorist rocket is the Russian-made RPG-7. It is simple, yet fires a destructive rocket that can quickly be reloaded in a few seconds. Virtually every terrorist group outside North America seeks this weapon system. Both American M-72 light anti-armor

M-136 AT-4 anti-tank
rocket launcher with night
vision device.

weapon (LAAW) and RPG-7-type rockets have been used several times in high-value assassination attempts to defeat executive limousine armor.

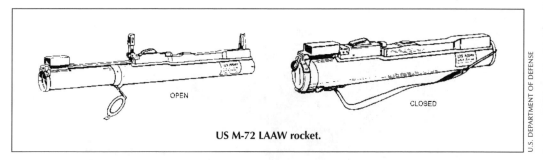

OPEN

CLOSED

US M-72 LAAW rocket.

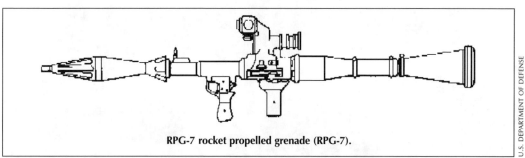

RPG-7 rocket propelled grenade (RPG-7).

Sample of Known Anti-Tank Rockets Used by Terrorists

Weapon	Maker	Usage	Known Groups	Region
RPG-7	RU	Very common	Various	All regions
RPG-16	RU	Common	Various	Russia, Middle East
M-72 LAAW	USA	Occasional	ASG, IJO, PIJ	Middle East, Asia
M-3 bazooka	USA	Occasional	N-17, FARC	All regions
RPO Shemel	RU	Rare	Chechen rebels	Russia

M-240 squad automatic weapon.

U.S. DEPARTMENT OF DEFENSE

INDIAN ARMY

Sample of Known Anti-Tank Gun/Recoil-less Rifles Used by Terrorists				
Weapon	**Maker**	**Usage**	**Known Groups**	**Region**
Carl Gustav RR	SW	Occasional	LTTE, LET	Middle East, Asia
SPG-9 RR	RU	Occasional	ASG, AQ, IJO	All regions

Mortars

Terrorists use mortars as standoff weapons launchers to project large bombs over distances of one to two miles. Mortars are the most common system terrorists use to bombard facilities and people from a distance, because they are difficult to locate without actually seeing the launch position. The Japanese Chukaku-ha and Anti-Imperial International Brigade (AIIB), PIRA, and other terrorist groups have converted vans and trucks into mobile concealed mortar launchers.

Production-Made Mortars

- 60mm mortar.
- 81mm mortar.

Homemade/Improvised Mortar Systems

These systems are made in a workshop and use various methods of projecting the explosive, including compressed gas, slingshots, and catapults. Some improvised examples include:

- **Propane gas bottles:** These improvised rounds have been used by the PIRA, the FARC of Colombia, and Nepal communist rebels as large-area explosives. Some propane gas tank mortar attacks have knocked down armored reinforced buildings.

- **Scuba tanks:** The PIRA used discarded scuba tanks launched from compressed air launchers hidden inside vans to bombard British army bases in Northern Ireland.

Top left, Colombian FARC terrorist standoff weapon launcher. Top right, FARC propane mortar shell. Bottom left, purpose-built U.S. 81mm mortar. Bottom right, Pakistani-backed Kashmiri terrorists used this 60mm mortar in operations against India.

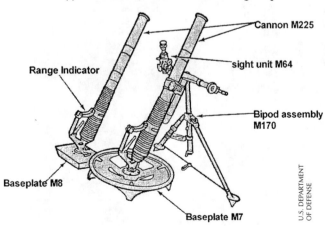

(a) M225 cannon, consists of the following components.

Range Indicator

Cannon M225

sight unit M64

Bipod assembly M170

Baseplate M8

Baseplate M7

Arab mujahideen in Afghanistan.

Surface-to-Air Missiles/Man Portable Air Defense Systems (SAM/MANPADs)

These missiles are designed to be carried on a person's shoulder and fired at aircraft passing within one to two miles. The missile has a chemically cooled seeker that hunts heat sources produced by jet engines. The warhead is actually very small and shoots down an airplane by damaging the engine and blowing holes in the fuel tank. The plane then crashes. Hundreds of civilian passengers and crew have been killed by MANPADs in Africa and Afghanistan in recent years.

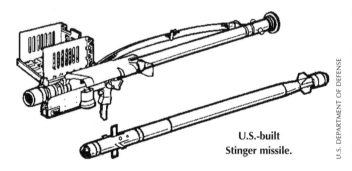

U.S.-built Stinger missile.

The Stinger missile and the SA-7 may have been responsible for killing hundreds of airline passengers and UN flight crews in Angola.

Known MANPAD Missiles Used by Terrorists

American-Made MANPAD Missiles

- FIM-43 REDEYE.
- FIM-92A STINGER.

Russian-Made MANPAD Missiles

- SA-7a/b (aka GRAIL, Strela-2M).
- SA-14 (aka GREMLIN, Strela-3).
- SA-16 (aka GIMLET, Igla-1).
- SA-18 (aka GROUSE, Igla M).

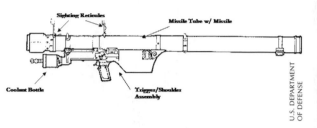

Other Foreign MANPAD Missiles

- Mistral (France).
- Blowpipe (UK).
- HN-5/5A/5B (Chinese-built SA-7 with combined Stinger and Igla technology).
- Anza (Lance) Mark 1/2 (Pakistani-built SA-7 with combined Stinger and Igla technology).

Top right, SA-7 Strela missile built by Russia. Right, Strela missile built by Russia was used by terrorists in Rome in 1973 in an attempt to shoot down an El Al airliner. Below, SA-18 Igla-2 missile built by Russia. It is the equivalent to the US Stinger.

12

NUCLEAR, BIOLOGICAL, AND CHEMICAL WEAPONS: EFFECTS AND ASSOCIATED EQUIPMENT IDENTIFICATION

Chemical and Biological Warfare (CBW) Associated Equipment

Gas Masks

Protective masks are a pre-incident indicator of preparation for WMD usage or a precaution against riot-control agents. A good indicator that some form of chemical agent is being prepared by a professional terrorist group is careful planning to ensure that all members have a mask within reach or at a centralized spot near chemical workbenches. A combination of masks, test equipment, and chemical precursors is a serious indication of a clandestine chemical or bioweapons laboratory. The most common gas masks available on the commercial market include:

- MSA Advantage 1000 commercial masks.
- M-17A1 gas mask.
- M40 gas mask.

U.S. DEPARTMENT OF DEFENSE

- MCU-2P gas mask.
- M9A1 (copies include the Swedish Skyddsmask-51, the Finnish m/61, and the Yugoslavian M-1).
- M-24A1 U.S. Army crew gas mask.
- M-25 U.S. armed forces gas mask.
- Israeli Simplex civilian-issue gas mask.
- East German Schutzmaske M10M gas mask.
- British S-10/SF-10 gas mask.
- Russian GASM or BN gas mask (Egyptian/Iraqi copies).

Protective Clothes, Chemical Decontamination, and Detection Kits

Suits or chemical decontamination kits, if open and accessible in a safe house, are a sure indication that chemical weapons are being stored or prepared somewhere nearby. The detection kits give an early alarm if some of the chemicals escape. Terrorist operatives who travel with bundled gas masks, chemical protective clothing, or skin decontamination kits are another indicator of possible imminent usage.

- Chemical, biological, radiation protective clothing.
- Chemical agent detection kit.
- Industrial splash aprons.
- Industrial or medical splash-guard face masks.
- Industrial rubber gloves.
- Medical rubber gloves.
- Toxic gas detectors, portable or fixed (such as Russian-made GSP-11 chemical agent detector/alarm, CHP-71 chemical analyzers).
- Wet chemical detection kits (M9/M256).
- Skin decontamination agent kit.

Testing and Development Equipment

Cryogenic ampoules, test tubes, or other containers—especially those designed for use with liquid nitrogen at low-temperature storage, or for rapid thawing of biological materials are the research, testing, and development equipment that give away a bioweapons lab. Other indicators include:

- Liquid nitrogen and containers.
- Grinding powder or milling machines.
- Freeze-drying system.
- Biological culture fermenting systems.
- Animal cages and/or animals—for testing biological agents.

- Baths or circulators—for a variety of liquid heating, cooling, and mixing purposes.
- Vacuum chambers—for use as controlled environment chamber and freeze drying.
- Petri dishes or other containers—especially those designed for storage and/or growth of bacteria and viruses.
- Incubator—to regulate and stimulate bacterial growth.
- Evaporation system—for toxicity testing and environmental analysis.
- Industrial microscopes.
- Funnels.
- Industrial ventilation hoods and underground bunker ventilation shafts.

Storage and Preservation Systems

- Refrigeration equipment.
- Cryogenic storage containers.
- Glass or Nalgene plastic beakers.
- Glass medical storage containers.
- Honda-style backup generators or other backup power source rigged solely to refrigeration and testing equipment.

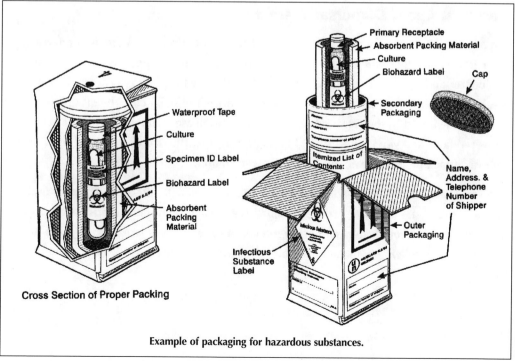

Example of packaging for hazardous substances.

CENTERS FOR DISEASE CONTROL (CDC)

Chemical or Biological Agent Dispersal Systems

Chemical and biological agents must be processed in order for them to be used as an effective weapon. The process, called weaponization, transforms the agents into either of two states: liquid or dry. The former is easy to prepare and offers good qualities of dispersal. Dry forms are difficult to create and require expensive equipment, but they tend to have better dispersive capabilities. Chemical or biological weapons are dispersed in two fashions:

1. Line-source distribution or dispersal systems distribute agents that are carried by the wind. Agents distributed this way are sensitive to weather changes and climate.

2. Point-source distribution systems release agents into small weaponized packages such as envelopes, bomblets, or exploding containers. Aum Shinrikyo's attack on the Tokyo subway used a point-source system in the form of small packages that, when punctured, released the nerve agent into the subway.

CASE STUDIES

Terrorist Agent Dispersal Systems

Japan: The Aum Shinrikyo cult trained a pilot to use a helicopter to distribute nerve gas over Tokyo and other cities. AUM was believed to have been in possession of a Russian helicopter and possibly two drone aircraft to be fitted with spraying systems. Shoko Asahara wanted to spray a nerve agent over an entire industrial city. The group also created and deployed in the Tokyo city subway three briefcases with side vents, battery-powered fans, and vinyl tubes to hold biological agents. This attack preceded the Tokyo subway attack by three days, but no agents were found.

United States: The al-Qaeda organization's Mohammed Atta questioned agricultural pilots in southern Florida regarding the spray system and flight characteristics of crop dusting aircraft. Crop dusters and other industrial spray systems would have given these terrorists an excellent chemical or biological distribution system.

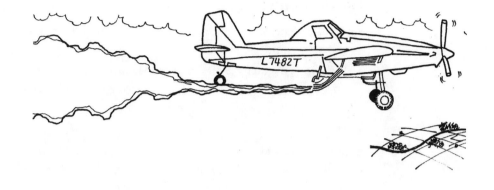

MARYSE BELIVEAU/AUTHOR

MARYSE BELIVEAU/AUTHOR

MARYSE BELIVEAU/AUTHOR

Examples of Improvised Chemical or Biological Agent Distribution Systems

- Aerosol spray cans opened up and resealed to insert CBW agents and sprayed by hand.
- Envelopes, including letters, Express Mail envelopes, and Fedex or UPS packages that have plastic liners or containers readied for insertion of agents.
- Handheld bug spraying tank.
- Vacuum-packed plastic bags with agents inside.
- Scuba tanks with a modified regulator replaced with a gas or oxygen demand valve to act as a rudimentary fogger.
- Modified water tubing and sprinkler systems.
- Industrial aerosol fogging system (in or on a vehicle or aircraft).
- Deceptive containers marked with some other inert contents or material.
- Induced industrial chemical accident to act as a weapon.

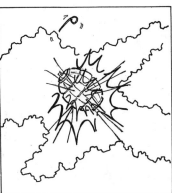
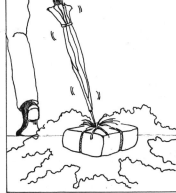

Why Chemical or Biological Warfare Agents for Terrorists?

This tongue-in-cheek but accurate list of why terrorist may use biological agents was compiled and disseminated by the U.S. Army Medical Research Institute of Infectious Diseases (USAMRIID) in its annual conference and telecast on "Biological Weapons in Terrorism." Although these were oriented to biological weapons, the comments relate to chemical weapons as well.

1. *"Available in stores everywhere":* Terrorists can acquire chemical and biological agents easily from public sources. Until recently, biological cultures could be ordered over the Internet.

2. *"Everyday low discount prices":* Unsophisticated CB weapons and equipment can be acquired for a small amount of money compared to the effort necessary for a nuclear weapon.

3. *"No roaming charges":* Small quantities of CBWs can create a mass effect over a broad area as well as mass destruction. However, many types of CBWs don't need to be spread over a broad area, but will spread themselves through contact transfer, airborne carry, or human infection.

4. *"Tastes great, less filling":* Most CBWs have little or no taste, order, or color.

5. *"Won't harm carpets":* Unlike explosive devices or nuclear weapons, CBWs affect people; nearby areas and surfaces can usually be decontaminated after use.

6. *"Works while you sleep":* CBWs don't need to stop working when people do. The persistence of CBWs is an attractive factor in their use as weapons. If terrorists want to punish an enemy, they can rest assured that the punishment won't stop immediately unless an effective antidote or containment is available.

7. *"Tested and effective":* Most advances and information on offensive CBW capability came from the military defense programs. These programs have been organized for more than a century, and the effects are well known.

8. *"What we don't know will kill us":* The first indicator of terrorist CBW attack may be the mass effect of the weapon starting to kill or incapacitate.

9. *"Four out of five doctors recommend":* The scientific community is in agreement that CBWs are highly effective terrorist tools.

10. *"Be the envy of your friends":* Although the capability exists for terrorist use of CBWs, the number of serious incidents have been small. According to the 2002 SRSI Corp. study of terrorist tactics, CBW development and usage is second only to nuclear weapons as the highest skills level attainable by terrorist groups.

CASE STUDIES

Terrorist Usage of Offensive Chemical Weapons

Iraq: In 1989, dictator Saddam Hussein made use of a particularly horrifying example of governmental terrorism by killing citizens within his own country by using weapons of mass destruction. He ordered chemical weapons containing mustard gas and the nerve agents Sarin, Tabun, and VX dropped from aircraft and helicopters on Kurdish people in the towns of Halabja, Khormal, Dojaileh, and their surrounding small villages, killing more than five thousand civilians.

Japan: The cult Aum Shinrikyo or "Aum Supreme Truth" made several terrorist attacks in Japan, the first of which was an assassination of a Japanese citizen using nerve agents. The attacks were ordered by cult leader Shoko Asahara (born Chuizo Matsumoto) in the belief that he would topple the government of Japan and establish a new global society led by his cult members. Asahara ordered the cult to develop Sarin gas in 1993. AUM then created a large nerve gas production complex located outside of Kamikuishiki, which became operational in March 1994. Additional advanced labs were founded in Naganohara and the group's Mount Aso camp. There is evidence that the group may have leased a sheep ranch in Australia and tested its nerve agents on the animals. Traces of Sarin and industrial pesticides were found to have been given to them. Asahara taught the philosophy that killing people who had committed "sins" was an act of "salvation." He came to apply this to all people living in the modern world, and was his justification for indiscriminate mass murder.

The first incident occurred in June 1994 in Matsumoto, Japan, when Sarin gas was released in the city during the night from an improvised truck spray system. This attack killed 7 people and injured 253. The most notorious attack was on the Tokyo subway system, where 12 people were killed and 5,510 people were injured. The group used a diluted solution of Sarin nerve agent (GB). The nerve agent was developed in-house by AUM members and dropped into the crowded Tokyo subway in an effort to divert attention away from the cult's activities. The bags of nerve agent were dropped into subway cars and then punctured with umbrellas to release the gas. More interestingly, AUM also produced small quantities of mustard gas, Tabun, Soman, hydrogen cyanide, and other chemical agents.

Offensive Chemical Weapons (CW)

The following are common chemicals that can be manufactured and weaponized. The U.S. Army *Field Manual 8-285* and the U.S. Army Medical Research Institute for Chemical Defense manual *Medical Management of Chemical Casualties* define *chemical agent* as "a chemical substance . . . intended for use in military operations to kill, seriously injure, or incapacitate humans (or animals) through its toxicological effects." Chemical agents are different from biological agents in that they are nonliving chemicals and not diseases such as bacteria, viruses, and fungi. Toxins are chemical compounds synthesized by living organisms and "occupy a netherworld between chemical and biological agents." Both manuals *exclude* the following from the list of offensive chemical warfare agents.

- Chemical herbicides (Agent Orange, Agent Blue, Agent White).
- Smoke and flame materials (fog, oil, petroleum oil smoke, diesel fuel, red phosphorous, white phosphorous, FM, FM and HC white smoke).
- Riot-control agents (CS, CN, CR, OCP pepper spray).

Nerve Agents

Nerve agents are colorless, odorless chemical weapons that "short-circuit" the central nervous system (CNS) within seconds to minutes of exposure. The most recent offensive usage was by Iraq, which used Tabun (GA) and Sarin (GB) in a military conflict against the Iranian army in the 1980s, killing and wounding tens of thousands. The first indications of use are the rapid onset of the below-listed symptoms or witnessing the actual application of the agent such as an exploding device or an innocuous spray. Without immediate treatment, these weapons kill within minutes. These agents may come in vapor or liquid form. Subjects exposed to nerve agents present the following four stages of symptoms:

1. Runny nose, tightening in the chest, constriction of pupils.
2. Difficulty in breathing, drooling, nausea, loss of control of bodily functions.
3. Twitching, jerking, coma.
4. Ultimately death due to suffocation from convulsive spasms.

Tabun (GA)

- Colorless to brown liquid.
- Colorless vapor with no odor when pure; fruity otherwise.
- Nonpersistent (dissipates in days).
- Absorbed primarily through the skin; inhalation is also dangerous.
- If a lethal dose is received, death occurs anywhere from immediately to twenty minutes later.
- Tabun is the easiest nerve agent to produce.

Sarin (GB)

- Colorless liquid.
- Colorless, odorless vapor.
- Nonpersistent (dissipates in hours to days).
- Very volatile liquid.
- Absorbed through inhalation and skin contact.
- Direct ingestion of a small quantity can kill in one minute.
- Was previously used in a terrorist attack.

Soman (GD)

- Colorless liquid.
- Colorless vapor that smells of rotting fruit or camphor when impure.
- Nonpersistent (dissipates in days).
- If absorbed through the skin, death occurs after fifteen minutes.
- If inhaled or absorbed through the eyes, death occurs in one to ten minutes.
- Some forms of nerve agent treatments are useless against Soman.

Lethal Agent (GF)

- Colorless to light brown.
- Can smell like peaches or shellac; musty or sweet.
- Absorbed through skin contact or inhalation.
- Nonpersistent.
- Death occurs within thirty minutes to eighteen hours.

Lethal Agent (VX)

- Colorless to amber liquid; looks similar to motor oil.
- No scent.
- Absorbed through skin contact or inhalation.
- Extremely persistent (dissipates in weeks to months).
- Much more powerful than "G" agents.

- Highly flammable under certain conditions.
- Death occurs within an hour or two. Effects are instantaneous if VX is gaseous and is inhaled.

Vesicants (Blister Agents)

Vesicants typically destroy exposed skin tissue.

Mustard

There are four types of mustard agents. The first three types are sulfur mustards; the fourth is nitrogen mustard. Mustard gases have been used since the introduction of sulfur mustard in the Battle of Ypres in World War I. Its use produced hundreds of thousands of casualties. Other instances of military usage include probable use by the Soviet Union, Italy, Britain, Spain, Egypt, and Japan. According to the United Nations, Iraq used sulfur mustard against the Iranian army and may have used it in a terrorist attack on the Kurds. The nitrogen mustards were developed in the 1930s in limited quantities for military purposes.

Subjects exposed to mustard exhibit delayed symptoms. Two to twenty-four hours may pass before there are any noticeable effects, but symptoms usually occur four to eight hours after exposure. Nitrogen mustards react quicker. Despite the delayed appearance of symptoms, tissue damage begins to occur immediately. HD and HN3 are the most dangerous due to chemical stability and vapor potential. The symptoms include:

- Erythema (a condition resembling sunburn).
- Skin irritation and blistering; conjunctivitis, corneal opacity, and eye damage; respiratory problems due to airway damage; gastrointestinal effects; and bone marrow stem cell suppression. Mustard is generally not lethal, though it could cause serious permanent damage, particularly to the eyes, which are the most vulnerable.

Sulfur Mustard (H)
- Oily liquid, light yellow to brown.
- Odor of garlic, onion, or mustard.
- Absorption through skin or inhalation.
- Persistent (days).

Distilled Mustard (HD)
- Absorption through skin or inhalation.
- Colorless to pale yellow liquid.

- Garlic or horseradishlike odor.
- Persistent (days).

Thickened Mustard (HT)

- Absorption through skin or inhalation.
- Mustard is thickened to contaminate equipment, terrain, aircraft, ships, and so forth to create a very persistent hazard.

Nitrogen Mustard (HN)

- Dark liquid.
- No odor, fruity odor, or musty/fishy odor, depending on type.
- Absorption through skin or inhalation.
- Faster acting than the sulfur mustards above.
- Absorption occurs through skin and inhalation. Skin contact is less of a danger.
- Persistent (days).

Lewisite (L)

- Colorless to brownish (liquid or solid).
- Odor varies, but may resemble geraniums.
- Generally considered less dangerous than mustards.
- Absorbed through contact and inhalation.
- Causes immediate pain to exposed areas (skin, eyes, lungs, et cetera), followed by erythema and blisters. Damage could occur to eyes, skin, and airways, similar to that from mustard.
- In addition to being a blister agent, it is also a toxic lung irritant and a systemic poison.
- In very high concentrations, Lewisite can kill in ten minutes.
- Nonpersistent (hours to days).

Phosgene Oxime (CX)

- White crystalline powder or colorless liquid.
- Sharp penetrating odor.
- Generally considered less dangerous than mustards.
- Absorption through skin contact or inhalation.
- Causes immediate burning and irritation, wheal-like skin lesions, eye and airway damage.
- Nonpersistent (hours).

Blood Agents (Cyanogens)

Hydrogen Cyanide (HCN, AC, Hydrocyanic Acid)
- Nonpersistent (minutes).
- Colorless liquid.
- Faint odor like peach kernels or bitter almonds.
- Highly volatile.
- Exposure through inhalation.
- Mild exposure: headache, nausea, vertigo, followed by complete recovery.
- Moderate exposure leads first to headache, nausea, vertigo, weakness in the legs; then to convulsions or possibly coma; the coma may result in central nervous system damage that could manifest itself as unalert reflexes, an ungainly gait, irrationality, and temporary or permanent nerve deafness.
- Serious exposure leads within a few seconds to a deepening of breathlessness; within twenty or thirty seconds to violent convulsions; within one minute to cessation of respiration; and in a few minutes to cardiac arrest and death.

Cyanogen Chloride (CK)
- Nonpersistent (minutes).
- Colorless liquid.
- Pungent biting odor.
- Highly volatile.
- Exposure through inhalation; irritation from contact.
- Irritation to eyes, lungs, and respiratory tract.
- Symptoms are very similar to hydrogen cyanide's, but many are exaggerated by the respiratory tract damage.

Choking Agents

These are the least dangerous of chemical weapons, but death can still occur if exposure is in concentrated form or lingers in one area. Gases such as phosgene and chlorine, which were both introduced in World War I, were used as choking agents on the battlefields. The effect of the attacks were more psychological than practical. However, a terrorist attack that uses or creates the release of these agents could have a devastating fear effect on a population and induce panic.

Phosgene (CG) and Di-Phosgene (DP)

- Under normal conditions, CG is a colorless gas.
- Under normal conditions, DP is a colorless liquid.
- Odor like newly mown hay.
- Exposure through inhalation.
- Easy to produce but unstable and thus needs to be refrigerated.
- Effects are immediate: coughing, choking, nausea, vomiting, tightening of the chest, or headache. These symptoms subside, and there is a two- to twenty-four-hour lull in which the victim feels fully recovered. After this lull, the patient may have a pulmonary edema.
- Nonpersistent (minutes to hours).
- Volatile.

Chlorine (Cl)

- Nonpersistent (minutes to hours).
- One-tenth as lethal as CG.
- Greenish yellow gas or amber liquid when compressed.
- Pungent odor.
- Effects are immediate: coughing, choking, nausea, vomiting, tightening of the chest, or headache. These symptoms subside, and there is a two- to twenty-four-hour lull in which the victim feels fully recovered. After this lull, the patient may have a pulmonary edema.

Indicators of a Possible Chemical Incident

Dead animals, birds, and fish Not just an occasional roadkill, but numerous animals (wild and domestic, small and large), birds, and fish in the same area.

Lack of insect life If normal insect activity (ground, air, and/or water) is missing, then check the ground, water surface, and shoreline for dead insects. If you're near water, check for dead fish or aquatic birds.

Physical symptoms Numerous individuals experiencing unexplained waterlike blisters, wheals (like bee stings), pinpointed pupils, choking, respiratory ailments, and/or rashes.

Mass casualties Numerous individuals exhibiting unexplained serious health problems ranging from nausea to disorientation, difficulty in breathing, convulsions, and death.

Definite pattern of casualties Casualties distributed in a pattern that may be associated with possible agent dissemination methods.

Illness associated with confined geographic area Lower attack rates for people working indoors versus outdoors, or outdoors versus indoors.

Unusual liquid droplets Numerous surfaces exhibit oily droplets or film; numerous water surfaces have an oily film. (No recent rain.)

Areas that appear unusually different to their environs Not just a patch of dead weeds, but trees, shrubs, bushes, food crops, and/or lawns that are dead, discolored, or withered. (No current drought.)

Unexplained odors Smells may range from fruity to flowery, sharp/pungent, garlic/horseradishlike, bitter almonds/peach kernels, and new-mown hay. It is important to note that the particular odor is completely out of character with its surroundings.

Low-lying clouds Low-lying cloud/foglike condition that is not explained by its surroundings.

Unusual metal debris Unexplained bomb/munitionslike material, especially if it contains a liquid. (No recent rain.)

Source: *Chemical/Biological/Radiological Incident Handbook,* Director of Central Intelligence, Interagency Intelligence Committee on Terrorism, Community Counterterrorism Board, October 1998.

Biological Weapons (BW)

In June 2001, the Johns Hopkins University Center for Civilian Biodefense, the Center for Strategic Studies, and other organizations conducted a large-scale exercise of the bioterrorism readiness system in the United States called "Dark Winter." In this scenario, a terrorist use of smallpox breaks out in Oklahoma City. The initial infection starts with only twenty people. By the end of the thirteenth simulated day, more than six thousand cases are discovered, fifty-five hundred new infections occur daily, and over a thousand U.S. citizens die. Even with maximum efforts by the U.S. government and the world community, more than three million infections occur within six weeks; the dead total almost one million. According to the Centers for Disease Control (CDC), the disease is asymptomatic at the time of exposure, with an incubation period of two weeks. There is no effective treatment once a person is infected, and more than 30 percent of all victims could die. Children may have much higher mortality rates.

The reason for the Dark Winter exercise and the dramatic response to the emerging biological weapons threat posed by anthrax is the realization that the United States is not prepared to deal with a serious WMD attack. Although much planning and training have been carried out for the first-responder community, including fire department hazardous materials (HAZMAT) teams, Federal Emergency Management Administration (FEMA) teams, and some federal support teams, little funding or consistent advice has been given to the true front-line soldiers in the war against WMD: the emergency room and hospital staffs that will be besieged by infected patients or policemen who will arrive on scene first.

In the most realistic case, such as was demonstrated by the five dead victims of the September 2001 anthrax attack, hospital staffs and doctors generally do not have the knowledge to rapidly identify a chemical, biological, or radiological attack soon after it occurs. Even those systems that do have that capability are still at risk to many types of disease such as smallpox and tularemia that are highly infectious and appear similar to common diseases. The misdiagnosis of anthrax by doctors as a common chest infection was a primary reason for the first deaths of U.S. postal workers in Washington, D.C. In the case of Thomas Morris, the postal worker who called emergency services when he was sent home after exposure to anthrax, he explained to his doctor that he had been exposed to anthrax. Still, the hospital staff didn't find his story credible, despite the fact that the detailed description he provided was a textbook anthrax infection. The patient died in the emergency room soon after calling his own ambulance. The one person who did believe him was the EMS dispatcher, who was knowledgeable about anthrax symptoms.

The first indication of a crisis is when patients present themselves and then subsequently die. Usually the autopsy or postdeath analysis of symptoms reveals the infection. Worse yet, a truly infectious disease may rapidly start to disable and kill the first responders, such as police, emergency medical technicians, paramedics, and fire department crews who respond to a routine medical distress call. If the disease is a highly infectious agent such as smallpox, the acute care or emergency room staff and first responders who have had contact with the patient may become incapacitated and die. In many exercises, hospital workers and doctors are victims at the end of the second generation of the disease. The nightmare of this scenario is that each person may become a vector for

BIOLOGICAL WEAPONS CASE STUDIES

United States: In September 2001, just weeks after the 9/11 attacks, a terrorist sent highly refined anthrax through the mail to political and media targets in America. The terrorist, widely believed to be an American or a group of Americans with extensive bioweapons experience, launched the first major biological weapons attack on the United States.

The attack killed five people and directly infected seventeen others; thirty-five thousand people were forced to take doses of prophylactic medication. (See page 160 for more details.) Contrary to the popular belief that this was perpetrated by a sole scientist to "send a message" regarding the unprepared state of U.S. biodefense preparedness, the type, quantity, and purity of the anthrax used indicate that the attack was designed to kill or incapacitate the entire U.S. Senate and may have come from defense stocks.

Japan: Aum Shinrikyo attempted to weaponize numerous forms of biological weapons as well as chemical agents. The group may have carried out as many as nine failed biological agent attacks. AUM researched and attempted to create weapons from studies on the toxin of the green mamba snake; tried to develop Q fever from horse sera, which were found on the Australian sheep ranch; made repeated failed attempts at cultivating botulinum toxin; attempted to create aerosolized anthrax; and even went to Zaire, Africa, in 1992 under cover of a humanitarian mission but to actually to acquire samples of Ebola for weaponization.

A New Potential Terrorist Tactic: Human-Deployed Biological Weapon Systems (HUMANBIOWEPS)

A potentially new terrorist tactic is the deliberate infection of a live human being with a contagious disease. The person acting as the disease vector may be infected knowingly or unwittingly. In history, there have been examples of spreading a disease successfully through human contagion, but most cases involved corpses. In 1346, for example, the Tartars laying siege to Kaffa (now Fedosia in the Crimea) launched plague-ridden human corpses into the enemy's siege lines to spread the disease. Infected people surviving this siege may have been responsible for starting the Black Death plague pandemic that killed millions in Europe. The Russians are known to have used the same tactic against the Swedish in 1710.

In the "French and Indian War," the Indians loyal to the French were infected with smallpox through infested blankets, as ordered by Sir Jeffery Amherst. This was a variation on the human-deployed bioweapon theme. This same tactic was employed even by the U.S. government on rebellious indian tribes in the nineteenth century.

The greatest non-nuclear threat to the continental United States may be the deliberate use of humans carrying inside them highly contagious diseases such as smallpox. These HUMANBIOWEPS would travel and infect as many people as possible before they died of the illness. If they were unwitting victims, their day-to-day activities during the infectious period would further spread the disease. Weaponized diseases such as smallpox—believed to be in the hands of rogue regimes such as North Korea—would be the most deadly if deployed as a terrorist weapon. Terrorists could secretly infect unsuspecting populations or travelers with smallpox in an act to punish the United States and actually get into history.

Worse yet, suicide cells from al-Qaeda or any other group could deliberately infect themselves with smallpox. A single person acting as a deliberate vector could theoretically infect hundreds of other people in the Middle East or Europe and still guarantee that the United States and the world would suffer millions of deaths. Europe, Turkey, and Arab allies could easily become the first victims of bioweapons attacks, and eventually America itself would succumb.

Based on the casualty projections from the Dark Winter exercise, the United States could in a matter of weeks end up with tens of thousands of citizens dead and millions infected. The closing of borders, ceasing of trade, and quarantine of large sections of the global population would be required.

the disease, infecting coworkers, family members, and every other person he or she meets until the symptoms reveal themselves. Hence, the horrible projections of one million people dead in just six weeks in "Dark Winter."

This exercise and the lessons of the September 2001 anthrax attack should demonstrate that biological WMDs are a lethal option for terrorists without the resources of a nuclear weapons program.

Potential Biological Weapons

The following is a partial list of the most likely biological weapons that may be employed by terrorists.

SMALLPOX

Known to Be Weaponized

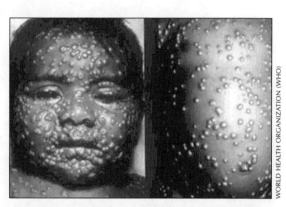

Examples of smallpox infection.

WORLD HEALTH ORGANIZATION (WHO)

The disease transmission: Smallpox is a serious, highly contagious, and sometimes fatal infectious disease. There is no specific treatment for smallpox disease, and the only prevention is vaccination. The name is derived from the Latin word for "spotted" and refers to the raised bumps that appear on the face and body of an infected person.

Two clinical forms of smallpox have been described. *Variola major is the severe form of smallpox,* with a more extensive rash and higher fever. It is also the most common form of smallpox. There are four types of variola major smallpox: ordinary (the most frequent); modified (mild and

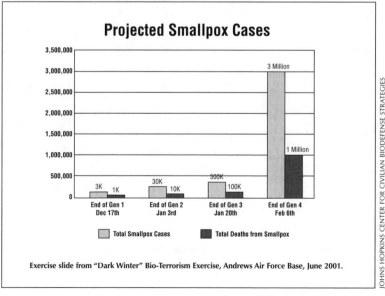

JOHNS HOPKINS CENTER FOR CIVILIAN BIODEFENSE STRATEGIES

occurring in previously vaccinated people); flat; and hemorrhagic. Historically, variola major has a case-fatality rate of about 30 percent. However, flat and hemorrhagic smallpox, which are uncommon types, are usually fatal. Hemorrhagic smallpox has a much shorter incubation period and is likely not to be initially recognized as smallpox when presenting to medical care. Smallpox vaccination also does not provide much protection, if any, against hemorrhagic smallpox. *Variola minor is a less common clinical presentation, and much less severe disease* (for example, historically, death rates from variola minor are 1 percent or less).

Frequency of outbreaks: Smallpox outbreaks have occurred from time to time for thousands of years, but the disease is now extinct after a successful worldwide vaccination program. The last case of smallpox in the United States was in 1949. The last naturally occurring case in the world was in Somalia in 1977. After the disease was eliminated from the world, routine vaccination against smallpox among the general public was stopped because it was no longer necessary for prevention.

Smallpox is caused by the variola virus that emerged in human populations thousands of years ago. Humans are the only natural hosts of variola. Animals and insects do not carry or spread the variola virus. Except for laboratory stockpiles, the variola virus has been eliminated as a disease. However, in the aftermath of the events of September and October 2001, there is concern that the variola virus might be used as an agent of bioterrorism. For this reason, the U.S. government is taking careful precautions to be ready to deal with a smallpox outbreak.

Smallpox can be caught through direct contact with an infected person; it cannot be caught from animals or insects. Generally, direct

Smallpox Disease

Incubation Period	Exposure to the virus is followed by an incubation period during which people do not have any symptoms and may feel fine. This incubation period averages about 12 to 14 days, but can range from seven to 17 days. During this time, people are not contagious.
Initial Symptoms (Prodrome)	The first symptoms of smallpox include fever, malaise, head and body aches and sometimes vomiting. The fever is usually high, in the range of 101 to 104 degrees. At this time, people are usually too sick to carry on their normal activities. This is called the prodrome phase and may last for two to four days.
Days 1-4 Rash distribution:	A rash emerges first as small red spots on the tongue and in the mouth. These spots develop into sores that break open and spread large amounts of the virus into the mouth and throat. At this time, the person is the most contagious. Within 24 hours, a rash appears on the skin, starting on the face and then spreading to the hands and legs and then to the hands and feet. Usually the rash spreads to all parts of the body within 24 hours. As the rash appears, the fever usually falls and the person may start to feel better. By Day 3, the rash becomes raised bumps. By Day 4, the bumps fill with a thick, opaque fluid and often have a depression in the center that looks like a belly-button. (This is a major distinguishing characteristic of smallpox.). Fever often will rise again at this time and remain high until scabs form over the bumps.
Days 5-10	Over the next five to 10 days, the bumps become "pustules" -- sharply raised, usually round and firm to the touch. They feel like there's a small round object under the skin. People often say it feels like there is a beebee pellet embedded under the skin.
Days 11-14	The pustules begin to form a crust and then scab. By Day 14, most of the sores have scabbed over.
Days 15-21	The scabs begin to fall off, leaving marks on the skin that eventually become pitted scars. The person is contagious to others until all of the scabs have fallen off. Most scabs will fall off after three weeks.
After Day 21	Scabs have fallen off. Person is no longer contagious.

and fairly prolonged face-to-face contact is required to spread smallpox from one person to another. In a terrorist attack, exposure to smallpox could occur by breathing airborne virus. A person who has been exposed to smallpox becomes infectious, or contagious, when a rash appears. After the appearance of a rash, the infected person is contagious until the last smallpox scab falls off.

- **Incubation:** Seven to seventeen days.
- **Symptoms:** Prodrome of high fever, malaise, prostration, vomiting, delirium. Followed in two to three days by musculopapular rash progressing into pustules and scabs, mostly on extremities and face.
- **Lethality:** 30 percent in unvaccinated people.
- **A vaccine** exists and can be effective if given within twenty-four hours of exposure.

ANTHRAX

Used and Known to Be Weaponized

Anthrax is a very lethal BW agent, though it exists in nature and is considered a "great disease of antiquity." There are three variants on anthrax: inhalation (known as "wool sorter's disease"); gastrointestinal, which is acquired from tainted meat; and cutaneous, which comes from contact with the anthrax spores and is rarely fatal. Prior to the 2001 anthrax attack on the U.S. Senate, there were only eighteen cases in the twentieth century. In the Soviet Union, a major anthrax outbreak occurred in April 1979 when a military microbiology center (Military Compound No. 19) released hundreds of pounds of anthrax in the Sverdlosk-Oblast region (now Yekaterinburg). This created an anthrax cloud more than thirty miles long downwind of the site that may have killed between two hundred and a thousand people. The 2001 U.S. Senate and media attack was less destructive—infecting dozens of people and killing five—principally because the material was confined quickly upon discovery.

> **"The doctor thought that it was just a virus or something, so we went with that and I was taking Tylenol for the achiness. Except the shortness of breath now, I don't know, that's consistent with the, with the anthrax."**
>
> —Thomas Morris, first U.S. postal worker to die in the 2001 anthrax attack on the U.S. Senate and media.

- **Incubation:** One to five days.
- **Infection** through inhalation, ingestion, or cutaneous contact by spores. Anthrax is resistant to white blood cells and uses other cells as a taxi to the lymph node. It creates two toxins: edema toxin and lethal toxin.

- **Symptoms:**
  - **Inhalation:** Anthrax is marked by fever, fatigue, nausea, headache, chest pain, and other symptoms associated with the flu. This is followed in two to five days with respiratory distress, mediastinitis, sepsis, or shock.
  - **Gastrointestinal** (ingestion): Anthrax symptoms are nausea, vomiting, bloody diarrhea, sepsis, abdominal pain.
  - **Cutaneous:** Anthrax features evolving skin lesions progressing to vesicle, depressed ulcer, black necrotic lesions.
- **Lethality:**
  - **Inhalation:** Once respiratory distress develops, 90 percent fatality if untreated.
  - **Ingestion:** Lethality approaches 50 percent if untreated.
  - **Cutaneous:** Is 20 percent lethal if untreated.
- **Vaccine** exists (six shots, yearly booster).
- **Treatment:** Intravenous cyprofloxin, doxycycline, and oral floxacin.

CASE STUDY

BW Assassination Attempt on the U.S. Senate

On September 17, 2001, a series of four letters, mailed to government leaders and news media personalities, infected mail facilities throughout the eastern United States. Each envelope mailed to Senators Tom Daschle (D-SD) and Patrick Leahy (D-VT) contained a highly sophisticated variant on weapons-grade anthrax. Press reports on the analysis of the anthrax state that it featured ten times more spores per gram than any grade previously made in the entire U.S. and Russian bioweapons program of the Cold War. The 1.5 grams of anthrax mailed to Senate Majority Leader Tom Daschle and Senate Judiciary Committee Chairman Patrick Leahy contained more than one trillion anthrax spores; usually five to ten thousand spores are necessary to kill a healthy person. Each envelope sent to the Democratic senators thus contained enough spores to infect and potentially kill almost one hundred thousand people. The amounts sent to the U.S. Senate were clearly designed to kill not only the addressees but also their staffs and everyone else working in the two senate office buildings. Additionally, hoax letters were mailed almost simultaneously from Florida in an effort to confuse the receivers into disregarding both the real weapon and subsequent mailings. In the end, the minuscule releases of the powders killed five people not related to the targets, through trace amounts passed through the envelope. Had these envelopes been more effectively dispersed, the entire U.S. Senate and its staff would have been incapacitated or killed. The Federal Bureau of Investigation does not discount the possibility that there may be future attacks using this same strain of anthrax.

Types of Anthrax Infections (Courtesy Centers for Disease Control, CDC)

Type	Exposure	Transmittal and Characteristics	Symptoms
Cutaneous	Skin	Cutaneous anthrax is the most common naturally occurring type of infection. It usually occurs after skin contact with contaminated meat, wool, hides, or leather from infected animals. The incubation period ranges from 1 to 12 days. Infection is introduced through scratches or abrasions of the skin.	Skin infection begins as a raised bump that resembles a spider bite. Within 1 to 2 days, the infection develops into a blister and then a painless ulcer, with a characteristic black necrotic (dying) area in the center. The lesion is usually painless, but patients also may have fever, malaise, and headache. Lymph glands in the adjacent area may swell.
Inhalation	Inhalation	Anthrax spores must be aerosolized to cause inhalation anthrax, which is contracted by inhalation of the spores. It occurs mainly among workers handling infected animal hides, wool, and fur. The number of spores that cause human infection is unknown. The incubation period of inhalation anthrax among humans is unclear, but it is reported to range from 1 to 7 days, possibly ranging up to 60 days.	Inhalation anthrax resembles a viral respiratory illness. Initial symptoms include sore throat, mild fever, muscle aches, and malaise. Symptoms may progress to respiratory failure and shock with meningitis. After an incubation period of 1 to 7 days, the onset of inhalation anthrax is gradual.

Types of Anthrax Infections *(Courtesy Centers for Disease Control, CDC)*

Type	Exposure	Transmittal and Characteristics	Symptoms
Gastrointestinal	Ingestion	Gastrointestinal anthrax usually follows the consumption of raw or undercooked contaminated meat and has an incubation period of 1 to 7 days.	Gastrointestinal anthrax is characterized by acute inflammation of the intestinal tract. Initial signs are nausea, loss of appetite, vomiting, fever followed by abdominal pain, vomiting of blood, and severe diarrhea.

BRUCELLOSIS

- **Incubation:** Five to sixty days (usually one to two months).
- **Symptoms:** Fever, headache, weakness, fatigue, anorexia, nausea, constipation, diarrhea. Osteoarticular complications likely.
- **Lethality:** Less than 5 percent fatality, even if untreated—brucellosis incapacitates rather than kills.
- **No human vaccine** (an animal vaccine exists).

CHOLERA

Cholera is known to have been explored for a biological weapon but not known to have been weaponized. Due to its difficulty in transmission, its use as a terrorist weapon would require contaminating large quantities of drinking water.

- **Incubation:** Four hours to five days (normally two or three days).
- **Symptoms:** Acute onset of vomiting, headache, intestinal cramping, "voluminous" diarrhea. Death may result from severe dehydration, hypovolemia, and shock.
- **Lethality:** 50 percent if untreated.
- A **vaccine** exists (50 percent protection).

GLANDERS AND MELIOIDOSIS

- **Incubation:** Ten to fourteen days after inhalation.
- **Symptoms:** Fever, rigors, sweats, myalgia, pleuritic chest pain, cervical adenopathy, headaches, splenomegaly, and generalized pustular eruptions.

- **Lethality:** Almost always fatal without treatment.
- **No vaccine.**

PLAGUE, PNEUMONIC (YERSINIA PESTIS)

Used and Known to Be Weaponized

Plague is responsible for at least three global pandemics: the Justinian plague in 541, the "Black Death" in 1360, and the modern pandemic in 1898. The Japanese army weaponized and used fleas to disperse plague in China during World War II. The Soviet Union weaponized large quantities of the plague for aerial disbursal in intercontinental ballistic missiles (ICBMs). Of the three types of plague—bubonic, primary septicemic, and pneumonic—pneumonic is the most fatal and offers the best potential for weaponization.

- **Incubation:** One to ten days (usually two or three days).
- **Symptoms:** "Acute onset of flu-like prodrome," fever, myalgia, weakness, headache. Within twenty-four hours of prodrome, symptoms may include chest discomfort, cough, dyspnea. Within one to two days, symptoms may include cyanosis, respiratory distress, and hemodynamic instability.
- **Lethality:** Almost 100 percent if untreated; 20 to 60 percent if treated within eighteen to twenty-four hours of symptoms.
- **A vaccine** exists.

Q FEVER

- **Incubation:** Two to fourteen days (up to sixty days possible).
- **Symptoms:** Chills, cough, weakness, fatigue, pleuritic chest pain, pneumonia.
- **Lethality:** 1 to 3 percent (survivors may have relapsing symptoms).
- **A vaccine** exists.

TULAREMIA, PNEUMONIC

Known to Be Weaponized
- **Incubation:** One to twenty days (usually three to five days).
- **Symptoms:** "Sudden onset of acute febrile illness," weakness, chills, headache, body aches, dry cough, chest pain. As the illness progresses, symptoms include greater weakness, malaise, anorexia, weight loss, potential for sepsis or organ failure.
- **Lethality:** 30 to 60 percent if untreated.
- **A vaccine** exists.

VIRAL HEMORRHAGIC FEVERS (VHFS)

Congo-Crimean hemorrhagic fever (CCHF), Ebola virus, Hanta virus, Lassa fever, Marburg virus, Rift Valley fever, yellow fever.

- A **vaccine** for yellow fever exists.
- **Symptoms:** Fever with mucous membrane bleeding, petechiae, thrombocytopenia, hypotension, myalgias, malaise, headache, vomiting, diarrhea.
- **Lethality** is variable depending on the strain—from 15 to 25 percent for Lassa fever up to as high as 90 percent for Ebola.

VIRAL EQUINE ENCEPHALITIS (VENEZUELAN, VEE; EASTERN, EEE; WESTERN, WEE)

Known to Be Weaponized

Venezuelan equine encephalitis was weaponized by the United States in the 1950s and 1960s, even though the other variants are more dangerous.

- **Incubation:** VEE: Two to six days.
  EEE, WEE: Seven to fourteen days.
- **Symptoms:** Systemic febrile illness, encephalitis in some populations, generalized malaise, spiking fevers, headaches, myalgia. Incidence of seizures and/or neurologic deficits may also increase after biological attack.
- **Lethality:** VEE: Less than 10 percent.
  EEE: 50 to 75 percent.
  WEE: 10 percent.
- Several IND **vaccines** exist, though they are poorly immunogenic and highly reactogenic.

Biological Toxins

BOTULINUM

Used and Known to Be Weaponized

Botulinum toxin is considered by USAMRIID to be the most lethal substance known to humankind. It is easy to find and cultivate in a laboratory environment. It was used in World War II to assassinate the Nazi leader Heydrich. Iraq weaponized botulinum and reported to the United Nations that it had more than nineteen hundred liters in its possession, including a hundred bombs (five hundred pounds each) filled with the agent.

- **Incubation:** One to five days (usually twelve to thirty-six hours).
- **Symptoms:** Initially blurred vision, diploplia, dry mouth, ptosis, fatigue. As the disease progresses, acute bilateral descending flaccid paralysis and respiratory paralysis occur, resulting in death.
- **Lethality:** 60 percent without ventilatory support.
- A **vaccine** exists (not available to the public).
- **Protective measures:** Improvised inhalation filters such as doubled-up T-shirts and painter's masks have been known to be effective.

RICIN

Used and Known to Be Weaponized

The Ricin toxin has been used as an assassination and murder weapon. In 1978, Bulgarian intelligence assassinated dissident Georgi Markov in London by stabbing him with an umbrella tipped with Ricin toxin. In 2001, the al-Qaeda terrorist training complex at Darunta was known to have developed and trained terrorists to make small quantities of Ricin. In February and March 2003, British authorities discovered an al-Qaeda Ricin laboratory in London. Ricin can come in powdered or liquid form.

- **Incubation:** Eighteen to twenty-four hours (acute symptoms may occur after four to eight hours).
- **Symptoms:** Weakness, tightness in chest, fever, cough, pulmonary edema, respiratory failure, circulatory failure, hypoxemia resulting in death (usually within thirty-six to seventy-two hours).
- **Lethality:** High with extensive exposure (specifics not available).
- **No vaccine.**

STAPHYLOCOCCAL ENTEROTOXIN-B

- **Incubation:** Three to twelve hours.
- **Symptoms:** Acute onset of fever, chills, nonproductive cough, headache.
- **Lethality** is probably low, but few data on respiratory exposure exist.
- **No vaccine.**

T-2 MYCOTOXIN

Believed to Be Weaponized

- **Incubation:** Minutes to hours.
- **Symptoms:** Abrupt onset of mucocutaneous and airway irritation, pain (skin, eyes, gastrointestinal tract); systemic toxicity may follow.
- **Lethality:** Severe exposure can cause death in hours to days.
- **No vaccine.**

Indicators of a Possible Biological Incident

Unusual numbers of sick or dying people or animals	Any number of symptoms may occur. As a first responder, strong consideration should be given to calling local hospitals to see if additional casualties with similar symptoms have been observed. Casualties may occur hours, days, or weeks after an incident has occurred. The time required before symptoms are observed is dependent on the agent used and the dose received. Additional symptoms likely to occur include unexplained gastrointestinal illnesses and upper respiratory problems similar to flu/colds.
Unscheduled and unusual spray being disseminated	Especially if outdoors during periods of darkness.
Abandoned spray devices	Devices will have no distinct odors.

Source: *Chemical/Biological/Radiological Incident Handbook,* Director of Central Intelligence, Interagency Intelligence Committee on Terrorism, Community Counterterrorism Board, October 1998.

Nuclear-Related WMD Equipment and Components

There are several forms of radiation. The most common types of ionizing radiation are alpha, beta, gamma, and neutron. Nuclear and X-ray radiation are both extremely useful—they are both high-energy radiation and very penetrating. Both forms are commonly called ionizing radiation, because of what they do to atoms. Radiation sources include:

- **Radioactive isotope sources:** Forms of elements that emit nuclear radiation from the nucleus of atoms are called radioactive (isotopes). Uranium and radon are common, naturally occurring radioactive elements. Uranium can be refined for nuclear reactor fuel. The energy from ionizing radiation from the uranium in reactors produces electricity. Sources include uranium-238 and plutonium.

- **Commercial or medical radioactive sources:** Radioactive cobalt, radioactive cesium, and radioactive iodine produce ionizing radiation used by doctors in hospitals to treat serious diseases such as cancer.

  - Cobalt-60 is found in food irradiation plants.
  - Radium is used in X rays and cancer treatments.
  - Cesium-137 is also used in X rays and cancer treatments.
  - Strontium-90, from nuclear batteries.

- **Low-level industrial radiation sources:** Tritium, americium, and radioactive nickel are employed in military equipment for such useful purposes as lighting without batteries and chemical agent detection. According to the U.S. Army, these are used in very small quantities and are not threatening sources.

Explosive Dispersal of Radioactive Material (EDRM)/Radiological Dispersive Device (RDD)— "Dirty Bomb"

Although occurrence is a remote possibility, radiological terrorism may involve several different scenarios. Their identification requires knowledge of exactly what type of material may be involved and where and when this may be dispersed effectively. Attacks may involve seizure of a nuclear facility or vessel, or theft of radioactive material and explosives to disperse the material.

This plutonium from a radiation smuggler was recovered in Germany in 1994.

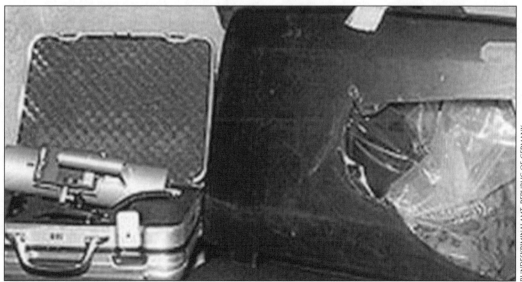

BUNDESKRIMINALAMT, REPUBLIC OF GERMANY

Nuclear Fission Weapons (Atomic Bombs)

Construction

There are two types of crude nuclear weapons construction:

- **Gun type:** A subcritical piece of fissile material is fired into another subcritical piece of fissile material to combine and create sufficient supercritical mass, which results in a nuclear explosion.
- **Implosion type:** A precise layer of high explosives (HE) is wrapped around a piece of fissile material of subcritical density within a shell. The HE, when detonated, is contained, causing an implosion that compresses the fissile material to a supercritical density, which results in a nuclear explosion.

Size and Weight

Unlike a sophisticated nuclear weapon—which could fit into a briefcase or the trunk of a car and weigh up to a few hundred pounds—a crude device would weigh a ton or more and require a large vehicle for transportation. Such a weapon, if detonated properly (which is unlikely without testing), would result in a one- to ten-kiloton blast.

Materials

An implosion-type weapon would require a critical mass of uranium (U-50) of roughly fifty-five pounds, as well as uranium oxide (UO_2), plutonium (Pu) of ten to thirteen pounds, or plutonium oxide (PuO_2). A gun-type weapon cannot be built with plutonium. It requires highly enriched uranium (HEU) in large amounts to achieve a critical mass. It is not known whether oxide powders can be used in this form or whether they need to be converted into the base metal form—a costly and highly technical requirement. Either way, it would take a good amount more of an oxide to create a critical mass than the pure metal form. The use of uranium oxide powder in a gun-type weapon, though possible, is improbable due to the large amount of fissile material that would be required.

Detection of Terrorist-Associated Equipment

A fission device is a sophisticated system that requires an extremely safe location for its assembly. The following types of equipment, if found, may be indicative of a fission bomb safe house:

- Personal dosimeter badges (worn on a coat to measure radiation absorbed by the body).
- Electronic dosimeter reader.

- Handheld radiometer.
- Advanced electronics bench.
- Heavy medical or improvised lead shielding.
- Lead radioactive materials containment box.
- Lead handling gloves and lead X-ray-type chest protector.
- Boxes, instructions, and wrappers for radiological hazards.

Expertise Necessary

The knowledge and skills required are so great that under ideal circumstances, a world-class team of three or four nuclear and engineering specialists would be needed to design a viable weapon. Many nations have this level of knowledge. In all likelihood, it would take dozens more engineers and tens of millions of dollars to start down the path to acquire just the basic components. If the weapons are to be made with plutonium, they require a much higher level of technical expertise and greater experience with conventional explosives and electronics. The tip-offs to this activity would require the resources of a national counterintelligence agency or international police effort.

Components and Equipment

Nuclear weapons require such a degree of precision that few, if any, of the components can be improvised from easily accessible sources. This means that many of the components must be machined, which in turn requires a large quantity of specialty precision equipment and a large allocation of time. Equipment needed from outside to inward includes:

- Container and transportation. Only part of this can be easily improvised—truck, trailer, cargo container.
- Lead shielding is a good indicator of radioactive material. It prevents radiation from interfering with the detonator and other components.
- A chassis supports the fissile material and explosives.
- Precision-measured high explosives, which spark the fissile material.
- A trigger to initiate the explosion of the high explosives.
- Radioactive fissile material.

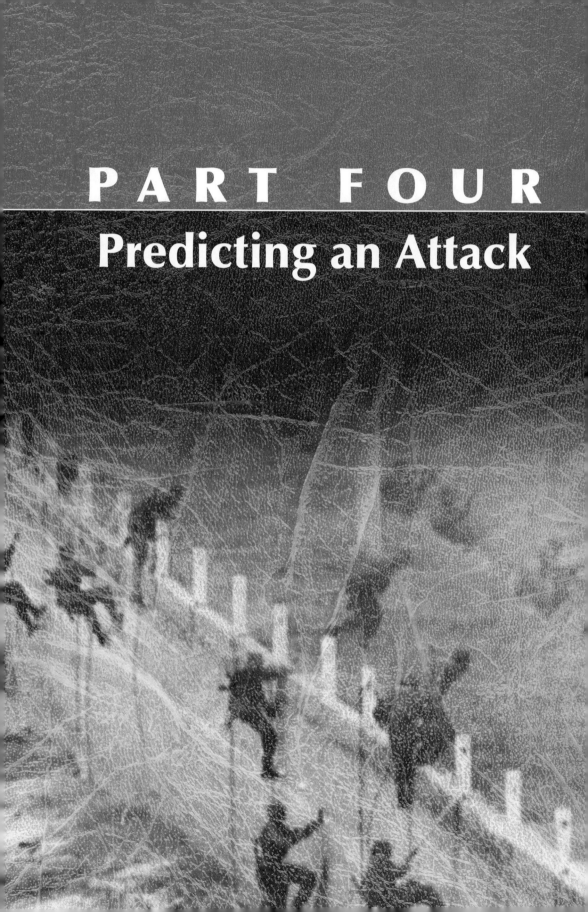

PART FOUR

Predicting an Attack

13

TERRORIST SURVEILLANCE TECHNIQUES

The purpose of this chapter is to introduce the street-level observer to the basic ways in which terrorists approach surveillance. Apart from the attack itself, the most predictable and observable part of a terrorist attack process is when terrorists conduct surveillance on a potential target. Surveillance is necessary for many reasons, the foremost being to decide if the target is actually worthy of attack and if the security is too heavy for an attack to be successful. If cell members do not conduct surveillance and move on a heavily defended target, they may be gunned down by an alerted force even before the attack begins. Although we said in a previous chapter that an attempted attack may be considered successful even if security stops it, a conscientious cell leader will want to know, at the very least, if the group can make it to the immediate vicinity of the target and inflict casualties before security can come into play. This requires surveillance.

All terrorist organizations possess an intelligence cell. Its members may be dedicated, experienced intelligence officers sent in especially to select and observe a target, or just auxiliary personnel who have been given surveillance duties. Anyone can be an intelligence collector. Children, supplementing a professional Hezbollah intelligence cell, were tasked to watch the U.S. Marine headquarters at Beirut International Airport months before the 1983 bombing that killed 241 marines. Terrorists have posed as policemen, census takers, and have used people with access to enter the target and build a detailed surveillance picture.

The *TRH* does not go into great detail on how to conduct surveillance. This manual has left out details on sophisticated surveillance, technical surveillance, communications intelligence, and the details of law enforcement countersurveillance efforts. That information is widely available to those who are cleared and have a specific need to know. The terrorist intelligence cell reads books and manuals like this to learn how the counterterrorism community works.

Will You Come Under Surveillance?

In order to determine if you or potential targets are being surveilled for attack, you need to study the potential surveillants. To do this, you need as much information as possible on the opponents who may conduct surveillance:

- Study the history of local terrorist surveillance and the recent surveillance history of international terrorist groups for indications about terrorists' premission surveillance techniques.
- Determine the proximity to areas of high criminal activity where criminal surveillance may mask terrorist surveillance or be subcontracted by terrorists.
- Coordinate with law enforcement countersurveillance teams. Know where professional personal protection, antinarcotic, or counterterrorist surveillance is in your jurisdiction so that it won't confuse the intelligence picture.
- Study classified and open-source histories on the capabilities and sophistication of any domestic terrorist group that has or may operate within your country, as well as international terrorist groups. This is a formidable task, but you must know who the potential opposition is before you can see them watching you.

Who Conducts Surveillance?

- **Terrorist groups** conduct surveillance to develop target intelligence and assess the psychological impact of a successful attack.
- **Criminals** such as murderers, rapists, stalkers, kidnappers, drug dealers, burglars, and the mafia with its enforcers conduct surveillance to detect the actions of law enforcement and victims.
- **Foreign government intelligence services:** Surveillance that is observed may be that of foreign government agencies attempting to commit espionage or our own government attempting to detect national security threats.
- **Homeland security and law enforcement agencies:** Surveillance is necessary to catch criminals as well as terrorists, and to watch for activities that may lead to a terrorist act.

Methods of Surveillance

Surveillance entails two basic methods:

- **Overt surveillance:** This is open observation carried out in a blatant manner (such as a man with a pair of binoculars) or using an overt ruse (say, posing as a news team).
- **Discreet surveillance:** Here, the surveillant does not want to be seen or recognized. This could be a person watching from a balcony

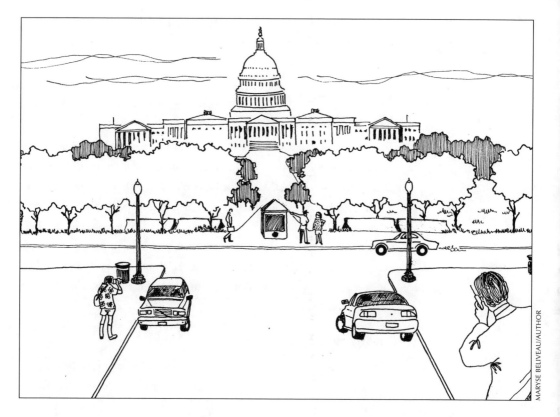

MARYSE BELIVEAU/AUTHOR

while sunbathing, a couple on a bench, or a family visiting a site as tourists—anyone observing in a surreptitious manner from a building or vehicle.

Terrorist surveillance comes in all forms. Every person in this illustration is a potential surveillant.

The methods of surveillance can also be classified in the following ways:

- **Sophisticated:** This surveillance is used by governments and police agencies, which may use sophisticated combinations of many types of surveillance against one or more targets. This form is very difficult to detect.
- **Unsophisticated:** Most terrorist surveillance is unsophisticated: The terrorists use improvised, one-dimensional methods until they build up a good idea of their target. Unsophisticated surveillance is also easier to detect.
- **Fixed:** Terrorists select a surveillance point where operatives don't move. This may be a rented apartment or hotel room, a sidewalk bench, an observation pit dug into the ground, or any other location where someone can comfortably watch a target for long periods of time.
- **Mobile:** Terrorists using people on foot, vehicles, boats, or aircraft may "orbit" or loiter around a target. This type of surveillance

becomes obvious when multiple sightings (called hits) are noted over a period of time. It can be enhanced with any of the following types of collection.

Types of Surveillance
Visual Surveillance

Terrorists observe a facility with their naked eyes or eyes enhanced by optics. A variety of optics could be used, depending on the training that terrorists have received. Most use binoculars, but others trained in sniper or sniper–observer skills may use high-powered professional spotting scopes or rifle scopes, perhaps enhanced with night-vision devices, thermal imagers, or even high technology such as radar imaging. Terrorists generally have a bigger budget with more discretionary spending than the average police force, so don't be surprised if they demonstrate a high level of sophistication.

Imagery Surveillance

There are two types of imagery surveillance: still imagery (photography) and video imagery. This technique is used to study the patterns or details of a potential target.

1. Still imagery surveillance:

Still imagery is critical for the terrorist targeteer's intelligence collection and target selection process. Terrorists may use still film or digital photo cameras for photo surveillance. The al-Qaeda publication Encyclopedia of the Jihad instructed photography teams to take panoramic photos of targets or—if that proved impossible due to security or high visibility—to take or acquire photographs of the area as a whole, as well as multiple photos of the target street. Terrorists acquire still imagery from the following sources:

- **Taking photos at the target:** This requires operating near the target and conducting photography. This is the riskiest type of imagery surveillance.
- **Hiring a professional photographer:** A less risky type of imagery surveillance. Hiring a professional photo firm may not gain pictures on areas of interest but may still yield useful images.
- **Purchasing satellite imagery:** This is becoming increasingly popular for use in long-range planning. French, U.S., and Russian firms routinely sell high-quality satellite imagery with resolutions that can show details of a target as small as three feet across. If

OVERT SURVEILLANCE CASE STUDY

Terrorist Still Photography of U.S. Military Aircraft

In December 2001, a terrorist supporter was arrested in Singapore conducting surveillance at the airport for a group that is associated with al-Qaeda. A technical maintenance man for Singapore Technical Air Services was caught taking photos of American aircraft. A search of his house found photos of more than fifty U.S. military aircraft that had landed in Singapore. Later that same month, police raided safe houses of Singapore's al-Qaeda supporters and found videotapes of visiting U.S. Navy personnel and the buses in which they rode to tourist sites. It is believed these videos were designed to select the appropriate place for a bomb attack.

acquired through a friendly intelligence source or corporation, such photos may also be virtually untraceable. Commercial requests for satellite imagery can lead to indicators of a potential target.

- **Using open-source or Internet photos:** Photos of selected targets that may have been in the news or have been the subject of a professional photographer can often be found on the Internet or purchased.

2. Video imagery surveillance:

When terrorists want to track routes or see procedures in action, they may use a video camera. The Liberation Tigers of Tamil Eelam engage in extensive, detailed videotaping of each terrorist act. In 1983, Hezbollah and Iranian intelligence both photographed and videotaped their near-simultaneous attacks on the U.S. Marines, the French Foreign Legion, and the Israeli army.

OVERT SURVEILLANCE CASE STUDY

Terrorists Videotape U.S. Embassy

Guards at the American embassy in Nairobi, Kenya, saw one of the suicide attackers with a video camera, days before the 1998 bombing attack, standing across the street from the embassy while videotaping the guards and the entrance. On the day of the attack, he was recognized in a van attempting to penetrate the embassy grounds but was told to go to the rear entrance. The van exploded minutes later at the rear entrance, killing 250 people.

The LTTE takes videos both to create popular support and to learn lessons from its many attacks.

3. Technical Surveillance

Electronic recording and monitoring devices are commercially available at electronics shops and Internet "spy shops."

- **Television:** The news media provide an unsophisticated form of technical surveillance to terrorists by transmitting live images from the area of a target. SWAT blackouts—agreements to not transmit live images—have been adopted by many media organizations.

- **Communications scanners:** These are portable radios that intercept radio signals. They are used to find out local police procedures and responses. The German terrorist group Red Army Faction used bomb hoaxes to carry out an attack on the opposite side of a city while employing police frequency scanners to confirm movements.

- **Video scanner:** There are commercial scanners that intercept video transmissions of internal and external security cameras. Terrorists could use these handheld intercept systems as a form of internal video surveillance without penetrating a facility.

- **Bugs:** Terrorists or terrorist sympathizers can place simple or sophisticated electronic devices on or in a target to eavesdrop on private conversations of a victim. Some bugs are extremely sophisticated. Foreign intelligence agents (Class I terrorists) would be best equipped for this method.

- **Wiretaps:** Physically or electronically connecting in a surreptitious manner to the telephone communications of a victim. Like bugs, this is a good way to gain personal information on a target.

- **Spikes:** Spikes are deliberately placed microphones or pinhole cameras inserted in walls. These systems are used for long-range intelligence collection and would be most likely used by a foreign intelligence agency or a very sophisticated terrorist group.

- **Standoff listening devices:** "Deer Ears"-type parabolic reflectors can listen in on conversations from as far out as one hundred yards. Directional pen microphones can listen in on conversations from up to ten yards. These, too, would be used to collect personal information on victims or their movements, as gleaned from conversations.

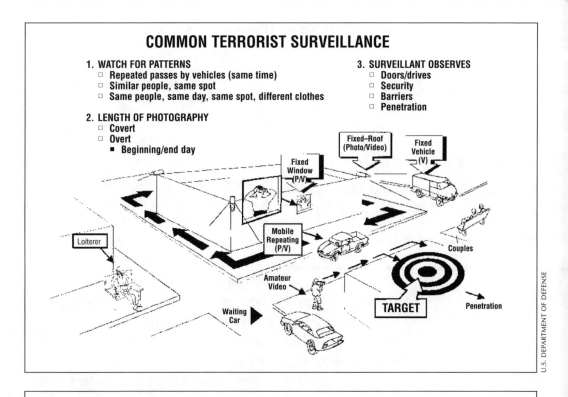

COMMON TERRORIST SURVEILLANCE

1. WATCH FOR PATTERNS
- Repeated passes by vehicles (same time)
- Similar people, same spot
- Same people, same day, same spot, different clothes

2. LENGTH OF PHOTOGRAPHY
- Covert
- Overt
  - Beginning/end day

3. SURVEILLANT OBSERVES
- Doors/drives
- Security
- Barriers
- Penetration

U.S. DEPARTMENT OF DEFENSE

Surveillance Detection Checklists

Ask These Basic Questions

- ❏ Why would this site or sites within your jurisdiction be under surveillance?
- ❏ Who would target a site such as this?
- ❏ From where and how would they best observe this site (in the open or discreetly)?
- ❏ What is the purpose of such a surveillance—initial target selection, last-minute walk-through, criminal activity?

Reporting: Report Suspicions Immediately! Take Action!

- ❏ Report activity to law enforcement or to a joint terrorism task force.
- ❏ Investigate *IMMEDIATELY* all suspected contacts.
- ❏ Call a security alert if suspicious.
- ❏ Raise security to next highest level.
- ❏ Conduct aggressive observation for terrorist security, drivers, or cell commanders.

Stop and Interview the Individual

- ❏ Log information in a careful interview with the individual.
- ❏ Polaroid photographs at close range if you confront the person.
- ❏ Follow arrest or detention protocols.

Detecting Surveillance

Look out for unusual behavior patterns that may appear normal.

- Rapid video or still camera usage at nontourist sites (the suspect arrives, videos, and departs quickly).
  - People observing at particular sites, then taking down notes or calling on a mobile phone.
  - People carefully pacing off distances.
  - Vehicles parked with passengers.
  - Unusual encampments of characters not associated with the areas they occupy (seemingly homeless people, campers, picnickers, bus stop loiterers).
- Ruses (news crews videotaping without a van or permission, out-of-jurisdiction plainclothes police or sheriff).
- Deliberate penetration attempts.
- People observing or climbing on perimeter fencing.
- A sense, supported by above detection, that you are under surveillance.

Detecting and stopping a terrorist intelligence cell on surveillance is the simplest way to stop an attack.

14

DETECTING INFILTRATION AND SPECIAL MISSION TECHNIQUES

Terrorists are often specially trained in skills to infiltrate borders, difficult targets, secure places, and checkpoints. Knowing the potential methods of infiltration and the targets that require special mission training and equipment will help you take necessary security measures to stop surveillance or an attack.

As in chapter 13, on surveillance, this handbook will not go into great detail on the subject of infiltration, but will provide direction to recognize the terrorist's options and techniques.

Terrorist Operatives: Special Cultural Survival Skills

To infiltrate a country or target area, terrorists will try to have good skills allowing seamless operation in society, with little contact with the police or government. Operatives must behave in such a way that they don't give themselves away by being misfits in the local culture. Therefore they need to learn and utilize several types of cultural survival skills:

Plausibility in community: Terrorists may temporarily adopt the values and behaviors of the nation they intend to infiltrate and carry out a mission. Why were the 9/11 skyjackers seen at a strip club before the attack? They were establishing plausibility in the community. More than likely, they were working out details in a place a Westerner would never look for fundamentalist Muslims. No American who saw them would think they were radical extremists with this behavior, so why not? As stated earlier, the oldest rule of terrorism is, in effect, "Do whatever it takes."

Plausibility near target: Terrorists must be able to fit into the scene of the target until the launch of the attack.

Use of legal identity infiltrators: Citizens, embassies, or naturalized immigrants may provide more than adequate support for a terrorist group to infiltrate a country legally. These operatives, once they infiltrate successfully, may become active terrorists, supporters, or sleeper cell members waiting to be activated and to strike.

PLAUSIBILITY NEAR TARGET CASE STUDY

LTTE Dress as Locals

In July 2001, a group of LTTE "Black Tiger" terrorist cadres, dressed as Sinhalese locals and playing local music on a radio, assembled near a security fence next to Sri Lanka's Bandaranaike International Airport. Locals weren't fooled and reported the terrorists to military police. They said some nonresident Tamils were acting strangely and checking out the airport. The police didn't listen. Minutes later, the fourteen suicide commandos stormed the airport, blowing up nine military fighter aircraft and three Air Lanka Airbus passenger jets.

Indicators of Trusted Agent Infiltration or Intelligence Collection

A trusted agent is a person who has official access to a potential target and gives terrorists entry to this location. Like spies, sympathetic baggage handlers, security guards, senior executives, law officers, and even bodyguards have used their positions to allow terrorists to gain access to sensitive, high-security locations. Often, these people supply critical intelligence on targets as well. Look for:

- Attempts to obtain information without a need to know (usually repeated or outside the scope of someone's job).

LEGAL INFILTRATION CASE STUDY

Al-Qaeda Uses U.S. and British Citizens

Jose Padilla (aka Abdullah Al Muhajir), a suspected member of the Usama bin Laden Organization's al-Qaeda terrorist group, was an American citizen of Puerto Rican descent. He was born in Brooklyn, New York, and converted to Islam in prison. In May 2002, Padilla was arrested entering the United States on his valid American passport as an intelligence cell member to select targets for future attacks. In December 2001, British citizen Richard Reid (aka Abdel Rahim) used his valid British passport to take a flight from Paris to the United States. He was stopped attempting to blow up a passenger plane by lighting a fuse attached to explosives in his tennis shoe. He is believed to have been the lone tactical operations cell member on an al-Qaeda suicide/martyrdom mission.

- Unexplained and excessive use of copiers (outside normal routine).
- People living beyond their means or experiencing sudden reduction of large debts.
- Unusual travel patterns (unexplained trips of short duration to same locale).

Cover Story and False Identity Usage

Use of "Clean" Operatives

Many terrorist groups, when attempting to penetrate difficult borders, may opt to use operatives who have no history of terrorism support. These operatives are considered clean and may have some of the following characteristics:

- Specifically trained for special onetime missions.
- Selected from people who do not seem the terrorist type.
- Encouraged to maintain normal lives and professions.
- Kept in tight isolation from other terrorists when in training.
- Usually hand selected by the terrorist leadership.
- Contacted and supported by a special covert communications pathway.
- Rarely have direct contact with "dirty" (known) terrorists.
- May infiltrate the enemy's security apparatus.

Detection of Clean Operatives

Clean operatives pose a serious detection challenge. They are selected by the terrorist group because they have no apparent or traceable terrorist links. They may possibly be detected by:

- **Identification of behaviors:** These operatives behave as terrorists once on a mission and can be detected through activities at safe houses or near targets.
- **Detection of terrorist liaison:** It is impossible to screen every person in a country. Excellent intelligence collection is necessary to find the points where clean operatives interact with the dirty ones. Meetings, communications, and other intersections where the clean operative and dirty operative cross paths are good identifiers of this method of infiltration. National counterintelligence efforts are critical to pinpoint such operatives due to the large amount of intelligence, analysis, and surveillance needed to successfully prosecute the search.

Use of False Identity (Dirty) Operatives

Most terrorists have some contact with the law enforcement systems of their nations. To cover their original identity, they assume a false life. These operatives may have been arrested for criminal, political, or terrorist activities in the past and have become too dirty to use their real names or life histories. So they adopt a new name (an aka—also known as) and travel on one or several different false stories called cover stories. Some well-known terrorists such as the Islamic Jihad Organization's Imad Mugniyeh have resorted to plastic surgery to change their appearance.

Detection

Dirty operative detection may include:

- Finding absolutely no documents on suspects or at residence (this extremely clean operative may be known as a "ghost"). Note: undocumented illegal immigrants not associated with terrorism are very common as well.
- Finding forged or changed passports.
- Finding multiple passports with similar photos and different names and/or nationalities.
- Finding multiple legal identity documents (driver's licenses, national identity cards, Social Security cards).
- Positive identification through fingerprints or biometric systems.

CLEAN OPERATIVE INFILTRATION CASE STUDY

Al-Qaeda Infiltrates the U.S. Special Force School

Egyptian native Ali Mohammed came to the United States in 1985 and spent three years as a supply sergeant assigned to the U.S. Army Special Operations Command's John F. Kennedy School of Special Warfare in Fort Bragg, North Carolina. He became the first defendant to plead guilty to conspiracy charges in connection with the 1998 Kenya and Tanzania embassy bombings. Mohammed admitted that, starting in 1989, he helped train al-Qaeda terrorists in the U.S. and Afghanistan. His access to advanced weapons knowledge, military contacts, legal weapons, and combat skills gave al-Qaeda excellent resources and a reliable intelligence source to judge the U.S. Special Forces' efficiency in stopping Bin Laden, as well as increasing al-Qaeda's own combat skills.

- Observing terrorist behaviors (surveillance, supply, and so forth) in conjunction with other evidence.

Special Mission Tactics and Techniques: Defeating Border Controls and Customs

How do terrorists get into the area of a target or a nation where they are to carry out operations? They must penetrate the nation's borders or— if they're already in the country—the security of the facility. Here are some methods they use to infiltrate:

- **Foot infiltration:** Terrorists can enter a nation by crossing borders on foot. They often walk from Afghanistan to Pakistan, for instance, and from Pakistan to India. Both the Mexican and the Canadian frontier with the United States can be easily crossed on foot. The best method of detection is watching for people who apparently are in the area solely to cross the border; you can also use inform- ants and empower locals such as hunters, fishers, and campers to observe for obvi- ous infiltration that they may usually ignore.

> **Unless you have a specific intelligence profile of the terrorist operative, all these infiltration techniques require you to look for behaviors of a terrorist suspect.**

- **Air infiltration:** Terrorists can infiltrate through regular airport controls or via charter aircraft, executive jets, or small air- planes, where customs controls are not as stringent.
- **Vehicle infiltration:** Infiltration by train, car, bus, or truck over land is another method. Terrorists can drive or be passengers in a vehicle or other transportation. Armed Islamic Group (AIG) ter- rorist Ahmed Ressam was arrested coming into the United States from Canada on a car ferry. His arrest stopped the planned year 2000 millennium celebration bombing of the Los Angeles International Airport. The customs agent noticed that he took a wide, circuitous route to get the ferry to cross at weaker customs posts instead of the direct route from Vancouver, British Columbia.
- **Sea infiltration:** Terrorists can infiltrate on scheduled cruise, mer- chant cargo, or container ships. They can enter as crew members, passengers, or stowaways. (See page 193 for an excellent example of using a container cargo for infiltration.)

Special Mission Tactics and Techniques: Defeating Airport Controls and Aviation Transportation Security

Authorized Access with Valid Identification

As noted before, clean operatives enjoy a significant chance of getting into a country if they have no terrorist contacts, no previous arrests, and a plausible reason for entering. The September 11, 2001, skyjackers were a classic example. Sixteen of the nineteen hijackers came legally to the United States to carry out their mission.

The hijackers had appropriate visas, travel documents, and places to go after arrival. At that time, it was believed there was no specific intelligence connecting them to al-Qaeda. In fact, two of them had been identified, but lapses in intelligence reporting allowed them to move freely in the United States.

Illegal Access

Operatives who need to defeat airport security controls have several high-risk methods of doing so. Each has benefits, but in the post-September 11 environment many airports worldwide have stepped up measures to stop these kinds of infiltration.

- **Foot penetration** involves terrorists who attempt to penetrate the inner security belt that leads to passenger lounges and jetways. The two principal methods of illegal access by foot are:

  1. Calm infiltration: Skyjacking or facility attack detection usually starts on the street from the point of checking in. Skyjackers may travel together or singly and meet up on the aircraft. Modern professional skyjackers may not be nervous, sweating, middle-aged men clutching bags tightly to their chests or young fiery-eyed holy warriors with belts of explosives. They're more likely to be younger, cooler, well dressed, and capable of passing security with minimal scrutiny. Those attempting to infiltrate weapons, explosives, or knives may be slightly nervous before heading into security, but by the time professional operatives run through the procedure, they more than likely have calmed themselves and trust their instincts and training to get them through. As is now widely known, the 9/11 skyjackers were calm because they knew they were operating within the rules of the airline and had little to fear. They entered the lounge after passing security without raising suspicions, just like every other passenger.

CALM INFILTRATION CASE STUDY

On April 12, 1999, five Colombian National Liberation Army skyjackers—smartly dressed as rich businessmen and the last to board Avianca Airlines Flight 9463 from Bucaramanga to Bogotá—commandeered the aircraft ten minutes after takeoff. They had smuggled in guns and hand grenades and took all the passengers and crew as hostages.

2. Gate crash: The skyjackers or attackers arm in the ticketing area or baggage claim and rapidly assault through security controls to gain access to the passenger boarding lounges and jetways. This technique is the least preferred method of infiltration, because it provokes an immediate armed response.

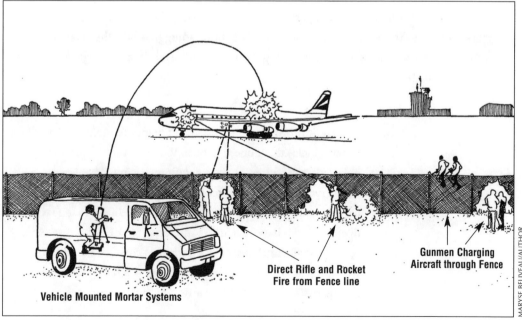

Vehicle Mounted Mortar Systems

Direct Rifle and Rocket Fire from Fence line

Gunmen Charging Aircraft through Fence

MARYSE BELIVEAU/AUTHOR

Airport facility ground attack and breaching techniques.

GATE CRASH CASE STUDY

On December 17, 1973, Palestinian terrorists stormed and penetrated the security barriers at Rome's Roma-Fiumicino Airport. The terrorists entered the airport and drew weapons, then commenced firing on civilian passengers in the ticketing area. They fought their way past the security checkpoint and entered the main terminal. The five hijackers entered the jetway of a Pan Am Boeing 707 named Clipper Celestial and threw at least two hand grenades into the passenger compartment. The subsequent explosions and fire of the fueled and loaded aircraft killed thirty-two people. The gunmen then took local ground crew and pilots in the terminal as hostages and skyjacked a Lufthansa Boeing 737. The hostages were eventually released, but the hijackers escaped.

3. Air infiltration: A unique tactic to infiltrate airport security control is to come in from the air on a scheduled airliner, or chartered or private aircraft, and seize a facility or aircraft.

AIR INFILTRATION CASE STUDY

In 1999, Pakistani Islamic extremists skyjacked an Indian Airlines Airbus with 210 passengers and crew. The terrorists had access to weapons smuggled into the baggage claim at the lower-security Kathmandu Nepal airport and used them to skyjack the aircraft to Afghanistan.

- **Vehicle infiltration:** Terrorists can attempt to infiltrate flight lines using vehicles that appear to be authorized, such as airport or local police, flight services, or safety equipment. In many airports, all that is required is an access code on an authorized person's ID card. In many small third-world countries, vehicles that get on the flight line only have to act with authority to effect the ruse. A person who deliberately assists the terrorists can be a member placed within the airport or someone who accepts a bribe. Additionally, stolen, lost, or misplaced ID cards and flight line passes have been a commonplace security lapse.

VEHICLE INFILTRATION CASE STUDY

Karachi Airport Flight Line Penetration:

In September 1986, terrorists associated with the Abu Nidal Organization accessed the flight line at Karachi Airport in Pakistan and seized a Pan Am 747 with 375 passengers. The terrorists were dressed as airport security police and drove a vehicle that resembled an authorized car. They accessed the flight line and drove right up to the boarding steps.

U.S. DEPARTMENT OF DEFENSE

Special Mission Tactics and Techniques: Defeating Maritime Security

Maritime security requires a multidimensional posture. Terrorist threats can emerge from land, on the sea, under the sea, and the air. In October 2000, the guided missile destroyer USS *Cole* (DDG-67) was attacked by two terrorists using a small boat and the ruse that they had been assigned by the port to tie the ship up to a fuel point. They performed this task and then exploded alongside of the destroyer.

Terrorists have learned to adapt to changes in security, especially in the post-9/11 environment. They have carried out dynamic attacks in a range of spectrums, from infantry-style raids on harbors to suicide combat swimmers who blew themselves up against their targets. Detection of each event is as simple as being aware that these attacks could occur. Each visitor, high-speed vessel, or sighting of bubbles surfacing nearby should be immediately evaluated as a potential terrorist threat. Due to the high risks of disaster in a maritime attack, it is imperative that everyone be aware of the potential of terrorists.

U.S. DEPARTMENT OF DEFENSE

Infiltration of Harbors

Terrorist teams could enter harbors through various methods. The methods of penetrating a harbor or facility that have been used by terrorists in the past include:

1. Infiltration by sea:

The terrorist penetrates and attacks using:
- Rowed boats, skiffs, canoes, or sea kayaks.
- Inflatable rubber raiding craft, dinghies (Zodiac types were used in the USS Cole attack).
- Commercial or military high-speed boats (HSBs).
- Deceptive fishing vessels.
- Floating debris.
- Vessels disguised as Coast Guard, pilot, police, or the like.
- Large commercial vessels marjacked by terrorists.
- Commercial vessels or mother ships. Another tactic is a mother

ship on which Zodiac-style rubber raiding craft are carried with a commando team and launched as they near an enemy's shore. Israel routinely stopped ships and attacks such as these from the 1970s through the 1990s. Libyan intelligence used the roll-on/roll-off merchant ship *Ghat* in 1984 to lay mines in the Red Sea.

- Mini submarines or electric-powered human-guided torpedoes. The LTTE operates homemade, human-guided torpedoes; the PLO trained in Lebanon on mini subs.
- Purpose-built Stealth-design suicide craft. The LTTE builds high-speed suicide boats that incorporate low radar observability or stealth designs. Video of one such craft was featured in the *Jane's Intelligence Review* of March 7, 2001.
- Small submersibles as weapons are known to be in the hands of national intelligence agencies such as Iranian, Libyan, and North Korean intelligence and the LTTE. Groups such as Hezbollah and al-Qaeda could easily gain this capability. The FARC and the drug lords of Colombia have tried to build, modify, or use both full-sized surplus and newly built diesel-electric-powered submarines to smuggle drugs into the United States. These could easily move agents or supplies.

Terrorists and counter-terrorist forces, like these German KSK commandos, can board vessels in port or underway through numerous techniques.

2. Infiltration by swimmer or scuba diver:

Terrorists could swim in towing or wearing explosives and weapons or dive underwater using scuba gear. These profiles include:

- **Recon swimmer:** Swimmer without weapons (with gear or without).
- **Combat swimmer:** Swimmer with goggles, fins, and weapons.
- **Combat diver:** Scuba diver with open-circuit breathing system (creates bubbles) and weapons.

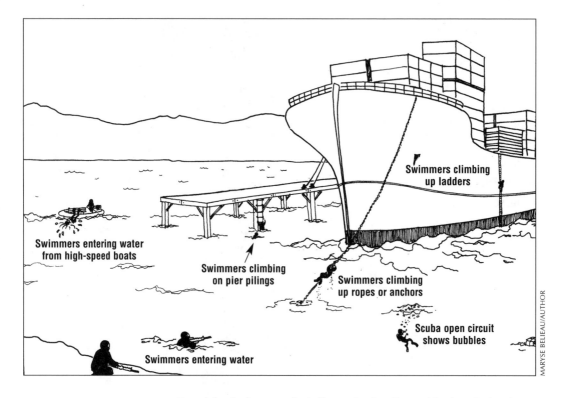

Swimmers climbing
up ladders

Swimmers entering water
from high-speed boats

Swimmers climbing
on pier pilings

Swimmers climbing
up ropes or anchors

Scuba open circuit
shows bubbles

Swimmers entering water

MARYSE BELLEAU/AUTHOR

- **Special mission combat diver:** Scuba diver with closed-circuit breathing system (Drager or other bubbleless rebreathing system) and weapons.

3. Infiltration by land:

Terrorists may infiltrate the maritime facility through legal or illegal means. They have demonstrated the ability to infiltrate via the following methods:

- **Valid identification:** The marjackers of the cruise ship *Achille Lauro* purchased valid tickets for their sea cabin. Others have used valid ID cards and passes.
- **Authorized access:** The terrorist could be an authorized person or crewman (trusted agent) who has infiltrated the facility or vessel.
- **Illegal identification:** False identity cards. These can be sold by criminal elements of the illegal immigrant community, and are often used to gain employment on the seafront.

4. Infiltration by air:

Aircraft and helicopters can be used to insert terrorists into a maritime facility. Parasails, hang gliders, ultralights, and parachutists are potential infiltration or attack methods.

SEA INFILTRATION CASE STUDY —

Purpose-Built Container Ship Infiltration

In a significant potential infiltration tactic, Amir Farid Rizk, an Egyptian-born Canadian citizen, was arrested in Italy on October 28, 2001, after arriving inside a cargo container from Egypt. The steel shipping box was modified specifically for his infiltration into a ship leaving for Canada the next day. He had a sleeping area, chemical toilet, laptop computer, satellite telephone, maps, and airline tickets.

U.S. Navy forces search containers on a suspected terrorist vessel off of Pakistan.

U.S. DEPARTMENT OF DEFENSE

Special Mission Tactics and Techniques: Defeating High-Value Target Physical Security

Given adequate manpower and weapons, no matter how secure a facility is, there is always a way for a determined group to penetrate it. Most terrorist groups do not have a full Ranger battalion to expend on a mission to take major U.S. military command posts or frontal assaults against the White House. Yet these facilities will always have weaknesses so long as there are humans working in them. Terrorist attacks are generally symbolic. Against some high-value targets, the loss of all the terrorists is necessary to demonstrate that the group has the power to flex its operational muscles and take on the hardest challenges. Basic physical security controls such as gates, fencing, and access points can all

be defeated by a group that takes careful surveillance and uses appropriate force.

- Nuclear power plants, sensitive research facilities, military, police, and homeland security command and control facilities or vehicle command posts may be specifically targeted to create a disaster, threaten a disaster, or hinder response to a real attack.

- The greatest threat to an HVT is the person with authorized access. Infiltrators with valid identification can get assaulters or reconnaissance teams into the entryway or the checkpoint of the HVT.

- Illegal or false document attempts have been used as well. In January 2002, for example, two people were arrested attempting to penetrate the Petten nuclear research facility in the Netherlands with false identification.

15

THE LAST CHANCE TO STOP AN ATTACK: THE DECISION AND ATTACK SEQUENCE

Ten-Phase Sequence of Terrorist Action

Many past studies have simplified the stages of terrorist action into three or five stages. When broken down further, however, virtually all terrorist events are actually comprised of ten distinct phases. These phases are made up of the logical actions inherent in any group's decision-making process. All terrorist operations have a predictable sequence. No matter how many members of a terrorist organization are involved, the operation will eventually include some visible component of the following phases:

Phase 1 Decision-Making Period

Phase 2 Intelligence Collection Cell Deployment and Infiltration

Phase 3 Final Target Selection and Planning

Phase 4 Tactical Operations and Logistic Cell Deployment

Phase 5 Tactical Operations Go-No Go Decision

Phase 6 Tactical Operations Movement to Target

Phase 7 Tactical Action Phase

Phase 8 Withdrawal and Extraction Phase

Phase 9 Regroup, Rearm, and Exfiltration

Phase 10 Negotiation/Credit/Debriefing and Lessons Learned

Real people are making real decisions that may eventually manifest into real action—which should motivate you to try to predict the events that will occur. If any part of this ten-phase sequence is observed, then you are forearmed with the knowledge of what should occur next.

Phase 1—The Terrorist Leadership Makes a Decision

Action: The terrorist leaders consider taking action against an enemy, receive a list of options and feasibility reports, then decide on a specific target or action.

Internal events: The leadership of an organization must decide on the specific political, ideological, or psychological goals of the group and the best uses of terrorist operatives. The leadership meets, debates, discusses, plans, and approves the best course of action. As with most groups, the leaders attend separate covert meetings that take place in a secure location. Decision makers' meetings are usually convened again after the receipt of a final target selection report from the intelligence cell (Phase 3).

Detectability: The decision-making period is rarely, if ever, detected unless there is successful intelligence collection by law enforcement or the intelligence services, or an inadvertent security breach in the terrorist organization occurs, such as lost documents or the arrest of key players who were present. A key indicator that this stage has been completed is the detection of cells conducting surveillance or deploying for attack. Additionally, the senior leader may decide to publicize an upcoming action through a written manifesto, a press release, a religious ruling, or an interview in which they specifically state that they have made a decision to act.

Phase 2—Intelligence Collection Cell Deployment and Infiltration

Action: A covert team of information collection specialists, or trusted agents, move into a target area to collect key intelligence around the best available targets.

Internal events: The intelligence cell will arrive, set up in a safe house, and start collecting information on potential targets. Individuals or teams scout out and collect information on the capability of the local security, actions necessary during the operations, and other safeguards. The cell may finish its evaluation on a specific place or select a series of suitable targets. It then passes a targeting recommendation to the senior leadership in the form of a bundle of information called a target options package (TOP).

Detectability: Intelligence cell operations in this stage may be very detectable (see chapter 13: Terrorist Surveillance Techniques). This stage is the best opportunity to stop a terrorist attack through counter-surveillance detection of the intelligence cell, visibly increasing security, and aggressively chasing leads. This may force the intelligence cell to select a softer target or even end the collection.

Phase 3—Final Target Is Selected

Action: The senior leadership receives the target options package and decides on the best target. After evaluating the intelligence cell's recommendation, a decision may be made at the highest level or left to a subordinate in charge of tactical operations. The intelligence cell will continue surveillance and collect more details.

Internal events: Once the leadership decides on the final target, instructions will be sent to the intelligence cell to start intensive information collection on a specific target. The cell leader will assemble a comprehensive final written, electronic, or verbal report called the target intelligence package (TIP). The team tasked to attack the target also gets a copy of this report via secret means.

Detectability: Intelligence cell operations in this stage remain very detectable due to the increased intensity of observation and intelligence collection near the objective (see chapter 13).

Phase 4—Terrorist Cell Activation: Sleeper Cells

Action: The teams designated to carry out an attack are sent to an area near the target. A team and/or people designated to supply the attack teams are sent to acquire or use existing safe houses, equipment, and weapons necessary for the mission's success. These teams or any other supporting team may be living secretly within the target area over a long period of time until called upon to do their duty. These cells are known as sleeper cells only when inactive.

Internal events—sleeper cell: Once activated, sleepers assume the role of a normal active tactical operations or logistics cell. This activation increases their detectability dramatically.

Detectability: A sleeper cell is generally detectable through intensive and cooperative counterintelligence efforts at the borders or through aggressive internal security. Sleeper cells generally use people with no criminal background or minimal involvement with illegal activities. Logistics personnel take those risks and support the sleeper cell. Sleeper cells are detectable through aggressive canvassing of criminal support elements, inaccuracies in their lifestyle, poor use of covert cover stories, and detection of professional tradecraft. Once activated, a sleeper cell is as detectable as any other terrorist cell.

Phase 4—Terrorist Cell Activation: Logistics Cell

Internal events—logistics cell: A dedicated logistics cell should arrive after the final decision is made to hit a target. The logistics cell usually arrives before the tactical operations cell but often after the intelligence cell departs (this is optional; it may arrive early to support both). The logistics cell prepares the safe houses and warehouses, and acquires weapons, explosives, and/or equipment necessary to support the tactical operations cell's mission. The logistics cell may remain after the operation is executed to provide supplies, security watchers, hostage guards, or follow-up intelligence collection before another strike.

Detectability: A logistics cell is detectable through intensive and cooperative criminal intelligence collection at the local and federal police levels. International counterintelligence efforts at the borders or aggressive policing also tend to detect logistics personnel because they are much closer to the criminal underground. Logistics cells generally use people who are involved with illegal activities. Such cells are specifically designated to take risks to support the other cells. Unusual behaviors of the logistics cells are *very* detectable (see chapter 10).

Phase 4—Terrorist Cell Activation: Tactical Operations Cell

Action: The action arm of a terrorist group is known as the tactical operations cell. The TACOPS cell is generally deployed after the final decision is made on the goals and objective of the mission. The logistics cell generally precedes the tactical operations cell's arrival and prepares a safe house for the members.

Internal events—tactical operations cell: The TACOPS cell arrives, sets up shop in a safe house, receives the weapons, explosives, and/or equipment necessary to support the mission, and starts the final planning, including collecting its own intelligence on the target to ensure that this is in agreement with the intelligence from the INTEL cell. Logistics cell members support the TACOPS cell operations and may be folded into the cell as security teams, drivers, or a follow-up intelligence collection organization.

Detectability: The TACOPS cell is most detectable if its members carry out "GO-NO GO" surveillance of the target (see Phase 5). This is a last check to ensure that the information they have received is accurate. They may be seen in the same places and roles, near the target, as the intelligence cell members who preceded them.

Phase 5—Go-No Go Decision

Action: The tactical operations cell leader makes a final decision whether to go forward with the operation ("go decision") or abort ("no go decision"). The abort may be permanent or temporary.

Internal events: The TACOPS cell leader makes a final decision after all factors for success are considered. The leader may make this decision alone, on orders from above, or in conference with the TACOPS cell members. On a no go decision, the operation may return to Phase 4 or proceed to Phase 10 for a "lessons learned" briefing.

Detectability: Without specific internal intelligence (wiretaps, informants, or intercepted communications), the go-no go decision is generally undetectable until the attack is in motion (Phase 6).

Phase 6—Terrorists Move to the Target

Action: On a go decision, the TACOPS cell members will move on to the immediate target area. The cell may stop short of the target to consolidate and to launch the operation.

Internal events: Members at the safe house draw the weapons, explosives, and/or equipment necessary for the operation. Each member is given a final briefing on the proper position needed for the operation and final assurances as to the goals of the mission. Members then transport themselves to the target area. If they are transported by a separate team that does not take part in the actual operation, they are "inserted" via an "insertion team," which may consist of members from the logistics cell.

Detectability: Tactical operations cells are vulnerable to detection as they move to the target. They may move as a unit or in an observable tactical order (in line, column, wedge, or diamond formations). These formations may be spread over a hundred yards or more and may be difficult to identify at first glance until two or more attackers are seen. On the other hand, a firefight may stagger terrorist attackers out to where they can be interdicted if an accurate volume of fire is brought to bear as far away from the target as possible. Usually the weapons, explosives, and/or equipment for this stage are on their persons or ready for immediate use. Detectability may be as simple as observing armed people with masks approaching from a vehicle in an overt attack. Ruses, uniforms, or diversions may be employed at the initial moments of a covert operation. Unusual movements or behaviors may be indicators. (For more on specific attack stratagems, see chapter 18).

Phase 7—Point of Failure: The Terrorist Attack

Action: The terrorist operation is carried out. This stage ends the moment the operative withdraws from the target area (some operations do not expect the operative to withdraw).

Internal events: Cell members take position and execute the plan. This is the stage when an attack becomes generally detectable to everyone. Cell members may or may not communicate verbally or with radios with each other as the operation is carried out. Members may constantly check on reaction from police and authorities, check on their relative positions to the target and other members, and take armed action against victims or responders. Most terrorists do not use interteam radio communications. However, during the attack and the mass hostage taking at the Japanese embassy in Lima, Peru, the entire team of Tupac Amaru terrorists had VHF/UHF tactical radios to coordinate their attack and movements once inside.

Detectability: Depending on the operation, the tactical action phase may or may not be detectable until the cell members are sighted in the act or when they successfully carry out the act. In a terrorist bombing, the delivery of the bomb—not the subsequent explosion—is considered the terrorist act. Powerful images of people throwing firebombs or grenades, firing weapons, or laying hands on kidnap victims are examples of the attack stage in action.

Phase 8—Withdrawal

Action: Surviving cell members may attempt to depart from the target area whether the operation was successful or not.

Internal events: On a given signal or event, cell members execute a withdrawal plan. There may be a predetermined vehicle or transportation team to get them away from the target area. This is called an extraction. Some religious extremist terrorists do not plan any withdrawal and expect to die in Phase 7.
Note: If the mission goes badly, the members may become disorganized and carry out escape and evasion. E&E is a survival function and is an "every-man-for-himself" tactic.

Detectability: Like the movement-to-target phase, the withdrawal phase is one with a high level of detectability. Unusual people witnessed moving away from the target just after an incident, or vehicles rapidly departing, are strong evidence of escapes in progress.

Postattack—what to look for: Valuable information about the perpetrators of an attack could be gleaned from small bits of information collected immediately in the postattack period. Some of these may only apply to small incidents. Major incidents with great loss of life generally lead to an immediate, hasty, and complete departure from the incident area. Look for evidence or eyewitnesses who have observed:

- ❑ People running away with weapons or equipment in hand.
- ❑ Persons running away from the target before the attack occurred.
- ❑ Persons running away in unusual directions of travel.
- ❑ Vehicles speeding away from the target (may violate traffic patterns and laws).
- ❑ Suspicious vehicles in the "escape radius." If you note the time of the first alarm, you can calculate the escape radius of a vehicle traveling at sixty miles per hour (one mile per minute on highway or half a mile a minute in a city). This can give you an approximate radius of escape for a vehicle.
- ❑ People sighted rapidly changing one vehicle for another within five to ten miles of the target site.
- ❑ People quickly abandoning vehicles within five to ten miles of target site.

Phase 9—Regroup, Rearm, and Exfiltration

Action: Once successful withdrawal is complete, the cell may call a rendezvous at a safe house or predetermined rally point to prepare for additional operations, to treat any wounded, to secure hostages, or simply to rearm.

Internal events: When a terrorist cell returns to a safe house or, more likely, to an alternate safe house, members will make immediate preparations to depart to a safer area where they can debrief and observe the results of their work.

- **Rest and rearm:** Escaping operatives may rest together or individually in homes of supporters. If they plan another mission or a "restrike" of the same target, they may restart the ten-phase cycle from Phase 4.
- **Exfiltration:** If leaders have decided that the cell will leave the country, they may have planned for exfiltration. This is the systematic departure of the team via air, land, or sea. Detecting terrorist exfiltrators requires you to assume they may have a departure plan. Depending on the size of the incident, some groups may opt to leave behind the logistics cell, deactivate the TACOPS cell to assume sleeper status, and/or exfiltrate all operatives. The exfiltration process, when planned in advance and used every time a "bug-out" is necessary, is called an "exfiltration routine."

Detectability: Exfiltration is detectable by checking for illegal or legal departures across borders—illicit transportation or legally leaving a country. Ramzi Yusef of al-Qaeda, the cell leader and bomb master for the 1993 World Trade Center attack and the creator of the plan to blow up twelve U.S. airliners over the Pacific Ocean, always used an immediate exfiltration routine that put him on the next available flight out of the city in question, and generally directly to Pakistan.

Phase 10—Negotiation/Credit/Debriefing

Action: If the incident requires negotiation, it may be performed in one of two ways: negotiation on site or surrogate negotiation. *On-site negotiation* means the TACOPS cell will remain at the target, making demands and leveraging its power and control over people's lives for a concession. This strategy risks the destruction of a trained tactical operations cell. The *surrogate negotiation* is thus a favored tactic of terrorists: Here, the TACOPS cell leaves, and someone else negotiates. Most abductions and terrorist acts use surrogates who eventually get in touch with the victim's representatives and strike a deal. Some religious extremist groups never seek credit or negotiation but attack for the satisfaction of inflicting damage.

Internal events:

- **Negotiation:** Negotiation takes place on site or with a surrogate. Usually negotiations are made via telephone or radio. Sometimes a third-party surrogate such as the International Committee of the Red Cross (ICRC), a church, or a religious or prominent personality will participate in the negotiations.
- **Credit:** A call, letter, or interview is placed and a specific claim is made. Many groups will claim small-scale attacks that injure only a few, but attacks that get condemned due to heavy casualties are usually only claimed by the actual group. Some groups will even deny an attack if it appears they are going to lose support for their actions. When the Real Irish Republican Army (RIRA), a small splinter group of the mainstream Provisional IRA (PIRA), killed 28 people and wounded 220 in a double car bombing in the town of Omagh (the single worst bombing incident in the history of the "Troubles"), the PIRA immediately issued a statement insisting that the RIRA had actually performed the attack and condemning the action. Months later, the RIRA issued an "apology."

- **Debriefing:** The survivors of a mission may return to a safe location to officially recount their experiences, determine successes and failures, and document procedures that work or will work in the next attack. Most groups prepare a "lessons learned" report for the next operation and the terrorist leadership.

Detectability:

- **Negotiation:** On-site negotiation is immediately apparent by terrorists shouting demands through bullhorns or out of windows, or giving TV interviews. Surrogate negotiators can be detected through law enforcement wiretaps or informants, and verified by finding phone contacts—written codes that many groups often use to authenticate their messages.

> **At this point, the decision/planning/attack cycle begins again.**

- **Credit statements:** Many credit statements are made by telephone or mail.
- **Debriefing:** Debriefing detection is another function of an in-depth intelligence mission.

16

THE BASICS OF ANALYZING INTELLIGENCE AND PREDICTING TERRORISM EVENTS

People Are Predictable . . . So Is Terrorism

The intelligence failures in the September 11 attacks are legion. Virtually all the intelligence indicators that easily should have led the FBI and CIA to detect almost all of the hijackers and gain awareness of the plot were either ignored, not believed or left unreported. Take for example the May 16, 2002 comments by National Security Adviser Condoleezza Rice who stated "I don't think anybody could have predicted that these people would take an airplane and slam it into the World Trade Center, take another one and slam it into the Pentagon, that they would try to use an airplane as a missile." How could such a senior administration official with a brilliant intelligence and policy background not consider such a threat when a stolen light airplane was crashed into the west side of the White House in 1993 a few dozen meters from where her office is located? The intelligence community can hardly be blamed when the White House was briefed two months prior to the attack that "We believe that [bin Laden] will launch a significant terrorist attack against U.S. and/or Israeli interests in the coming weeks . . . The attack will be spectacular and designed to inflict mass casualties against U.S. facilities or interests. Attack preparations have been made. Attack will occur with little or no warning." In fact many global intelligence agencies and U.S. government organizations considered the possibility of suicide aircraft attacks. Israel shot down a Libyan Arab Airlines 727 in 1970 believing it was a flying bomb on a suicide mission. The 1994 hijacking of an Air France A300 to Marseille was halted when French counterterrorism forces learned the plane was going to be used as a cruise missile and crashed into the Eiffel Tower. So what happened on September 11? The facts are painfully simple. The political consumers did not view terrorism as a high national security priority and so they simply ignored the warnings. In fact, after the April 1, 2001 forced landing of a Navy reconnaissance aircraft in China the administration made a highly publicized change of the intelligence priorities from terrorism to National

Missile Defense. The National Security Advisor's comments reveal how simply terrorists can push the envelope of improbability for those who choose to ignore the asymmetric nature of their operations.

Could good intelligence analysis have predicted the September 11 attacks? The answer is clearly yes. Some of the earliest reporting concerning the plot appeared when FBI Special Agent Kenneth Williams from the Arizona field office noticed that people with anti-American tendencies and possible links to al-Qaeda were attending flight schools in the United States. He quickly associated the potential for al-Qaeda to use an aircraft for terrorist attacks. The investigation of suspected terrorist Zacharias Moussaoui led to his arrest and seizure of information related to the plot for the hijackings. However, the reporting on the actionable intelligence broke down and the skyjacking incident occurred according to the terrorists' plan.

This chapter will outline the process involved in effectively predicting a terrorist attack and provide you with some basic tools to analyze and make simple intelligence predictions while working in the field.

Most terrorist intelligence analysis courses offered by the U.S. government usually involve a course of instruction between two and five weeks long. A person in the field such as a detective, policeman, service member, force-protection officer, or even a casual observer may come across or be assigned to evaluate data related to a potential terrorist incident. Decision makers may have to evaluate the analysis of another person or agency. No matter what your role, having a basic understanding of the factors and fundamental techniques used in intelligence analysis will allow you to better evaluate intelligence that may be passed on to your organization. Terrorism intelligence analysis is conducted in order to:

1. Identify the existing terrorist threat conditions in your country or jurisdiction.
2. Rapidly identify terrorist attack pre-incident indicators (TAPI) that show changes in the existing terrorist threat conditions.
3. Accurately predict trends that may be building into an attack.
4. Direct conclusions to the relevant authorities for action.

To do this job well, you need to learn to carry out the never-ending process of collect, analyze, conclude, report, and respond (CACRR). CACRR is defined as follows:

1. **Collect** indicators and intelligence on terrorists from all sources.
2. **Analyze** the information and process indicators into a logical sequence.

3. Conclude the terrorists' potential courses of action.

4. Report rapidly up the chain of command.

5. Respond with overwhelming force or increased security measures.

Within this process, you will make a prediction based on information and evidence about where, what, when, why, and how you believe the terrorist will strike. You will also forecast the terrorists' potential attack options, known as their courses of action (COA), in an estimate. This estimate may give you a chance to provide intentions and warning (I&W) of terrorist attacks in an effort to provide the 3Ds of homeland security: detect, deter, and defend. COAs listed in an I&W estimate will give you the intelligence to detect the attackers in the planning stage, deter them through increased security, and/or defend against an attack. You need to be cautious and pause when indicators point to terrorist activity. Be mindful of asking intelligence-focused questions rather than queries from a law enforcement standpoint. Taking stock and asking the right questions will lead to better understanding and results.

The Collect, Analyze, Conclude, Report, and Respond process.

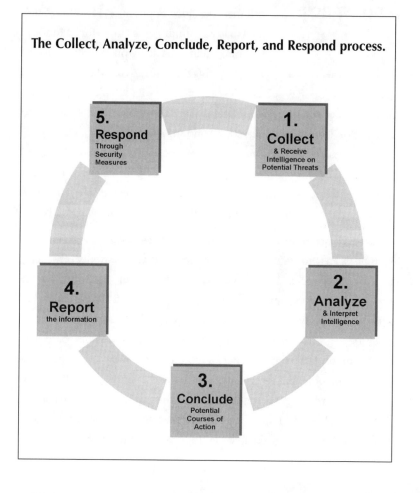

Estimating versus speculating: How do we know when a terrorist is going to attack? The short answer is, we don't. The long answer is, given that terrorists are human, they are predictable. This predictability—coupled with good intelligence collection and analysis—is the basis of making a trustworthy intentions and warning (I&W) projection of what the terrorists may do. Your projection of the terrorists' COAs will be based on known information about terrorist strategies and tactics; the weaknesses of potential targets in your area; and the fusion of intelligence reports, observations, and evidence into logical conclusions. This process is fundamentally different from *speculation,* which the *American Heritage Dictionary* defines as "Reasoning based on inconclusive evidence, conjecture or supposition" or *guess-timating,* "an estimate based on conjecture." This is the "analysis" you often see on news programs by the hundreds of "terrorism experts" who have cropped up since September 11, 2001. Such speculative punditry is fine for Monday-morning quarterbacking but not for current threats facing America. Avoid the guesses and conclusions you may see on television news. Avoid "September 12" terrorism experts and commentators. Counterterrorism analysis is too serious for TV morning talk shows and infotainment radio. Draw your own conclusions dispassionately, without political or personal bias, and based on *intelligence facts,* not speculative fiction. Intelligence facts are hard data fragments, indicators, or evidence collected and analyzed. Stick to where the intelligence facts lead you and try to avoid all bias.

> Avoid the guesses and conclusions you may see on television news. Draw your own conclusions dispassionately, without political or personal bias, and based on intelligence facts, not speculative fiction.

Making a prediction: The *American Heritage Dictionary* defines the verb *predict* as "to state, tell about, or make known in advance, especially on the basis of special knowledge." Again, what you are predicting are the potential courses of action for a terrorist group or cell. These courses of action are actually very limited. You must carefully learn the unique patterns of a group's demonstrated and potential capabilities based on known or projected intelligence. This information can then be compared to the potential targets in your area and the group's ability, manpower, and resources to conduct each of the twenty-one classes of terrorist attacks (see chapter 18: Points of Failure). This comparison should give you a fairly reliable envelope of terrorist potential as well as an idea of where and how they may strike. It is the unfortunate misperception that terrorist acts are completely random and that attacks cannot be predicted that stops efforts to project their COAs. In previous chapters, you have been introduced to the information that gives you the special knowledge you need about the terrorists; now you must integrate it with other information to stop the attack sequence.

Chapter 15 illustrated that all phases of the terrorist planning and attack process must occur in sequence. As you collect intelligence that indicates something is happening (during Phases 1 through 6), you must build a picture that gives you a chance to stop Phase 7, the attack—or, as it should be known, the "point of failure." Arresting and rolling the terrorists up in the postattack stages (Phases 8 through 10) is good strategically, but the tactical damage will have already been done. The goal of stopping the terrorists in the period preceding an attack is critical. In this chapter, you will learn the tools that will help you do exactly that.

The Basics of Predicting and Preventing Terrorism

While prediction is not a hard science, intelligence analysis is. By utilizing the steps outlined below, the chances of projecting the correct COA and preventing a terrorist act will improve. Let's examine the steps individually.

1. Collect

Terrorist intelligence collection is the gathering of any usable information related to a particular group or event by any method.

Collect Data Through Regular Intelligence Methods

Data can be collected through regular intelligence sources and methods. Many of these methods may be classified as well due to the critical need to protect the source and the special techniques necessary to gain that information. These data collection techniques include:

- Public information (aka open-source intelligence: press, television, literature).
- Professional exchanges (conferences, professional chat, roundtables).
- Interviewing public personalities.

- Interrogating criminal and terrorist personalities.
- Criminal informants or intelligence agency human assets.
- Covert or clandestine collection operations.
- Legal briefs or indictments.
- Tips from the public.
- Visual and technical surveillance.
- Captured electronic data processing.
- Imagery or photographic intelligence.
- Electronic intelligence.
- Leaks.

Classified U.S. Government Materials, Sources, and Methods

If you are a law officer, public decision maker, or other official, you quite possibly may come into contact with confidential information related to terrorist activities; usually it will be presented in one of three forms:

1. Sensitive intelligence from an external agency such as the FBI, NSA, CIA, or subagencies in the Department of Homeland Security.
2. Direct observation from a bystander, surveillance team, or other party.
3. Informant intelligence from someone very near or in the group.

The information may be "raw" intelligence, or it may be processed into an estimate. In most cases, it will be scrubbed of sensitive sources and methods to give you only the critical kernel of information that you need. For example, information from a sensitive source may be sanitized to simply state, "A terrorist act is planned for x date in x location by x group." You generally don't need to know anything else. For the purposes of this handbook, we will focus on information from the second two sources: direct observation and informant intelligence.

Never reveal intelligence because it is too good to believe or could make you look important.

Every case study in the *TRH* comes from open-source, unclassified information commonly found in the press, academic, and law enforcement, and military communities for the express purpose of keeping classified examples from being divulged inappropriately.

In the future, the FBI, CIA, and Department of Homeland Security may be sharing "sanitized" intelligence with local law enforcement and even the community. In the meantime, if you are entrusted with this information, you must learn to *keep it to yourself.* Security of the sources and methods of government collection is absolutely necessary when handling terrorist intelligence. An impressive article in the *Washington Post* based on intelligence facts could kill an innocent person or dry up valuable sources of intelligence.

Never divulge how or from whom data was collected. Only divulge information to people with an absolute need to know. In fact, it is far more satisfying to say, "I'm sorry but I can't tell you," or simply "I don't know," than to whisper a damaging fact to people who aren't cleared, or are cleared but don't need this information. Let them use their imaginations about how "superspooky" you are rather than to try to prove it and thus damage the national intelligence effort.

Study a group's history, operations, and targets: A good indicator of when terrorists are going to act is how they have acted in the past. Terrorism is violence or threat of violence with a purpose. Each act generally carries meaning and symbolism. If a group carries out a successful operation, you can be almost certain that you will see that attack recur in the future, if not by only one group, then by others that feel they can refine it or use it in a similar manner—copycatting, if you will.

Before you analyze specific terrorist group intelligence, you must gain a working background, a base of knowledge, about the people and culture from which the group is formed. This can be accomplished through reading summary reports, case studies, books, manuals, and newspaper and magazine articles; watching news broadcasts and videos; holding interviews; and attending professional seminars with university experts or people from similar cultures. Study terrorism in general and then slowly focus on specific groups that have a proven history of operating within your area of concern. The process of knowing your opposition is not quick, but as you continue to collect information, you will gain a clearer understanding of the specific terrorist group you are interested in, and the patterns will slowly emerge. Case studies in the previous chapters of this book and those in the bibliography will help you in this process.

Almost all terrorism has its roots in the complaints of a specific group or culture. To understand the grievances of terrorist groups and how these complaints translate into violence against innocent victims, you must try to set aside personal prejudices and understand the terrorists' perspective. One mental exercise is to imagine yourself or your family in the circumstances of a terrorist, projecting if, how, and why you would take up armed actions (see page 42).

Often law enforcement and members of the armed forces view and evaluate terrorists through their own perspective of good versus evil. While this may be applicable to the acts themselves, moralizing does not help, and may even hinder the analytical process. Good investigators can put aside their opinions and emotions to get inside the mind of the criminal—in this case, the terrorists. Assuming that the proper data has been collected, let's introduce the next step in the process.

Study the incident after the point of failure: If a terrorist act occurs in any part of the world, a good student of terrorism analysis should know about it. Terrorism "incident analysis," or the study of terrorism events, starts with tracking incidents as they occur globally, not just domestically. Every terrorist incident is a learning opportunity. As incidents occur, the analyst should start asking basic incident analysis questions in order to build a "query baseline." This is a standard series of questions that will serve as a yardstick for learning the fundamental patterns of global terrorism. Terrorists study what works, and so should you.

Study historical incident data: Additionally, when studying a terrorist group's history of incidents and attacks, you may want to ask baseline questions that should be compared from incident to incident to get a firm understanding of the group's operations. The questions may include:

- ❏ Is this event an act of terrorism (or found to be an act of terrorism)?
- ❏ Which tactic was used?
- ❏ How many operatives were involved in each stage?
- ❏ Was the mission a success or failure? (Attempts, even if they fail or the terrorists escape, are considered successes.)
- ❏ How long did the tactical operations phase (attack phase) last?
- ❏ What was the end result of the act?
- ❏ Were any members killed or captured?
- ❏ What were the intelligence profiles of the captives?
- ❏ Which group has demonstrated this capability and matches the captives?
- ❏ Has anyone claimed this incident?
- ❏ Does the claim match the capability of the group?
- ❏ Is this a new tactic, form of attack, or target of opportunity? (In the case of the July 2002 Hamas bombing of Hebrew University, seven of the ten people killed were Americans. Does this indicate

a shift in tactics against American interests in the region, or were they unfortunate victims in the wrong place at the wrong time?)

2. Analyze

The 9/11 attacks occurred despite data that, at the very least, should have led to accurate predictions about the method of attack, if not the actual participants and scope of the attack. Had these TAPIs been detected and given even the slightest credence, the attack more than likely would not have occurred. Had the data from Zacharias Moussaoui's computer been aggressively followed up, even the most rudimentary criminal intelligence division would have had little difficulty breaking the rest of the skyjack cells. On their face value, the Arizona and Minnesota FBI memos should have constituted a national security emergency. How do we ensure that such an intelligence breakdown never happens again? We must analyze better.

Analysis will help in predicting the who, where, when, why, and how of terrorist activities. *Analysis* is the study of all information contained within a complex problem and its placement into a logical sequence that points to a possible course of action. These COAs give us adequate I&W on the threats. Even if you have only a small role in your organization, there is a chance you may be called upon to analyze a situation, just as a centralized intelligence analysis center would. Terrorist intelligence analysis is not limited to a formal analysis center. When tips are received, observations are made, or you gain information that enhances your knowledge of terrorists, the focus on analysis must be there. Someone almost always sees or hears the indicators of an attack, but may not realize that this evidence is an intelligence indicator. The following terms will help you better understand some of the more common terms used in intelligence reporting and analysis.

Analytical Product and Components

The terrorist intelligence I&W estimate: The intelligence report that carries your pre-incident indicators, potential courses of action, and conclusions is often called an I&W estimate. An I&W estimate is a summary of evidence and information that often ends with a prediction on the courses of action available to terrorists. Many people believe that making estimates, especially those that have different or competing conclusions, is a waste of resources. This inherent distrust comes from past intelligence failures such as Pearl Harbor, the Tet Offensive in Vietnam, and both the first and most recent World Trade

Center attacks. In fact, each of these examples had many intelligence indicators, and if read correctly, they could have tipped us off to the attacks. Proper estimates are made up of evaluated pre-incident indicators. You start to connect the proverbial "dots" of the terrorist intelligence picture by completing an analysis and placing all the evidence in the estimate. Who is responsible for "connecting the dots"? The person who draws up the estimate should spell out the dot picture in the conclusion section of the estimate, but if you are the reader, you are also responsible for interpreting the data presented to you. Even if you didn't collect the data, you may have additional information or a different perspective that enhances the analysis. This means that everyone who reads the document and sees the indicators is responsible for connecting the dots and making the call.

> **"Incidents do not occur in a vacuum. They are planned, organized and carried out by individuals acting alone or in groups. The nature of the incident, its target, the level of force used, the types of weapons used , the number of people involved, and the behavior of the perpetrators will depend on the nature of the group."**
>
> **—U.S. Defense Intelligence Agency**

Terrorist Attack Pre-Incident Intelligence Indicators (TAPIs)

Every terrorist incident has pre-incident indicators. TAPIs are the individual bits or data fragments of intelligence information that produce patterns and allow the investigator to understand the potential courses of action. Law enforcement refers to these as evidence, tips, and hints. Pre-incident indicators can collectively or in part lead you to detect terrorist activities. They could be any of the detectable activities discussed in previous chapters.

Classes of Indicators

1. Group-related indicators are techniques, methods, equipment, or operations that give clues as to the group preparing to carry out operations. Groups may have areas of operations they specifically operate in, targets they specifically wish to strike, and weapons that they favor. Many groups declare terrorist "campaigns" or may strike on significant dates. The International Association of Counterterrorism & Security Professionals (IACSP) prints an annual calendar of dates significant to terrorist groups, which may help you identify group indicators.

Structural expansion is a group indicator that requires excellent intelligence of the terrorist group's baseline operations. It requires knowledge of the usual complement and makeup of a cell or day-to-day patterns of the group at each level. Accelerated recruitment or expansion of the number of members in a cell may indicate impending operations.

For example, if a suspected cell in your area is reported to contain three or four low-level logistics members, and your investigation discovers that several new members arrive with explosives and weapons training, it constitutes a localized structural expansion that may indicate preparations for an impending attack.

2. Target-related indicators are fragmentary or whole data that lead investigators to believe a specific target is under consideration for attack. Threats, manifestos, or declarations by terrorist groups are good target-related indicators, because they often specifically spell out who is at risk. However, noting that a building is under repeated surveillance by a consistent person or group indicates it is a potential target. For people who may be targets, actions by a potential victim, such as routine travel or regularly scheduled visits, may increase chances of attack. The Secret Service aggressively attempts to predict "target indicated" threats because the president and senior staff must so often travel to conduct business in public and on schedule.

> **Terrorist attack pre-incident intelligence indicators are data fragments that collectively or in part may lead you to detect terrorist activities.**

3. Incident-related indicators may be events or reported incidents that may not appear directly related to terrorist activity but may be a single link in the chain for a major incident. The 9/11 skyjackers' complete disregard for learning to land an aircraft—even abandoning an aircraft on a runway at a major aiport—was a clear indicator of suspicious activity. Dry runs and dress rehearsals either on the actual target or in a specific training base are also good incident-related indicators.

Quality of Indicators

1. Ambiguous indicators are tips or observations that do not clearly spell out a definable threat. These could be any of the detectable activities of terrorists that are not immediately identified. Most indicators are ambiguous. Example: A terrorist suspect is observed with a book on chemistry (may indicate planning).

2. Unambiguous indicators are tips or observations that show clear activities of terrorism. Example: A terrorist suspect is caught at a safe house exhibiting physical symptoms of both smallpox and inhalation anthrax.

3. Tip-offs are solid unambiguous intelligence indicators that give clear, uncontestable warning or clues to an imminent event. The airline tickets, completed bombs, and detailed plans found in a Philippines safe house were the tip-offs to Project Bojinka, the 1994 al-Qaeda plan to blow up twelve airliners simultaneously over the Pacific Ocean.

4. *Chatter* is an intelligence community phrase that refers to many intelligence sources providing indicators in an increasing crescendo of indirect indications that some event is imminent. Its origin is from Cold War signals intelligence, wherein enemy communications would increase as an event grew closer. In terrorism, this is not literal. The chatter may be increasing reports, observations, and tips.

While indicators are the basis of estimates, they are of no value unless filtered through three testing agents:

1. Pertinence (of indicator):

All information must be evaluated for pertinence or relevance. Indicators are like jigsaw puzzles: Data fragments may or may not appear related until the puzzle's picture firms up. Ask yourself: Does information you receive relate to the estimate you are making, or perhaps another estimate? Information comes from many sources, and seemingly unrelated data may be pertinent. Always keep seemingly obscure indicators in a database to be brought back up when you need them. For example, information that a suspected terrorist had selected a window seat on the left side of the plane during each flight from Hartford to New York might seem obscure or irrelevant unless the analyst considers that the individual might be attempting to become familiar with the landmarks, flight path, and approach to a specific target in New York.

2. Source reliability:

Each source of information must be evaluated for reliability. Additionally, the reporting agency should also be evaluated, using the same standard. (See the chart below.) The agency and source are always evaluated separately. Is this information and the person reporting, reliable? Does it hold up to scrutiny? The phrase *consider the source* is always valid when reliability and credibility are being considered. Government-generated terrorism reports usually give both a source information and an evaluation rating. An A-rated source is rare unless the source has deep and broad experience with the information to the point where it is

Source Reliability		Source Credibility	
Rating	**Meaning**	**Rating**	**Meaning**
"A"	Completely Reliable	"1"	Confirmed by other sources
"B"	Usually Reliable	"2"	Probably true (in essential parts)
"C"	Fairly Reliable	"3"	Possibly true
"D"	Not usualy reliable	"4"	Doubtfully true
"E"	Unreliable	"5"	Improbable
"F"	Reliability cannot be judged	"6"	Truth cannot be judged

Basic Data Evaluation Charts

unquestionable (for example, a foreign diplomat who has been 100 percent reliable in the past). B-validated information is more common.

For example, an undercover officer is a source for the Drug Enforcement Administration estimate you read. He reports an indicator of a possible chemical weapons factory at a house that was thought to be a crystal methamphetamine lab. The source has great experience in drug lab processing and is usually correct. Based on this information, the source may be rated as source reliability B. The source agency—in this case, the DEA—is also evaluated as B.

3. Credibility/validity source:

Credibility refers to the probable truth of the source information. This information must be evaluated by asking the following questions:

- Is it possible for the reported event to have taken place?
- Is the source information consistent with itself?
- Is the report confirmed or corroborated by different sources or agencies?
- Does the report agree or disagree with other information?
- If the report does not agree with other information, which is most likely to be true?

When seen in U.S. government intelligence reports, each source rating is given a numeric value that usually follows the reliability rating (see the chart) from 1 (most reliable) to 5 (least reliable).

Evaluating the ratings: The two rating scales are usually combined to come up with a letter-number symbol that summarizes the reliability and credibility of the information. If a source and its reporting agency are both rated as usually reliable (B) but the information reported is highly improbable (5), the source data is listed as B-5. A source that is F-6 (neither reliability nor credibility can be judged) may be completely accurate, when it is confirmed by other sources, and cannot be discounted. This system provides flexibility for the analyst evaluating the intelligence and the consumer of the information. Rating example: "DEA Los Angeles reports that they have discovered a chemical weapons factory in what was believed to be a methamphetamine laboratory 10 miles outside of Warner Springs, California." (B-2)

Analytical Process — Evaluation

Once information has been checked for reliability, accuracy, and pertinence, it must be turned into usable intelligence. This is done through a myriad of analytical processes, tools, and techniques. The heavy intelligence analysis techniques used by U.S. intelligence and law enforcement intelligence divisions, including matrix manipulation, visual investigative analysis charting, link analysis, time charting, and program evaluation review technique (PERT), are too advanced for a book of this scope. Many computerized intelligence analysis programs exist for these techniques and can enhance any analysis done mentally, especially when visualization is necessary. For the average reader, this manual offers the following simplified techniques that can be used on a daily basis and in every aspect of the job. Some of the techniques include:

- **Inductive analysis (aka plausible reasoning):** The U.S. Defense Intelligence Agency defines *inductive analysis* as "the process of formulating hypotheses on the basis of observation or other evidence." Inductive reasoning is learning from observing patterns and drawing a conclusion about the activity. A tragic example is the passengers of the fourth hijacked flight on September 11, who quickly induced that their plane would also be used as a suicide weapon after receiving cell phone calls informing them of the fate of three other hijacked aircraft.

- **Deductive analysis (aka demonstrative reasoning):** is the process of reasoning where a conclusion is reached from a theory. This method starts with a premise and comes to a logical confirmation of the theory through gathered evidence or observation. Let's look at this process as used by the author on the morning of September 11.

1. **Theory:** Usama bin Laden's al-Qaeda organization is using multiple simultaneous, spectacular attacks against American interests as a modus operandi.

2. **Observation 1:** On September 11, 2001, at 0832 two aircraft are

skyjacked and piloted by terrorists into both World Trade Center towers almost simultaneously.

3. **Observation 2:** In 1994, an al-Qaeda plan to blow up twelve U.S. airlines simultaneously over the Pacific Ocean on the same day they assassinate the pope in a suicide attack is stopped by an accident at the safe house.

4. **Observation 3:** In September 1998, the American embassies in Nairobi, Kenya, and Dar es Salaam, Tanzania, are attacked almost simultaneously and destroyed. More than 250 people are killed. America attacks terrorist camps with cruise missiles.

5. **Observation 4:** At 0900, two additional aircraft over the United States are missing and believed to be hijacked.

6. **Conclusion:** Al-Qaeda is probably responsible for this attack.

This example sounds simplistic in hindsight, but it is a good illustration of how little time an analyst may have to rapidly draw a conclusion from a standing theory in the field. Conclusions drawn during a terrorist incident may require you take action quickly. In this instance, resources in the government (after the Pentagon was hit) were concentrated on determining the likelihood of additional attacks and defending against those attacks: launching fighter aircraft, landing all airborne U.S. airliners, and evacuating Congress.

- **Simple key-word association:** This is the basic analytical process used for comparing words that may logically match a terrorist's capability to a group's potential path of options. It is based on words associated with indicators. We use these techniques every day. For instance, *sore throat + stuffy nose + body aches = cold or flu.* Key-word association helps the analyst focus on the logic of an assumption or come up with a realistic deduction. Earlier we used the example of associating *Usama bin Laden, al-Qaeda* and *pilot training.* In hindsight, it obviously spelled out *skyjacking: aircraft-as-flying-bomb* as illustrated in the graphic on next page.

A more precise key-word association might read like this:

> *Al-Qaeda + Pilot Training* = control of an *Aircraft.* This line of reasoning can lead to an estimate by proceeding from the initial conclusion. In this case, al-Qaeda's control of an *Aircraft* can be used for purpose of *Skyjacking* for goal of gaining a *Suicide Weapons System* aimed at *Destruction of a ground target* by way of *terrorists piloting aircraft.* Based on al-Qaeda doctrine and history this is a *high probability.*

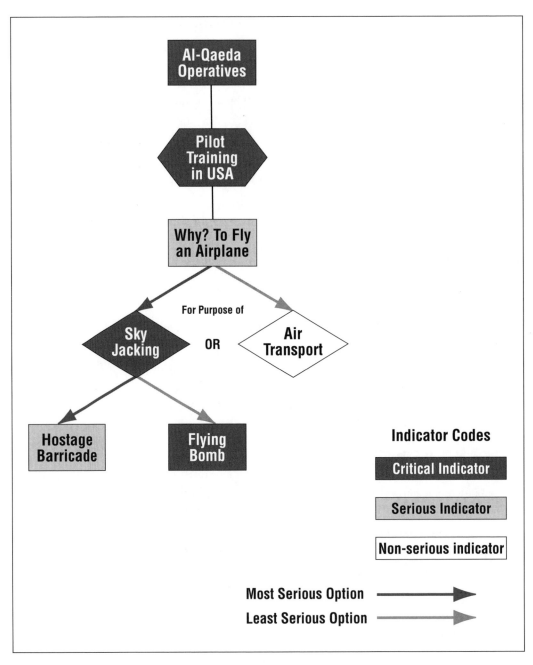

Al-Qaeda Operatives

Pilot Training in USA

Why? To Fly an Airplane

For Purpose of

Sky Jacking OR **Air Transport**

Hostage Barricade

Flying Bomb

Indicator Codes

Critical Indicator

Serious Indicator

Non-serious indicator

Most Serious Option ➡

Least Serious Option ➡

Key word association example.

This exact analysis was found in one FBI agent's report prior to the incident. Al-Qaeda's global capabilities, matched with Bin Laden's personal animosity toward America and a previous skyjacking for this purpose by a group associated with al-Qaeda (the skyjacking of an Air France airliner by the Algerian GIA in 1994), should have clearly constituted a terrorism emergency. Comparing a different group with goals and capabilities gives us an altogether different end result:

FARC + pilot training = possible *aircraft* seizure—for purpose of *skyjacking*—for *ransom* aimed at *release of prisoners*. Based on FARC doctrine and history this is a *high probability*.

Below are a series of key-word association options:

Group	System/Vehicle	For the Purpose of	For the goal of	Targeting
UBL/AQ	Bomb	skyjacking	publicity	high value targets
RIRA	Rocket	ransom	weapons system	symbolic value targets
HAMAS	Firearms	hijacking	theft	individual targets
LTTE	Vehicle	destruction	extortion	national infrastructure
ROHOWA	Train	damage	death	military targets
PFLP	Aircraft	seizure	cash ransom	
IJO	Ship	barricade	seizure	
PIJO	Submarine	hit and run	logistics	
FARC	Biological weapon	assassination	intelligence	
ELN	Chemical weapon	intimidation	demands	
FLN	Nuclear weapon			
	Human weapon			
	computer virus			

- **Weighting indicators:** Once the indicators have been collected and evaluated, they can each be given a subjective value. These values can be added up and given "weight." Once you have given an indicator a measure of credibility, it is piled onto the estimate. Unambiguous indicators have more weight than ambiguous ones. Tip-offs, such as captured plans and documents from the terrorists, have even greater weight. When the combined weight of the indicators exceeds the safety precautions that are in place, it crosses a "potential threat" line. This line is subjective and at the discretion of the analyst. If the indicators are overwhelming, they may move past the potential for an incident to an "imminent threat" line, which is also subjective but leads you to believe an attack is about to occur. Other risk value lines can be created as you deem appropriate. For our example, we have created a "national security emergency" line for incidents that occur within five miles of the president or the U.S. Capitol.

Sample key word association options.

Weighting indicators is not an analytical technique that is incorporated in the formal reporting document (the estimate), but at your desk or in your head it gives you a visual tool to weigh the risk factors as you see them. Weighing indicators may be tested by key-word associations and subjective values placed on each indicator.

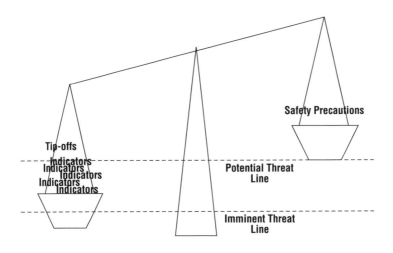

Subjective Risk Values

Potential Threat line:	50 points	
Imminent Threat line:	100 points	
National Security Emergency:	100 ponts if within 5 miles of President or US Capitol	

Source	Indicators/Data Fragments reported	Credibility	Value
Mossad	Hezbollah operatives heading to Wash DC	B-2	10+
US Customs	Hezbollah suspect is in US	A-1	50=60
			60=potential threat
FBI	Suspect's hotel room found with explosive residue and ball bearings in Gaithersburg	A-1	+50
			110=Imminent Threat
DC Police	Suspect's car found abandoned near White House on the Ellipse	B-1	+100
			210=National Security Emergency

Key-Word Association: Hezbollah + Human Guided Suicide Bomb = Realistic & High Possibility

Weighing intelligence indicators.

- **Escalation of threat (skills growth analysis):** A part of pattern analysis is observing the growth of terrorists' tactical skills level. This observation of increasingly skillful terrorist operations is called the escalation of threat. Terrorist groups generally start with operations of low skill such as fund-raising and arson. As they gain strength and experience, they move on to operations that require greater manpower, skills, and resources. There is usually a pattern in the development of these skills and tactics by evolving groups. Some well-funded groups start big, as with al-Qaeda's 1993 vehicle bomb attack on the World Trade Center, but most national and international terrorists generally adhere to the below-listed pattern of growth in tactics and techniques.

Least Threat & Skill

Tactics Menu

- **Fundraising**
- **Physical Intimidation**
- **Arson**
- **Fire Attack**
- **Pistol assassination**
- **Grenade bombing**
- **Simple bombing (pipe, package)**
- **Sophisticated bombings**
- **Abductions**
- **Light Infantry Weapon Attacks/Raids**
- **Stand-off bombings (Mortars, Rockets)**
- **Car bombings**
- **Maritime Attacks**
- **Suicide/Martyrdom Bombings**
- **Skyjackings**
- **Surface-to-Air missile attacks**
- **Mass Effect & Destruction Bombings**
- **Chemical Weapons**
- **Biological Weapons**
- **Nuclear Weapons**

Greatest Threat & Skill

Is al-Qaeda Getting Weaker or Stronger?

On October 15, 2002, the Washington Post ran a story titled "Weaker Al Qaeda Shifts to Smaller-Scale Attacks." The assertion by CIA and other officials was that, due to the successful war on terrorism, al-Qaeda had lost its key leadership and was in disarray. This confusion meant it had to resort to more "indiscriminate attacks." The article noted that smaller, more rudimentary attacks may be "a sign of weakness . . . but the simplicity of these attacks might make them more difficult to predict and prevent." The facts collected by the journalists who wrote the story are accurate. The information quoted from the former CIA official is also accurate. However, the story's conclusion may be inaccurate. This illustrates how correct data can sometimes lead different analysts to conclusions that may be radically different from one another.

Why is al-Qaeda growing stronger? In 2001, AQ conducted major attacks in Indonesia and the United States. In Asia, it performed a bombing wave by attacking more than thirty Christian churches. In the U.S., it performed a mass effect/destruction attack through hijackings of airliners.

In 2002, however, the loss of Afghanistan did force al-Qaeda to rely on regional field commanders to plan and carry out attacks using AQ resources and manpower. This reenergized the AQ international network and has led to a trend of smaller-scale attacks that show a distinct but increasing level of skills that had heretofore been seen only in special task groups of AQ operatives. The examples listed below (attacks either carried out, or planned but thwarted) indicate that AQ operations worldwide are trending toward attacks of increasing sophistication in many more geographic areas than we had seen before—which means al-Qaeda is getting stronger and gaining experience with more operatives.

Conducting the Analysis of Terrorist Skills Growth

Like many other forms of analysis, assessment of a group's increasing skills level can be performed with a subjective quantification of each category of terrorist attack. We have listed the classes of terrorist attacks below and have provided each class of attack with a number. The numbers represent a subjective level of risk that we believe each category poses. A terrorist group that conducts a series of criminal fund-raising activities (5), escalates to small pipe bombings (25), and moves on to car bombings (75) over the course of a year attains a skills level equal to the car bombing (75). This represents the overall skills level of this group. Attacks that were planned but thwarted during their execution are also considered in this analysis, because the attempt shows the level of skills achieved, even if the attack is stopped. Frequency of attacks is generally not taken into account for this type of analysis. That is done when you combine escalation of threat with pattern and frequency analysis (see below). An analysis of al-Qaeda trends in 2001 reveals that two major efforts occurred: a bombing wave in Indonesia against thirty churches by the al-Qaeda-backed Jamma Islamiya (JI), and the 9/11 hijacking. The AQ-JI effort yielded a skills rating of only 30 because even though there were more than thirty bombings, they reveal no increase in group skills level. In the 9/11 incidents, AQ demonstrated that it could perform mass destruction attacks on U.S. soil and is rated at 200 for skills. In 2002, however, many other AQ-sponsored or -inspired attacks occurred with varying levels of skills. The trend line shows attacks of increasing skills in many geographic areas. This is a sign of independent action by AQ regional cells with increasing skills. We can only expect this trend to continue.

Terrorist Activity Skills Value

Fund-raising	5
Physical intimidation	6
Arson	10
Fire attack	15
Pistol assassination	20
Grenade bombing	25
Simple bombing (pipe, package)	30
Sophisticated bombings	40
Abductions	50
Light infantry weapon attacks/raids	55
Standoff bombings (mortars, rockets)	60
Car bombings	75
Maritime attacks	85
Suicide/martyrdom bombings	100
Skyjackings	125
Surface-to-air missile attacks	150
Mass effect and destruction bombings	200
Chemical weapons	250
Biological weapons	400
Nuclear weapons	500

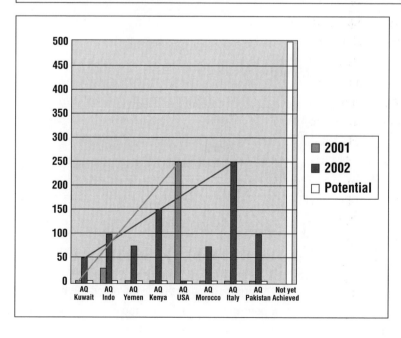

Skills value growth of
al-Qaeda by region.

- **Pattern and frequency analysis** is the study of certain characteristic patterns that can be identified and predicted. If a tactic is being used again and again as a group gains experience, a pattern is established, and the group may move on to a different tactic. Repeated observations of known terrorists entering the country, living with or meeting each other, conducting surveillance on the same target, or repeatedly purchasing legally obtained items that can be used to create terrorist weapons can all be pattern indicators. As you can see in the example, the terrorist group represented on our chart starts its campaign with two weeks of light infantry weapons attacks (LIWA) (an activity skills value of 55), followed by three weeks of bombings (40), and finishing with more LIWA. The first pause occurs in the seventh week but breaks with an increase in skills with the introduction of mortar attacks (60), followed by car bombings (75) and a continuation of regular bombings. This pattern continues, with the group continuing the attacks it has perfected. Predictably, the fifteenth week brings another increase in skills with a suicide bomb attack (100). Simpler bomb attacks occur with more frequency, and LIWA attacks, which are risk intensive, decrease. Part of the pattern is a pause prior to the introduction of a new skill. This may be a training period or a preparatory period in advance of a government response.

Pattern & Frequency Analysis—Escalating Threat:

Terrorist Group Activity Pattern

	Week 1	2	3	4
Month #1	LIWA	LIWA	Bomb	Bomb
Month #2	Bomb	LIWA	–	Mortar
Month #3	Car bomb	Bomb	Bomb	Car bomb
Month #4	LIWA	–	Suicide Bomb	Suicide Bomb

No matter which form of analysis process you find yourself using (and you probably use several unconsciously even now), you need to give weight to credible reports, indicators, and tip-offs against your current security posture. Putting this together with other intelligence is called integration. But before you do that, you must ask yourself a few questions and apply reason and logic to the process.

Analytical Process—Commonsense and Logic Questions

Are there other ways to collect and analyze data that can assist you in understanding the terrorist threat? Certainly. *Common sense* is the most disregarded intelligence analysis tool in our arsenal. Learning to apply common sense and logic to every thought about terrorism is the single best skill you can learn. However, you must consider whether your common sense is different from that of the terrorist group in question. Our culture has different boundaries than the rest of the world. The common sense of people from Central Asia is affected by their culture, environment, religion, and history, so don't apply American midwestern common sense to them. It may be completely unrealistic and unbelievable for reported terrorists to drink twenty shots of vodka before a mission . . . unless they are Russian ultranationalists. In America, it makes absolutely no sense to step onto a bus full of innocent people and blow

> **Common sense is the most disregarded intelligence analysis tool in our arsenal.**

yourself up with them; yet it is done on almost a weekly basis worldwide. Seen through another cultural lens, such an act not only makes sense, but is also respected and admired. So think twice before you make a final judgment about what is appropriate or inappropriate, sanity or madness, possible or impossible. Stick to the intelligence facts and factor the cultural facets of common sense into your analysis as well.

The following questions are designed to help you gain a commonsense-based baseline of information during the analysis process. The answers to these questions are considered the starting point from which to evaluate and interpret information. These questions should be asked every time a new threat is introduced or briefed to you. Don't go into the field during a potential terrorism alert without knowing the answers or at least having considered these questions—even if the answer is, "We don't know."

General Vulnerability Questions

These questions provide general information about the possibility of a threat on a broad scale:

- ❏ Is there really a threat?
- ❏ Are these threats strategic or tactical?
- ❏ Are the potential threat groups political, religious, criminal in ideology?
- ❏ Why would they target our assets?

General Threat Group Questions

☐ If a threat group has been identified as posing a risk, perform the following analysis:

☐ What does this group call itself?

☐ What is this group also known as?

☐ What tactics have this group demonstrated?

☐ What tactics have yet to be demonstrated by the group?

☐ Have undemonstrated tactics of this group ever been demonstrated or attempted by another group (Class I through V)?

☐ Based on demonstrated acts, what skills class of terrorist is this group considered?

☐ What is the most difficult security obstacle this group must overcome?

☐ What is its ability to adapt and overcome new security measures?

☐ Does it use and prefer suicide/martyrdom operations over all other tactics?

Terrorist Leadership Questions

Once these questions have been answered, you need to develop a picture of the leadership with this type of analysis:

☐ Who is the overall responsible leader of this group?

☐ Who is the spiritual and/or political adviser to this group?

☐ Who are the first-tier deputies or advisers (senior leadership)?

☐ Who truly runs the covert or militant wing of this terrorist group?

☐ Who constitutes the field leadership of this group?

☐ Have any on these members been detected in your area of concern in the last x number of years?

Tactical (Street-Level) Threat Questions

☐ Who are the specific terrorist groups known to us?

☐ When did they last plan, use, or attempt a lethal terrorist act?

- Which tactic was used?
- How many operatives were involved in each stage?
- Was the mission a success or failure? (Attempts, even if they fail, are considered successes.)
- Was any surveillance detected before the attack?
- What was the end result of the act?
- Were any members killed or captured?

☐ Which tactics have been most successful for this group?

☐ Which tactics does it prefer?

❏ Do its street-level operatives use a specific pattern of attack?

❏ How might they operate within my jurisdiction?

Post-Incident Analysis Questions

The following questions may guide an inquiry into an act of terrorism. Collect data through the following basic questions:

❏ Is this a conventional weapon or a weapon of mass destruction (WMD) attack?

❏ Is this a WMD attack made to look like a conventional attack?

❏ Is this the primary incident or a diversionary attack?

❏ Is this incident a potential trap for first responders?

❏ Where would a secondary trap be located?

❏ Is there a perimeter set to screen people departing?

❏ Have all witnesses within visual range been removed and corralled? (INTEL cell members may be in a nearby crowd.)

❏ If there was a terrorist security team or driver, which avenues of exit would they take?

❏ Which direction was the fastest way out to a major avenue of escape—subway, highway, rail, airport?

❏ Were people running away without regard to the incident (suspicious people escaping versus running for their lives)?

❏ Were people seen running away with weapons or equipment?

❏ What are the descriptions of people running or "moving with purpose" before the attack occurred?

❏ Do we have descriptions of escape vehicles (or vehicles moving without regard to the incident) and its occupants?

❏ Do we have descriptions of all vehicles speeding away from the crime scene?

❏ What was the direction of travel of escaping people or vehicles?

❏ Did we calculate an escape radius? Note the time since the first alarm and calculate the escape radius of a vehicle at sixty miles per hour (one mile per minute on the highway, or as slow as two miles per minute in a city). This is how Timothy McVeigh was captured after the Oklahoma City bombing: An aware state trooper realized that a potential bomber could be near his patrol point.

❏ Did witnesses observe anyone making rapid vehicle changes within five to ten miles of the target site?

❏ Did police visually inspect local alleyways and balconies within two miles and visual distance of the incident site for a possible command and control cell?

❑ Has EMS or an emergency room seen unusual victims (flash burns on hands and face, shrapnel only in back)?

❑ Are any audio recordings or video footage available that could assist in answering other questions?

Analytical Process—Integration

Raw data fragments, collected and summarized intelligence facts, photo imagery, and open-source information are not intelligence until they are evaluated and integrated with other sources of information into a usable summary. It is also known as multisource integration, intelligence fusion, or intelligence synthesis. Integration is a process that brings all facts and indicators together to produce a hypothesis. Information from imagery, visual surveillance, and wiretaps of the suspects would be integrated into a report along with other data to create a complete picture of the intentions of the terrorists. Integrated intelligence product should reveal to the analyst if the likelihood of an attack from terrorist action is increasing or decreasing. However, integrated intelligence is only considered "final product" when it has been evaluated against known or projected intelligence of the capabilities of the group of interest and all of the courses of action have been spelled out.

A simple method of integrating all of the key factors necessary in predicting potential threat courses of action is called Four-Ts technique. The Four Ts are: terrorists, targets, time, and tactics. This field analysis technique relies on placing what you know about the four categories into a logical sequence and then drawing a conclusion about the terrorists' COAs from the data at hand. It takes an enormous amount of the guesswork out of the analytical process by allowing you to see the key data in the critical categories.

1. Terrorists:

Collect and organize all known data related to the terrorist group of interest's culture, leadership, operatives, and goals, including:

• Evidence of operatives in your area.

• Intelligence indicators in order of discovery.

• Indicators of logistics operations.

• Known peculiarities and weaknesses.

2. Targets:

Collect and organize all data related to the known or estimated targets that may be or are believed to be destined for attack:

- List known targets that have been singled out by the terrorist.
- List targets that have been under surveillance.
- List target sets preferred by the group based on their history.

3. Time:

Estimate or collect information related to indicated or estimated attack time frames as favored by the terrorist group. Include estimated or known time lines for the following attacks:

- **Hasty attack** (developed and executed over hours or days).
- **Normal attack** (developed and executed over weeks).
- **Deliberate attack** (developed and executed over months).

4. Tactics:

Collect and list all data, testimony, evidence, or indicators of the terrorists' preferred or planned methods of attack:

- Include historical attack preferences.
- List known or estimated combat skills and training.

Predicting Terrorist Courses of Action

Before you can draw a conclusion, you must first evaluate terrorists' options. Here is another mental exercise: Knowing the potential targets in your area, what would you attack if you were a terrorist? Invariably, as nonterrorists, we want to use the most devious and technical Tom Clancy-like plan possible, but a real operative will almost always use the simplest, yet most innovative technique possible. For example: If the terrorist has only a pistol and one hand grenade, where would these be most effective? What action would gain the most publicity? Attacking Grand Central Station? Taking and executing hostages live on TV? Setting off the grenade in a suicide attack? It depends on the type of terrorist. A committed terrorist may do the most spectacular, media-grabbing attack. Terrorists of Classes I, III, IV, and V (intelligence agents, radical revolutionaries, guerrillas, and militias) generally conduct secretive attacks, escape, and make claims later. Class II terrorists (Islamic extremists) often prefer to conduct a spectacular attack without regard to loss of life, escape, or claiming credit. These are all factors in determining the course of action.

3. Conclude

Intelligence estimates as a whole are not subjective. The sections in which you predict the possible or probable courses of action may appear subjective, but in fact are deeply rooted in the indicators you've collected. Estimates are solid information and indicators. It should give you adequate intentions and warning on a given threat if you've collected good data and integrated them properly. Predictions of the terrorists' COAs are what may be found in the conclusion after the evidence is spelled out. It is how these indicators are analyzed and interpreted that may be somewhat subjective. As we've said before, stereotypes, lack of information, and lack of attention to indicators leads to speculation and unreliable conclusions. These forms of guessing and speculation are not considered intelligence.

Another problem, especially within the terrorism intelligence community, is that estimates are usually overly cautious. They rarely ever come to a conclusion that could be considered gutsy enough to actually provide adequate I&W for a real attack. Most reports are extensive summaries of highly detailed indicators yet leave readers to draw their own conclusions. This has to stop. Better that the analyst draw a poor conclusion and later reevaluates than to draw no conclusion and be misdirected by deception, politics, or those who don't have enough training or common sense to adequately interpret the information. On the other hand, estimates repeatedly reporting that the terrorist will inevitably attack somewhere, some day are useless. Analysts need to resist filling the reporting system with reports that are vague. It only reveals a level of unprofessionalism from the originating office. Sometimes it may be necessary to state the obvious, but terrorism is a human tactic that has been in use since the beginning of time. It will occur again in the future. If there is no threat, it must be stated that "We have no indications of a threat at this time."

People who need to read intelligence estimates assume terrorists will someday attack. Just as you want specifics, they want specifics. A lack of information may lead a decision maker to magnify the next inconsequential attack well out of proportion.

Worse than a bad call is having good information but developing no conclusion at all. No conclusion means no action. Decision makers want to be told what it is they are reading and how they should behave. Go ahead—that's what professionals are paid for. Prior to 9/11, many indicators of the skyjacking attack—some unambiguous, others pure tip-offs—were found to have been ignored by the FBI headquarters. After 9/11, a common defense heard was, "No one told me this type of attack was a realistic option, and I was waiting for more information before taking action." Concluding your report is only half the I&W picture. Now it must be reported to the decision makers.

4. Report
Unreported Intelligence Supports the Terrorists

The *warning* part of *I&W* requires that the estimate be disseminated to the appropriate level for action or consideration. Any finished estimate of a terrorist act or indicators should be sent up the chain of command using a "Flash" reporting system. If your agency does not have a system in place, one should be created. Cooperative reporting structures with the FBI, the Department of Homeland Security, or state homeland security agencies may be forthcoming and should be reported in the format they require.

What happens when decision makers don't get reporting? In the case of Zacharias Moussaoui, the alleged twentieth hijacker, a request to search his computer, which contained virtually all the core information necessary to stop the 9/11 hijacking plot, was denied. Why? The reporting of the intelligence collected was stopped at various levels of the FBI quite possibly for political or career reasons. It is not the job of intelligence consumers or their management to dismiss reports based on intelligence facts out of hand. It is management's job to ask the tough questions on what constitutes a real threat and to back up analysts if the facts warrant it. If the analysis is believed to be faulty, then other analysts can be placed on the job to do a quick scrub of the data and come up with a conclusion that may be more accurate—or that validates the original conclusion. Beware of anyone rejecting a report because it sounds implausible or unbelievable. Remember, *implausible* generally means someone else has found a solution to a problem you didn't think of first!

Agencies that receive good terrorism intelligence reports should make reading them a daily priority. More important, if you receive word that a terrorism I&W report that originated from lower down the chain of command is considered serious and time sensitive, then you should clear your desks and roll up your sleeves. Read it, sign off on it, and pass it rapidly up the chain of command. Never sit on a time-sensitive report. FBI Special Agent Coleen M. Rowley submitted such a report in the Zacharias Moussaoui case but was strongly blocked by a supervisory special agent. She believed that while the entire scope of the 9/11 plot might not have been prevented, had the reports been taken seriously then a major portion of the plot would have become known to the FBI months before the attack. Bottom line: Read the intelligence reports!

5. Respond

We've emphasized that the chain of command should take reports seriously and provide a vigorous and immediate response to indicators of a threat. So how do we respond without throwing the general populace into a panic? It's generally agreed that recent implementation of the Department of Homeland Security's terrorism alert system has generally created more fear than assurance. What response to terrorism intelligence can balance the needs of security without inducing more fear? Before we answer that, let us consider the words of British Prime Minister Tony Blair:

> The dilemma is reconciling warning people with alarming them; taking preventive measures without destroying normal life . . . if on the basis of a general warning we are to shut down all of the places that Al Qaeda terrorists might be considering for attack, we would be doing their job for them.

There lies the rub. It is not the job of the protective agencies to inculcate more fear. Terrorists seek such a response to their actions, but they don't expect a committed or coherent response. They thrive on confusion, and your overreaction will enhance their terror campaign. The dilemma that law enforcement faces is that a fear of "crying wolf" might inhibit a strong, effective response.

The whole purpose of analyzing and processing terrorist intelligence is to create a balanced response that protects lives. The response may come in the form of a warning to law enforcement only, a public warning, discreet vigilance, or even rarer—preemptive direct action. Everyone involved in this effort should take reports seriously and provide an environment in which vigorous and immediate response to indicators is job number one.

The key to an effective antiterrorism intelligence effort is to collect, analyze, conclude, report, and respond to the intelligence indicators.

When action is delayed or not taken in the face of the growing indicators, people are placed at risk. Terrorists recognize the slightest changes in security, so increasing security measures is never a bad call unless it is done so sloppily and superficially that the terrorists only become encouraged. In a time of tight fiscal resources, issues such as lower budgets, increased overtime, Homeland Security alerts, and public pressure may have a dramatic impact on your ability to sustained a series of responses. No matter what, however, should good intelligence come your way, you need to react aggressively to make terrorists reevaluate their plans or call off the attack in its entirety.

Integration and Interpretation Simulated Case Study

With the preceding overview of terrorism prediction, consider the following scenario and begin applying the principles and methods of analysis. The targets associated in the example are connected using the a basic link diagramming technique.

Monday 0800, situation: You get an indicator that an illegal gun runner in Los Angeles is providing a refurbished sixty-millimeter mortar launcher, twenty empty shells, and sixty propellant charge bags for a foreign client (B-3). A schematic of the relationship is shown here as intersecting boxes. The mortar is the hub of the relationship, so it is represented between the two people.

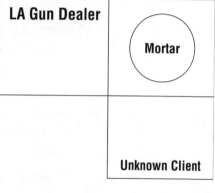

Monday 1000, indicator—tactic: Discussion with the Bureau of Alcohol, Tobacco and Firearms and the U.S. Army provides information on the mortar system. The operator can be approximately a mile and a half from a target to hit it accurately. (B-2)

Monday 2100, response: Surveillance is placed on the gun dealer.

Tuesday 1400, indicator—terrorists: Surveillance of the dealer reveals that the buyer is an unknown young Asian woman about twenty-three years old. She moves the mortar into a black SUV. After leaving, she conducts three hours of countersurveillance driving. Surveillance ends at a building subsequently identified as an Aum Shinrikyo office in Los Angeles. (B-1)

Wednesday 0600, primary group intelligence report: Aum Shinrikyo is a Japanese cult that was responsible for the 1994 Sarin gas attack on the Tokyo subway and four other nerve agent attacks in Japan. (A-1)

Wednesday 0900, indicator—terrorists: The next indicator is a foreign intelligence report received via the FBI that there is a former member of the Japanese Chukaku-ha terrorist group visiting an Aum Shinrikyo USA temple in San Francisco. (FBI C-2)

Wednesday 1000, secondary group intelligence: Chukaku-ha was a Japanese protest group that attacked by firing mortars in the 1980s, bombing economic conferences and a U.S. military base. The group generally used a van or car as a mortar launcher platform, removing the roof and replacing it with a paper or plastic copy so shells could be launched from inside relatively undetected. Members may have participated in a mortar attack with the Japanese Red Army on the U.S. embassies in Rome, Italy, and Jakarta, Indonesia, in 1986. (FBI A-1)

Wednesday 2100, indicator—target: A joint terrorism task force surveillance team installs a wiretap. Initial wiretaps indicate that AUM members are discussing visits and photography of the Hollywood Bowl and Santa Monica Mall. One person mentions revenge for Yu Kikumura, a Japanese Red Army operative arrested with explosives on the New Jersey Turnpike in April 1988. Kikumura may have been a close compatriot of the Chukaku-ha leadership. (FBI B-3)

Thursday 0300, indicator—time: A wiretap reveals a coded phone conversation between the Aum Shinrikyo offices in Los Angeles and San Francisco. The translated intercept reveals, "Our friend will plant the blossom in your garden between 3 and 7 P.M. Later, when the bucket is full, he will drop them in and the fish will die." The translator's notes indicate that the message could mean the mortar and shells will be delivered to the LA safe house and launched at a target crowded with people, with fatal results. (FBI B-3)

In the summary I&W report below, all the essential elements of intelligence are present, and action can be taken in the form of a SWAT team take-down of the terrorist cell and seizure of the weapons and equipment.

LA Gun Dealer — Mortar — ASG — JRA — Japanese Woman AUM (LA) — CHU — OEL-Qaeda

Wednesday 0310—Draft Terrorist Intelligence Intentions & Warning Estimate:

Subject: TERRORIST ALERT #001—POSSIBLE IMMINENT AUM SHINRIKYO (AUM)/CHUKAKU-HA (CHU) CHEMICAL MORTAR ATTACK IN LA AREA (FOUO = For Official Use Only, C = Confidential, S = Secret, TS = Top Secret)

1. **(S) Summary:** As of Tuesday 1400, a 60mm mortar system plus 20 hollowed-out shells and 60 propellant charge bags are believed to have been sold to an unidentified Asian woman related to the Los Angeles office of Aum Shinrikyo. This system can loft a shell approximately 1.5 miles.

   ◆ **Terrorists:** The involvement of AUM and CHU in the United States with a 60mm mortar, inert shells, and their history of chemical weapons usage indicates a terrorist threat emergency.

   ◆ **Tactics:** According to the FBI, the involvement of Aum Shinrikyo could possibly indicate the use chemical weapons in the mortar shells. (FBI C-2)

   - Indicator 1: Sale of mortar system to known AUM member.
   - Indicator 2: Chukaku-ha terrorist staying in AUM temple.
   - Indicator 3: Collection of intelligence on potential target and time.

   ◆ **Time:** An event should be considered imminent, as there are no definitive time parameters. The use of the weapon could take place at any time.

   ◆ **Target:** The indications are that several public venues may be targeted for attack.

2. **(S) Potential Incident Time Frame:** As early as Thursday 1500 if chemicals are already prepared and the shells are filled and ready. An experienced mortar gunner is necessary to fire the system accurately.

3. **(S) Terrorist Courses of Action/Options:** The terrorists have received the system and may be capable of using it as early as Thursday 1500. At this time we have no indications of use of the actual system. However, the presence of the mortar and the hollow shells indicates that they are actively planning and preparing for attack. We estimate that Aum Shinrikyo USA has the following courses of action (from most probable to least probable):

   A. They are preparing for imminent use of the weapon in cooperation with a Chukaku-ha operative.
   B. They are contracting this experienced terrorist to fire a mortar.
   C. They are receiving training from a former Chukaku-ha mortar gunner.
   D. They are stockpiling the weapon for future use.

4. **(S) Conclusion: A terrorist mortar attack, possibly with chemical weapons, is imminent (within the next 11 hours) in the Los Angeles area by unknown members of AUM SHIRIKYO/CHUKAKU-HA. Estimate the attack may occur after 1500 today at the Hollywood Bowl, Santa Monica Mall, or other crowded venue. Launcher may be as far away as 2 miles from impact point.**

5. **(C) Recommendation:** Recommend immediate enforcement action in cooperation with FBI and BATF to recover this system and its shells while it remains in the safe house.

17

POINT OF DANGER: LAW ENFORCEMENT TRAFFIC STOPS AND ENCOUNTERING TERRORISTS

I . . . solemnly swear I will support and defend the Constitution of the United States against all enemies, foreign and domestic . . .

—*Oath of office for members of the U.S. armed forces, government, and law enforcement*

During a recent training session of the Georgia State Homeland Security Agency's SWAT team, an officer asked, "We now know everything there is about a terrorist except what we may find or see during a traffic stop. What is there to know?" In an effort to answer this question, this chapter will outline the pre-incident indicators an officer can use to recognize a potential terrorist operative, either foreign or domestic, when pulled over for a traffic violation.

Law enforcement has had much experience recognizing and apprehending terrorists and potential terrorists of American origin from the antigovernment movement. There also has been considerable experience detecting potential terrorists in the United States from foreign organizations. Al-Qaeda, Hezbollah, the Irish Republican Army, and the Japanese Red Army have been stopped and arrested in the U.S., or their operations exposed due to diligent local law enforcement. On the other hand, law enforcement has stopped many members of these same organizations who exhibited no reason to detain or question them. This is in no way a failure of law enforcement but an example of how seamlessly some terrorists fit into society.

Other countries with extensive antiterrorism experience have found that local law enforcement is critical to stem the flow of equipment and collect intelligence on terrorists within their area of responsibility. England has extensive antiterrorism experience against the Irish Republican Army. France has waged a nearly never-ending war on terrorism, starting with defense against French-Algerian terrorists in the 1950s, Palestinians in the 1960s and 1970s, radical leftists in the 1980s, and Islamic extremists presently. In the 1970s and 1980s, Germany was terrorized by the Baader-Meinhof Gang (aka the Red Army Faction or RAF), whose members became notorious for shooting policemen during traffic stops. In Britain, France, and Germany, traffic stops and police control checkpoints are carried out professionally, courteously, but cautiously because they have been dealing with terrorism risks for decades. Europe's aggressive antiterrorism effort is labeled "guarded vigilance"— a sustained level of antiterrorism readiness and awareness that is imbued in all officers. I believe that the guarded vigilance concept is a better law enforcement doctrine than our current method of spiking to heightened alert levels. On the other hand, in Middle Eastern countries such as Israel the risks are always considered imminent, and so they maintain a very high state of readiness. Local police agencies need to be aware of the most critical factors in their antiterrorism effort: knowledge that there are terrorists out there, they are active, and you can run into them at any time.

Terrorists and the Patrol Officer

It is certain that the most dangerous part of a law enforcement officer's job is stopping vehicles. The traffic stop is a common part of the policeman's job, but may be the first step in a chain of events that could lead to the detection of active terrorists. In the post-September 11 environment, we need to be more vigilant about activities that may precede a terrorist attack. Most officers, if they think about it, already know the indicators of terrorist or illegal activity. Terrorism is a crime, and terrorists are criminals. We must be on constant lookout for criminal activity that may be part of an active terrorist cell's planning or logistics functions. Even though terrorists may be active in a country, they occasionally must use transportation for their activities. If they're well trained and living as clean operatives, then they will have to be rooted out using counterintelligence by officers trained specifically in this skill. Other terrorists may surface through their criminal association and activities. Ahmed Ressam, the logistics chief and bomb master for al-Qaeda's planned millennium bombing in 1999, was known in the Montreal criminal underworld. He was involved in smuggling and petty theft of electronic equipment. According to their own doctrine, al-Qaeda teams in the Western world are required to work and raise funds for operations on their own as well as use AQ resources. Many do so in the petty criminal world. Ressam and his partner Abdul Majed Doumanhane were both known to Canadian police, but authorities did not watch them despite intelligence that they were known members of the Algerian Armed Islamic Group, a support group of al-Qaeda. Ressam was arrested crossing into the United States carrying urea nitrate and other bomb components in an effort to blow up Los Angeles Airport during the millennium. An alert U.S. Customs agent noticed that he took a circuitous route to get to Seattle, instead of a direct one. The philosophy that "Everyone is a potential terrorist" holds up well because at U.S. Customs, "Everyone is a potential smuggler." Ressam was caught on that principle.

The difficulty lies in identifying people who may be preparing for an attack but have generally clean backgrounds. This cannot be done with racial profiling alone unless you are focused on a very specific and ethnically homogeneous terrorist group. As stated earlier, this may not work for al-Qaeda, whose members hail from virtually every society and ethnicity.

That said, improper enforcement of the law creates a cycle of hatred. Every Middle Eastern male who is stopped in the United States on the basis of race alone contributes to the propaganda effort of groups such as al-Qaeda. Many in the American Muslim communities now perceive that they are being unjustly harassed. A terrorist group can adopt such perceptions into its propaganda. When Muslims overseas read or hear about this propaganda, many may be persuaded that Bin Laden may be wrong in his methods, but is telling the truth about this one fact. This is how terrorists gain new followers. One small facet of truth based on an injustice can quickly snowball into a terrorist act. We don't need to give terrorists more ammunition. There is a smarter way of doing business. It requires officers to throw out their stereotypes of who is a terrorist and stick to intelligence about what kinds of terrorists have been known to operate in the immediate area. If you have specific intelligence about terrorists from Yemen, then you can look for people who may originate from the Red Sea region, but if you have no intelligence on terrorist presence you cannot focus solely on Muslims. Surprisingly, Muslim extremists are not your greatest day-to-day terrorist threat. American extremist terrorists are present in far greater numbers and are more likely to seek violent confrontation.

Terrorist Intelligence Profiling and the Traffic Stop

How do you deal with the possibility of encountering a terrorist on a traffic stop? Simple. History shows that if you do your duty as a law officer, you are already conducting a highly critical antiterrorism mission. Run traffic stops, searches, and intelligence collection in accordance with your agency's protocols. If you have specific intelligence about a specific terrorist, cell, or group operating in your area, then use intelligence profiling (as outlined in chapter 3) on every person you stop. Ethnicity is but one of fourteen factors in that profile. The drunk driver you stop to arrest may be an antigovernment extremist who is more likely to shoot you than is an al-Qaeda sleeper cell member. The AQ operative is generally trying to blend into society and avoid confrontations with police, so the likelihood of hitting the gas and running is low.

There were at least three examples of known terrorists involved in the September 11 skyjacking being stopped by state or local police and cited for traffic violations prior to the mission. These terrorists, well aware of what they intended to do against America, calmly took their traffic violations and went about their business of making America pay on a much larger scale. A violent confrontation was not necessary or in the terrorists' interests. Unfortunately, one of them is reported to have been known to U.S. intelligence as an al-Qaeda planner. The question that arises is "How can I possibly detect a terrorist like this?" The short answer is that you cannot unless you know who you are stopping, see something in the vehicle, or note suspicious behavior such as suspects using words that would lead you to believe they are threats and possibly involved in suspicious activity. On the other hand, antigovernment extremists often openly seek confrontation and openly violations of traffic safety and laws.

Profiling and stopping a terrorist suspect requires specific intelligence, such as a known name, description, or photograph circular that may be collected at a higher level than the street. Now more than ever, specific intelligence about potential or known terrorists needs to be pushed down from the intelligence community to the joint terrorism task force level and from there directly into the jurisdictions that may make contact with the individuals. That means the police officer on the street is the new front line of the antiterrorist effort. Note I used *antiterrorism*. No one should adopt a mind-set of counterterrorism. After 9/11, everyone should agree that terrorism must be stopped or deterred before it occurs.

An active program that is being billed as an antiterrorism effort for police is to train officers to stop people whom they think fit a certain "drug courier" profile. Efforts by the drug enforcement community to rework their efforts into the terrorism world are doomed to failure without real-world counterintelligence information. Drug profiles cannot be changed into "terrorist profiles." Criminal profiles do have some common elements with terrorists, but unless programs such as this adopt classified counterintelligence models from a national intelligence agency, they are merely feel-good efforts.

Indicators of Foreign Terror Suspects During the Traffic Stop

This section will list what we do know in the unclassified realm of foreign terrorists who have operated within the United States. We have no need to reveal to future terrorists our precise information, so this section is based solely on incidents in which terrorists have been captured or encountered.

Driver may attempt to enter through minor border checkpoints: There have been numerous attempts of terrorists being stopped at border crossings and checkpoints. Prior to 9/11, many of these checkpoints were unstaffed and conducted through remote video teleconference. The reason behind this indicator is that foreign terrorists often attempt to access a country legally. That may change in the future, but professional groups may still attempt to enter cleanly and legally.

Driver mainly drives rental cars: Foreign terrorists, even those with U.S. residency, will want to use transportation that is reliable, changeable, and relatively difficult to trace. Vehicles need to be easily picked up and dropped off as the mission requirements change. Purchasing a car leads to increased documentation and violations that could be traced by law enforcement, whereas rental cars are self-contained and require less documentation. Terrorists including the 9/11 skyjackers and Japanese Red Army member Yu Kikumura were stopped in rented cars. These vehicles were rented from small agencies where the terrorists would get less scrutiny and be more difficult to trace quickly than would be the case at a larger dealer.

Driver generally adheres to major interstates: Foreign terrorists appear to use the simplest, most direct travel routes between cities. Unlike domestic terrorists who can blend into smaller towns, foreign terrorists are limited to major interstates for movements that don't attract much notice. As demonstrated by the 2002 Washington, D.C., sniper case, a terrorist can practically live in rest stops, mall parking lots, and on the highway between operations.

Driver and passenger are nervous and attempt to hide evidence: Nervousness on the part of the driver or passenger may be distinctly heightened when the suspect has weapons or is en route to a mission.

In Israel, the personal behaviors of a suspected bomber or terrorist when being questioned are the core of the antiterrorism effort. The details of these personal behaviors are better left for a formal training program for your agency. The instincts of an experienced law enforcement officer are more than adequate to recognize the deceptive or masking behaviors of criminals en route to a crime.

Driver and/or passenger may travel on valid U.S. driver's licenses or state ID cards: Foreign-born terrorists operating in the United States are well aware that to live here, they need to be under legal cover. Al-Qaeda terrorists living in the U.S. have it written in their doctrine that they should acquire legal documents using false identities as soon as possible. The license you find on a suspect may be completely legal. Again, counterintelligence efforts are necessary to match legal entrants of known or suspected terrorists in the U.S. with the state identification system.

Driver and/or passenger may possess legal and checkable foreign passports: As stated above, foreign terrorists want as little contact with government as possible—and even less involvement with law enforcement. Even if the identity is false, legal documents are a critical logistical requirement for operatives in the United States. Legal passports from foreign allies such as France, Britain, Japan, Germany, Sweden, Canada, and Saudi Arabia were given far less scrutiny than those of less developed nations.

Driver and/or passenger often have invalid or expired visas: Anyone working at the Immigration service can tell you that the most common offense for foreign-born nationals living illegally in the United States is staying in the country on expired tourist and work visas. There may be as many as eleven million immigrants with no documents or expired documents in this country. Mohammed Atta, the leader of the 9/11 plot, traveled out of the U.S. to Germany for several planning missions on an expired tourist visa. This information may become known during a stop and may be a lesser indicator in the intelligence profile of a terrorist suspect.

Driver and/or passenger may have false Social Security cards and associated documentation: The Social Security card is a passport into the American economy and legal system. Many legal documents can be manipulated, copied, printed, or sold on the black market or even on the Internet.

It's difficult to distinguish terrorists from illegal aliens: The two previous examples reveal how hard it is to discern terrorists in sleeper or active cells from illegal immigrants. If a suspect is believed to be a terrorist, supporting counterintelligence evidence may be necessary to verify the supposition. Many criminal activities in the world of illegal immigrants could appear to be terrorism related but may not be related at all.

Vehicle contains weapons, propaganda, or explosive devices: The clearest indication of terrorist activity is evidence obvious to the eye, such as primed bombs, weapons, or plans. However, there may be other evidence that would lead you to believe a vehicle is involved in terrorist activity. Weapons and propaganda found in a vehicle after an attack, such as in the McVeigh case, as well as actually finding explosive devices or components as with Ahmed Ressam or Yu Kikumura are distinct possibilities.

Vehicle plates differ from driver's license or legal documents: As we stated earlier, terrorists on a mission need transportation that is reliable and disposable. Terrorists using a vehicle for surveillance, logistics, or mobility may change the vehicles often. The driver's licenses may indicate the locale where terrorist suspects have a safe house, while the rental area of the vehicle may indicate the area where the operation (whether a meeting, supply pickup, or attack) is occurring. An example is 9/11 skyjacker Zaid Jarrah, who was stopped and cited in northern Maryland coming from Springfield, Virginia, and driving a rental car from Newark, New Jersey. Many, many legal reasons could be found for such a combination of events, and this might be considered in conjunction with other evidence. The same profile was seen with hijacker Hani Hanjour—New Jersey plates and Florida license. In all of the cases of the three 9/11 skyjackers who were stopped by law enforcement, however, there was no evidence to indicate their future intentions. Authorities let each go with a citation.

Traffic Stop Indicators and Warning Signs for American Antigovernment Extremists and Terrorists

The following is a list from the Anti-Defamation League designed to train law officers in the indicators when stopping vehicles that may be associated with the antigovernment, neo-Nazi, or militia movement members. More information can be found at the ADL Web site: http://www.adl.org/mwd/trafstop.asp.

1. Peculiar license plates:

These include, but by no means are limited to plates claiming to be from the British West Indies, Republic of Texas, Washitaw Nation, Kingdom of Heaven, Dominion of Malchezidek, Republic of Nicaragua or similar non-existent entity. They also include numerous variations on the themes of "sovereign citizen," "sovereign American," "common law," "UCC1-207" (or other UCC themes; these refer to passages in the Uniform Commercial Code), "Republic of [any state]," "militia," and biblical passages. Some plates display volume and page numbers for a document filed in a county recorder's office somewhere. Others quote some phrase in a statute or legal writing. The quality of such plates range from homemade cardboard plates to stamped metal plates that look very legitimate. And of course some will use no license plate at all.

2. Peculiar bumper stickers:

There are bumper stickers and then there are bumper stickers. Some companies market stickers to anti-government extremists and these are readily identifiable. Examples include: AND THE LORD SAID (LUKE 11:46, 52) "WOE TO YOU LAWYERS"; FREE THE SLAVES, ABOLISH IRS AND THE FEDERAL RESERVE; OUR DANGER ISN'T FALLOUT—IT'S SELLOUT; KNOW YOUR ENEMIES: THEY ARE YOUR LEADERS!; REAL AMERICANS DON'T WEAR U.N. BLUE; JOE MCCARTHY WAS RIGHT; and so on.

3. Decorations:

Other strange car decorations, including homemade placards and signs in windows or along tailgates. Cars might display "militia identification numbers" on them.

4. Vocal Resistance to Documentation:

Objections to requests for registration or license on the basis that they are not driving a commercial vehicle. Many extremists claim that the laws requiring such documents apply only to vehicles used for commercial purposes. Strange statements from the driver or passenger, particularly in response to requests for license, registration, proof of insurance or other form of identification. Any references to these documents as "contracts" should be a warning sign; so too should any statement to the effect that they are not required to have them. If they self-identify themselves as "sovereign citizens," "non-resident aliens," "sovereigns," "common law citizens," "state citizens," "freemen," "constitutionalists," or claim some other pseudo-legal status, they are providing police with valuable information about their nature. Any suggestion that the

Constitution or the Bible gives them an absolute right to travel unregulated, or if they present the officer with a Bible as a drivers' license, can be considered a warning sign. Belligerent requests for the officer to produce an arrest warrant can also be a sign. The subject attempts to audiotape the conversation.

5. Anti-Government Literature:

The subject hands the officer political literature or strangely threatening documents for him to read or sign. Anything that reads "Notice to Arresting Officer" or "Form CRIF 2PA95" or which purports to explain the law to the officer should be taken as a warning sign.

6. Anti-Government Documentation:

The subject produces some sort of identification which seems to identify him or her as some sort of strange-sounding law enforcement officer, such as a "Special U.S. Marshal," a "Constitution Ranger," or agent with the "Civil Rights Task Force."

All of the above are examples of some of the possible warning signs. Certainly there can be others as well. The individuals described here tend to believe one or more of the following:

- The government, federal and state and perhaps local as well, is illegitimate.
- They are members of another system of government, which could be a "common law" system, a "township," the "Kingdom of Heaven," or any of a number of other varieties.
- They have an absolute right to completely unfettered travel.
- They can elude or escape the consequences of the law by creating bogus documents such as identification cards, vehicle-related documents, or flyers to give to police officers.
- They are morally and/or legally justified in taking extreme action to protect the rights that they perceive are in jeopardy. Given these circumstances, you can imagine other possible statements, documents, or actions that such mind-sets could produce.

Case Studies of Terrorist Traffic Stops Before and After Terrorist Acts

2002, al-Aqsa Martyrs Brigade Suicide Bombers, Versus Israeli National Police: An Israeli mobile police patrol near the central Israel town of Hadera became suspicious of two young men in a Mazda sedan when they observed different front and rear license plates. The officers conducted a terrorist traffic stop by cutting off and blocking the suspect vehicle. The passenger emerged from the vehicle and engaged the officers with an AK-47 rifle and two explosives devices. One officer was wounded but the other officer killed the assailant. Since it was apparent to the police that they had stopped a terrorist cell en route to a mission, the Israeli police entered a high-speed chase and gun battle with the driver. The terrorist vehicle later exploded after stopping at an intersection. The Israeli National Police believe that the cell was on the way to a combined weapons and suicide bomb attack when they were stopped.

2001, Mohammed Atta, al-Qaeda 9/11 Skyjacker, Versus Florida State Police: September 11 skyjacker and cell leader of the anti-U.S. tactical operations cell Mohammed Atta was stopped by police in July 2001 in Tamarac, Florida. Atta was ticketed for an invalid license. He ignored the ticket, and a bench warrant was later issued for his arrest. But when he was stopped for speeding a few weeks later in a nearby town, the officer, unaware of the bench warrant, let him go with a warning. Atta is believed to have piloted American Airlines Flight 77 into the World Trade Center's north tower.

"There was nothing evident that gave any hint of what Jarrah was about to be involved in."

—Col. David Mitchell, Maryland State Police

2001, Zaid S. Jarrah, al-Qaeda 9/11 Skyjacker, Versus Maryland State Police: A second 9/11 skyjacker, Zaid Jarrah, was stopped on September 9, 2001, for a traffic violation. Maryland State Police Trooper Catalano cited Jarrah for driving ninety miles per hour in a sixty-five mph zone—a $270 fine—on a rural section of Interstate 95 at Pikesville in Cecil County, near the Delaware state line. In a classic example of how clean operatives keep materials and intelligence away from law enforcement, Trooper Catalano reported that he looked over the car both times he approached it, and saw "nothing evident that gave any hint of what Jarrah was about to be involved in." Catalano said the incident was "a regular, routine traffic stop, no different from any other traffic stop." In the video made by the trooper's dash camera, Jarrah's Virginia driver's license listed his address as 6601 Quicksilver Drive in Springfield, Virginia, and he can be heard with Catalano on the tape verifying that address. Jarrah was driving a red 2001 Mitsubishi Gallant that was owned by Garden State Car Rental at Newark, New Jersey's, International Airport. The car was found at the airport after the September 11 hijackings, and the citation written by Trooper Catalano was still in the glove box.

2001, Hani Hanjour, al-Qaeda 9/11 Skyjacker, Versus Arlington Virginia Police: Police in Arlington, Virginia, stopped and ticketed Hani Hanjour in August 2001. He was another 9/11 skyjacker who was aboard the American Airlines flight that struck the Pentagon. Hanjour was driving a Chevrolet van with New Jersey plates and surrendered a Florida driver's license to the policeman who stopped him. He was stopped for going fifty miles per hour in a thirty mph zone.

1999, ETA Terrorists, Car Bomb En Route to Drop-off, Versus Spanish Police/Guardia Civil: On December 21, 1999, Spanish police stopped a cell of Basque separatist terrorists from carrying out a major car bombing attack on Madrid. Police intercepted a van that was a large vehicle bomb with nearly six thousand pounds of explosives ready and primed for detonation. The vehicle was stopped because of a minor traffic violation near Calatayud, about 140 miles from Madrid. The van had false Spanish license plates and had been stolen in southwestern France. A criminal check on the driver, Jose Maria Novoa Arroniz, revealed that he was linked to ETA.

1999, Ahmed Ressam, Millennium Bomber, Versus U.S. Customs/Border Patrol: On Saturday, December 18, 1999, U.S. Customs charged al-Qaeda-backed terrorist Ahmed Ressam with bringing more than thirty ounces of highly flammable, explosive nitroglycerine into the United States. Ressam possessed two Canadian driver's licenses (each in a different name), bomb-making ingredients in the trunk of his rental car, and airline tickets to New York and London. He had reserved a room at the Best Western motel a few blocks away from the Seattle Space Needle and the Seattle Center, the site of the city's millennial New Year's Eve celebration. He was arrested in Port Angeles, Washington, after running from a U.S. Customs agent who asked him about his circuitous route by ferry from Victoria, British Columbia. It was a 140-mile drive that does not require a trip to Vancouver Island, a ferry ride, or a stop in Port Angeles. He fled after inspectors searched his car and was caught several blocks away.

1999, Lucia Garafolo, Possible al-Qaeda/AIG Active Supporter, Versus U.S. Customs/Border Patrol: Another incident involving a suspected al-Qaeda/Armed Islamic Group logistics person is the arrest of Lucia Garafolo. A Canadian national, Garafolo appears to have been designated as a transporter/smuggler of operatives from Canada into the United States. On December 21, 1999, a few days after the capture of Ahmed Ressam, a man believed to be an Algerian national tried to enter the United States in the company of Lucia Garafolo. Garafolo allegedly tried to smuggle in Buoabide Chamchi, age twenty, also a Montreal resident. Garafolo was known to have ties with the Armed Islamic Group. She is married to an Algerian national and had contact with Said Atmani, who allegedly forged documents for the GIA. Atmani appears to have been the logistics and false documents cell leader for the GIA. He and Ahmed Ressam were once roommates. According to press reports, "Beecher Falls agents became suspicious because Garofalo had crossed the border on Dec. 6 in the company of her son and an unidentified man whom she said was Canadian. Several days later, Garofalo in the same new Chrysler, reentered Canada with her son and the same man whom Canadian authorities identified as Mustafa Roubici, an Algerian national." Investigation showed that Garafolo made several trips to the United States in the same manner. On December 15, she attempted to cross the border at Pittsburg, New Hampshire, a remote post that is not staffed twenty-four hours a day where off-hours entries are conducted via video equipment. She identified herself to an immigration official in a video conference. The man with her identified himself as Ahmed Saheen and said he was a Canadian citizen born in Pakistan. But Saheen had no identification, and they were denied entry and told to report to a staffed border crossing. They did not. At the time of her arrest, Garafolo was carrying a cell phone registered to a man believed to be connected to the Algerian Islamic League and driving a car co-registered in his name. Garofalo and her husband have "clear links to the GIA, a known Algerian terrorist organization," a Vermont prosecutor said. She was later convicted of minor immigration charges.

1994, Timothy McVeigh, Oklahoma City Bomber, Versus Oklahoma Highway Patrol: Second Lieutenant Charles J. Hanger of the Oklahoma Highway Patrol stopped terrorist Timothy McVeigh seventy-five miles outside Oklahoma City just ninety minutes after the explosion that killed 168 innocent people—the worst act of terrorism perpetrated by an American terrorist within the United States. Trooper Hanger was looking for suspicious vehicles heading away from Oklahoma City, realizing that a speeding vehicle could be in his approximate area. He spotted a run-down yellow Mercury Marquis without license plates—an indicator of antigovernment extremists. Trooper Hanger pulled McVeigh over and approached carefully. McVeigh was "very calm and polite." The trooper noticed a bulge under McVeigh's jacket, and McVeigh told him he had a gun. In fact, he was carrying a concealed .45-caliber Glock pistol. Hanger said he grabbed the bulge and put his own gun to the back of McVeigh's head. McVeigh said, "My weapon is loaded." Hanger replied, "so is mine." The handgun was loaded with Black Talon "cop killer" bullets. In the car, Hanger found an excerpt from *The Turner Diaries,* a novel written by Andrew MacDonald, a pen name for William Pierce, leader of the National Alliance, the largest neo-Nazi group in the United States. The book advocates a violent uprising against the government starting with a truck bombing of the FBI headquarters in the same way the Murrah Building in Oklahoma City was bombed. During the trial, the excerpt was read to the jury: "The real value of our attack lies in the psychological impact, not in the immediate casualties." The T-shirt McVeigh wore at the time of his arrest broadcast his intentions with an image of Abraham Lincoln and a quote from Thomas Jefferson: "The tree of liberty must be refreshed from time to time with the blood of patriots and tyrants." Police found traces of residue from a detonator cord on McVeigh's shirt, in the pockets of his pants, and on a set of earplugs found in his pocket.

1988, Yu Kikumura, Japanese Red Army Bomber, Versus New Jersey State Police: On April 12, 1988, a New Jersey state trooper stopped Japanese Red Army terrorist Yu Kikumura for a motor vehicle violation in a service area. On inspection of the vehicle, the officer observed several gunpowder containers and cans of lead shot in a bag on the backseat of Kikumura's car. He also saw a cardboard box containing three red cylinders with black tape and wires on them. On questioning, Kikumura invited the officer to examine these items. The officer concluded that they might be bombs and arrested him. Kikumura was later indicted on several counts of interstate transportation of explosive devices and passport violations. He was convicted on November 29, 1988, and is currently serving a sentence of 262 months. The three red cylinders and other evidence from Kikumura's car were sent to the FBI laboratory for examination. The FBI confirmed that powder from the red cylinders was a mix of six identifiable types of smokeless powders and one unidentified smokeless powder. Three pea-sized objects found in a paper bag in the car were "prills" of ammonium nitrate. According to the indictment, "The red cylinders were fire extinguishers that had been emptied and refilled with about three pounds of gunpowder, wadding, about three pounds of lead shot, and a flashbulb connected to some wires running out of the top. On one of the bombs, there was an assembled fusing system made from an electric timer, a toggle switch, some batteries, and jack connectors. This timer . . . would allow the bomb to be detonated up to an hour after it was set. The car also contained materials from which similar fusing systems for the other two bombs could be made."

1972, Andreas Baader, Baader-Meinhof Gang—Red Army Faction, Versus Cologne Police: In the early 1970s, the German terrorist group Baader Meinhof gang (BMG) and its spin-off group the Red Army Faction (RAF) engaged in a wave of gun battles with German law enforcement. Many occurred while routine antiterrorism traffic stops were being conducted. Andreas Baader, founder of the BMG, was pulled over while driving a BMW 2000 with Berlin plates in the city of Cologne by a traffic policeman. A police circular noted that the Baader-Meinhof gang preferred fast BMWs. The policeman grew suspicious and drew his weapon to cover the driver. When asked for identification, Baader drew a pistol from the glove box and shot the officer. Baader escaped, and the policeman escaped serious injury.

1971, Petra Schlem, Baader-Meinhof Gang—Red Army Faction, Versus German National Police: Petra Schelm, age nineteen, was one of the younger members of the RAF. On July 15, 1971, Schlem, in the company of an unidentified RAF member, was driving a blue BMW when she was ordered to stop by police for a traffic violation. Schlem choose to run and led the police on a high-speed chase. When the police cut the vehicle off, Schlem stopped. The male passenger got out and opened fire. Police ordered the pair to surrender. Both Schlem and the passenger continued firing on the police, who returned fire with pistol and submachine guns. Covering the passenger—who escaped on foot— Schlem kept up sustained fire. She was finally killed by a burst of SMG fire to the head.

1971, Holger Meins and Margrit Schiller, Baader-Meinhof Gang— Red Army Faction, Versus German Local Police: On September 25, 1971, police officers noticed an incorrectly parked car and thought they were conducting a routine traffic citation when Holger Meins and Margrit Schiller jumped out firing guns. One policeman was shot through the hand while the other sustained serious injuries. Both terrorists escaped.

Dangerous Terrorist Traffic Stops: Anti-Defamation League's Chart of Antigovernment Encounters

June 1994: White supremacist Robert Joos is charged with resisting arrest and carrying a concealed weapon following a traffic stop confrontation with Missouri State Highway Patrol officers.

July 1994: Steven Garrett Colbern is pulled over in a traffic stop in Upland, California, but resists arrest and has to be subdued by five officers. His car is found to contain an assault rifle, a silencer, and a part necessary to convert the rifle to full automatic fire (he is later briefly thought to be the John Doe #2 sought after in the Oklahoma City bombing investigation).

October 1994: A routine traffic stop of three Michigan militia activists near Fowlerville, Michigan, uncovers three loaded semi-automatic rifles, four other guns, armor-piercing ammunition, and night vision goggles. The militiamen are arrested but never show up in court for their trial (later, one of the fugitives allegedly murders another one).

Early 1995: Tim Hampton is charged with assaulting a police officer near Dallas, Texas, over an incident that occurred at a traffic stop.

May 1995: James Boran is pulled over because of outstanding traffic warrants in Massachusetts. Boran refuses to exit his van and instead drives away. After his path is blocked, he continues his escape on foot, barricading himself in his apartment. After he finally surrenders, police find bombmaking materials and militia manuals.

June 1995: Michael Hill, a militia and common law court activist in Ohio, is shot and killed by a Frazeysburg, OH, police officer after pulling a gun on the officer during a traffic stop.

October 1995: Donald Lee Smith, of Cherokee County, Georgia, is pulled over for a traffic stop, resists arrest and is found to be in possession of a concealed assault weapon.

November 1995: "Sovereign citizen" Reinaldo A. DeJesus of White Creek, New York, is arrested for numerous traffic and vehicle charges, and two charges of resisting arrest, following a traffic stop for a burned-out headlight.

January 1996: Larry Martz, a militia and common law court activist in Ohio, attacks a Highway Patrol trooper during a traffic stop near Cambridge, OH. Martz had 23 weapons in his truck.

February 1996: Washington militia leader Bruce Alden Banister is pulled over for expired license tabs. The confrontation which follows ends with him eventually convicted of third-degree assault of a police officer and resisting arrest.

August 1996: Kim Lee Bonsteel of Franklin, North Carolina, is convicted on 18 charges stemming from a 1994 incident in which he led law enforcement officers on a chase through three counties after he refused to produce his driver's license or get out of his truck at a traffic stop. The chase destroyed several patrol cars, injured three officers, and caused a sheriff's deputy to die of a heart attack.

January 1997: A routine traffic stop involving skinhead and militia leader Johnny Bangerter of Utah turns into a chase and brief standoff at a trailer park.

February 1997: Cheyne and Chevie Kehoe engage Ohio law enforcement officers in two well-publicized gun battles following a traffic stop in Wilmington, Ohio.

March 1997: Aryan Nations member Morris Gulett rams a police cruiser during a chase following an attempt to pull him over for going the wrong way down a one-way street. Gulett claimed he drove away because he did not have a driver's license and he "was just in one of those moods." One week earlier, another Ohio Aryan Nations member was arrested following a traffic stop during which police found that he had a loaded handgun stuffed in a beer carton.

August 1997: Carl Drega is stopped near a supermarket in Colebrook, New Hampshire, because of the rust holes in his pickup. Drega opens fire on the state trooper, killing him, then kills his partner as well. Drega then drives into town and kills two more people before fleeing into Vermont, where he has a final gun battle with police there. He dies, but not before injuring three more officers.

September 1997: Craig and Doug Brodrick, two brothers who had recently moved to Boise, are stopped for failing to signal. They begin a gun battle which results in their own deaths as well as the death of a Boise police officer and the wounding of another.

THE POINT OF FAILURE: TERRORIST OPERATIONS AND TACTICS

Recognizing the Point of Failure

The moment you realize that an attack is under way, you have reached the "point of failure" (POF). When a bomb explodes, terrorists storm a building, an airplane crashes, or a person is abducted, you have failed in the mission of detection and defense. Everything from this point on is just a response to the terrorists' plan, and no matter the end result, the terrorist holds the initiative thereon.

Law enforcement and Homeland Security need to learn their enemy's capabilities and intentions *before* the POF. This means detecting and engaging terrorists when they are most vulnerable. Walking into the POF blinded by stereotypes of incompetent terrorists is invariably fatal.

Imagine you are a SWAT team leader on the opposite side of a door from a suspected terrorist cell. Perhaps you don't know anything about this cell other than that there are suspected terrorists of x country origin, from x group, in x strength, who will do x if confronted. Your orders are to go arrest them. Many SWAT teams believe that superior training and tactics will overcome the terrorists. And if these are Class V American militiamen with no formal training, the task could be no more dangerous than a high-risk warrant. On the other hand, they could be tactical operations cell members from the Islamic Jihad Organization on a suicide mission. They have rigged the safe house with explosives, because that is what they use as a counter-counterterrorism technique (and have since 1982). Do you still want to go through the door without knowing their tactics?

Our Special Operations Forces are instructed to know "what's on the other side of the door." One thing that will surely kill them is a cartoon image of their opposition. They need to know who these people are, how they think, and what they will do once the assault team enters the room. Will they booby-trap the entire building? SEAL and Special Forces operators don't take chances. They learn to understand and respect the enemy . . . then they kill them using superior intelligence support and lethal training.

Terrorist Attack Profiles

The terrorist attack profile has two methods of entry. In a hard (or noisy) entry, the enemy "goes loud" immediately and assaults using firearms, missiles, torpedoes, or explosive boats. In a soft (or stealth) entry, the terrorists attempt to enter quietly so that the penetration is not known until the actual terrorist act occurs (the ship blows up, machine guns go off, or the building burns down).

Explosives Bombing Attack

The explosives bombing is the most widely used type of terrorist tactic. Explosives bombings are used in more than 75 percent of all terrorist attacks. The reason is that characteristics of bombs are favorable to creating the highest impact. Explosives bombings are recognized as:

- Universally available.
- Cheap.
- Featuring multiple, easy delivery methods.
- Highly concealable.
- Offering outstanding destruction-to-weight ratio.

U.S. Marine Corps Headquarters Beirut, Lebanon, blows up killing 241.

U.S. DEPARTMENT OF DEFENSE

Manual Bombings

Bombs that are placed by hand.

- **Drop bombing:** A bomb left or dropped off at a location.
- **Toss:** A bomb tossed at a target.
- **Drive-by:** A bomb tossed from a moving vehicle.
- **Courier delivered:** A bomb given to a second person who knows the device is a bomb and delivers it to the target.
- **Surrogate delivered:** A bomb given to a person who does not know it is a bomb and unknowingly carries it to the target.
- **Remotely detonated:** A bomb detonated by electronic control from a distance away.
- **Victim activated:** A bomb that explodes when the victim starts a vehicle or trips a detonation device.
- **Planted or landmine:** A bomb placed on a roadside or under a roadway that explodes when a victim steps on it or rolls over it.

Terrorist bombs can come in the most innocent looking containers. This shampoo bottle cap was found in a terrorist bomb-making safe house.

Standoff Bombing

Bombs that are launched from a distance.

- **Shoulder launched:** A bomb is shot from a rocket launcher that must be mounted on the shoulder of a terrorist.
- **System launched**: A bomb is fired from a system such as a mortar, vehicle-mounted rocket launcher, or other improvised device that shoots it a great distance.

Vehicle Bombings

Bombs that are attached to or target a vehicle or are the weapons itself.

- **Planted device or landmine:** A bomb is deliberately placed on or under a vehicle.
- **Booby-trapped on site:** A vehicle has a bomb attached to the chassis while it is at the victim's residence or office.
- **Booby-trapped off site:** A vehicle is turned into a bomb after the car is taken away by the terrorist, modified, and returned without the victim knowing it.
- **Remotely detonated:** A bomb is detonated from a distance, usually electronically.
- **Victim activated:** A car bomb explodes when the victim starts the vehicle, moves it, or sits in it.

Arson or Fire Attack

Arson is the simplest form of terrorism, a fire attack as an offensive weapon that results in a flame. It can be done by the most junior member of an organization. Setting fire to a building; gas station; ammunition dump; oil, fertilizer, or grain storage facility; petroleum refinery; or ship transporting flammable liquids can be an effective weapon of mass destruction. If carried out correctly, it could be very difficult to trace the act to a terrorist group.

- **Arson by hand:** This is the initiation of a fire by hand with lighter, matches, and/or accelerants such as gasoline and other fuels.
- **Device-initiated arson:** A mechanical explosive device is filled with an accelerant that creates and spreads a fire. Many are designed by professional arsonists. Samples of arson devices have been posted on the Internet by the Earth Liberation Front to encourage the use of arson in its cause by active supporters.
- **Device-activated fire attack:** Purpose-built devices such as Molotov cocktails, white phosphorus incendiary grenades, magnesium destruction devices, and more.
- **Vehicle-carried fire attack:** Flame grenades, incendiary mortar launchers, or flame throwers mounted on a vehicle chassis.

U.S. DEPARTMENT OF STATE

U.S. contractor Bobby Mozelle assassination. Turkey, 1991.

Assassination

Assassination is the tactic used to selectively eliminate a *specific enemy* of a terrorist group. Assassination may use techniques associated with other terrorist tactics (such as an explosives bombing or light infantry weapons attack) because the target is usually one or a small group of important people. The selectivity of the target makes assassination its own special tactic.

- **Blade assassination:** This technique was the primary terrorist assassination technique for centuries until the firearm came along. Sharp objects such as knives, daggers, swords, and other piercing equipment are used.

- **Poison assassination:** Poisoning is an ancient technique of introducing toxin into a victim until it cannot be counteracted. In 1978, Bulgarian intelligence killed Georgi Markov, a Bulgarian defector, with an umbrella tipped with the toxin Ricin, an extract of castor bean. The Usama bin Laden Organization was known to experiment with toxins in Afghanistan and may have succeeded in turning them into weapons of mass destruction, as opposed to personal assassination weapons.

- **Blunt force assassination:** Another time-tested technique is beating the victim to death with hands or a blunt object.

- **Hanging or garrote assassination:** A silent killing technique, strangulation by rope has been used in every period of history as a terrorist weapon. In modern terrorism, it is usually reserved for the execution of a victim already in captivity, execution of traitors, and on-the-spot assassinations. Kidnapped U.S. Marine Lieutenant Colonel William Higgins was shown to have been hung by the Hezbollah terrorist group, though evidence reveals he may have died from torture.

- **Firearm assassination:** Usually a small-caliber pistol is used in a firearms assassination: The killer steps behind or in front of the victim and kills with one clean shot to the head or multiple shots to the body. In 1987, four American service members were assassinated on the street or in their cars by Filipino New People's Army "Sparrow" assassination squads in this exact manner.

- **Sniper assassination:** The use of high-caliber bolt-action or magazine-fed purpose-built sniper rifles, or accuratized military or hunting rifles to kill a victim.

- **Explosives assassination:** The use of commercial, homemade, or improvised explosives to kill a victim with bombs delivered by booby trap, landmines, rockets, a suicide bomber, or another direct method that hits the target, usually while stopped.

- **Drive-by vehicle assassination:** The spraying a large quantity of bullets from an automatic rifle, submachine gun, or pistol when driving by the target in a vehicle.

- **Light infantry weapons assassination:** A surprise attack from a hidden place that combines a team of people using the full firepower of bombs, rifles, machine guns, and/or rockets to kill a victim and neutralize bodyguards.

- **Explosives ambush assassination:** A surprise bomb attack on the route the victim takes, exploding a device left on or near the road.

U.S. DEPARTMENT OF DEFENSE

Light Infantry Weapons Attack

Light infantry weapons assault (LIWA, pronounced *LEE-wah*) takes place when a small terrorist unit or cell assaults a target with light military weapons and explosives such as assault rifles, hand grenades, and shoulder-launched rockets.

These attacks reach for success by laying down a large volume of concentrated firepower. The effectiveness of a LIWA is the training that the terrorist cell has prior to the assault. Many terrorist groups create professional and well-trained infantry soldiers highly capable of conducting a LIWA. Some terrorist groups, such as the Hezbollah in Lebanon, have superb ground combat capability comparable to our Special Operations Forces. LIWAs with small arms and mortars by terrorist groups and paramilitaries drove the well-trained Israeli army out of Lebanon with numerous and increasingly effective assaults. All land warfare weapons and attacks can be used against our airbases, ships, piers, and facilities. The typical LIWA attack may take one of two forms.

LIWA assault: A LIWA assault is a concentrated, highly dynamic infantry-style attack on a target or victim. The assaulters in the terrorist cell will generally focus on either seizing and holding their target or just destroying and killing its occupants. In December 2001, a Pakistani-backed terrorist team stormed the Indian Parliament with a LIWA team and killed more than thirty-five people.

LIWA ambush: The weapons ambush can be done with assault rifles, anti-tank rockets, surface-to-air missiles, or explosives. The target can be anything or anyone. It will be unexpected, intense, fast, and extremely violent in execution. It is generally designed to kill the victims or neutralize security forces. The difference between the LIWA ambush and a weapons assassination (LIWA/combined arms) is that the LIWA is a full-scale attack where heavy volumes of fire are applied, as in a war, versus a precise single shot—though the result may be the same.

Armed Raid

Raids are military-style operations conducted generally to destroy a facility, seize weapons, or rob banks. They are often popular tactics for new groups and wannabe guerrillas who need to demonstrate a limited operations capability, or experienced groups that want to seize high-value targets for short periods. In a highly videotaped shootout in North Hollywood on February 28, 1997, two masked gunmen with several fully automatic assault rifles tried to rob a bank. The event led into large-volume gunplay between the police and the robbers, with the civilian population caught in between. Though not an act of terrorism, this typifies the armed terrorist raids prevalent in Latin America and Asia.

BRAZILIAN ARMED FORCES

- **Weapons seizure raid:** Amateur terrorists conduct armed raids on government armories, police stations, police outposts, or commercial gun shops to acquire guns, explosives, and ammunition.
- **Money seizure raid (bank robbery, et cetera):** Gunmen conduct robberies to acquire the funds necessary to pay active cadres and fund future terrorist attacks.
- **Destruction of garrison/personnel raid:** This raid is designed to completely destroy the buildings, equipment, and people at a government facility. In 2002, the government of Nepal suffered more than five hundred soldiers, police, and civilians killed in garrison raids by communist terrorists.

- **Decoy/feint raid:** The decoy/feint is conducted to draw police and law enforcement away from the actual intended target. Each attack a terrorist carries out should be evaluated as a potential decoy/feint. Police should stand by for a secondary attack.

Abduction (Kidnapping, Hostage Taking)

Victims of abduction are often kidnapped by terrorists for cash ransoms to fund other terrorist activity, or held hostage to gain political leverage over governments or to make a victim give them access to a secure facility. Victims are usually taken within a hundred feet of the front door of their office or home.

Kidnappers use many different techniques. Most victims are held by a special guard cell for as long as the negotiations continue. They are usually kept in poor conditions over a time span that may last from a few hours to several years. Most victims come out alive. Less than 1 percent of all hostages are killed once they have served their purpose. However, more than 2 percent are killed in rescue attempts.

- **Ruse abduction:** The use of police, military, or another false pretense to get the victim to comply with the abductor until it is clear that it is an abduction.
- **On-foot or on-street abduction:** Abduction occurs on the street, usually on foot, in a spot where the victim has been led or that is part of a victim's set routine, which the terrorist has discovered by surveillance.
- **Home invasion or surreptitious entry abduction:** Terrorists sometimes deliberately storm a residence and take hostages away. This is a home invasion. A surreptitious entry is when a terrorist stealthily enters a residence and quietly abducts the victim before anyone realizes the victim is gone.
- **Vehicle stop abduction:** When victims are on the road, it is absolutely necessary for terrorists to stop the vehicle to conduct the abduction. The stop can be done via ruse, such as a false police roadblock or creating an accident. The Red Army Faction pushed an empty baby carriage into the path of an abduction victim to force his convoy to stop suddenly.

- **Site abduction:** Terrorists conducting attacks on corporate work sites, remote infrastructure, and critical facilities may require a large force. In December 2000, the FARC of Colombia conducted a site raid in neighboring Ecuador seizing ten Western oil workers and a corporate helicopter.

- **Mass abduction:** An unusual tactic is the abduction of dozens, hundreds, or sometimes thousands of hostages without a barricade situation. In 1995 and 2002, the Chechen Muslim rebels who later became the al-Quaeda–supported Islamic Army of the Caucasus, conducted three mass abductions with thousands of hostages in Russia. They twice used them as human shields until they could escape. The ELN and FARC of Colombia have also conducted mass abductions of lesser numbers, but they kept most of these victims as hostages until the ransoms were paid.

Barricade or Hostage Barricade

Terrorists on a raid may seize, then barricade themselves in a facility to gain attention. They generally take hostages and may execute some of them to press their demands. This type of situation requires professional hostage negotiators and immediate containment by a competent security force.

ARMENIAN ARMED FORCES

- **Hostage barricade:** This is a common and dramatic tactic to confront a government with the fact that terrorists have seized a facility and taken hostages. At this point, the terrorists usually make grandiose statements before the news media. Hostage barricades can last for months. In the 1970s, most hostage barricades ended in favor of the terrorists. When the 1996 hostage barricade at the Japanese embassy in Lima, Peru, occurred, most nations learned to end these barricades with deadly offensive action.

- **Terrorist barricade (no hostages):** Terrorists seize a facility to demonstrate they have the power to do it but take no hostages. They may raise political banners, make demands, and engage in a suicide battle with police or law enforcement if they feel the demonstration has no further use.

Human-Guided (Suicide/Martyr) Weapon Attack

This is the most feared and rapidly expanding form of terrorism world-wide. There are two forms of human-guided (HG) weapon attack: the suicide attack and the martyrdom attack. The phrase *suicide attack* can refer to both types. The recent use of the phrase *homicide attack* is inac-curate, because it reflects the result rather than the tactics. Any fatal ter-rorist attack can be a homicide attack.

Suicide attack: This is a nonreligious, politically motivated terrorist attack whose operatives understand that there is little to no possibility of escape; the terrorists are prepared to die or will kill themselves at the end of the attack; or a terrorist's body is the explosive device's guidance system. This may include making plans to commit suicide before cap-ture or fighting until killed.

SUICIDE ATTACK CASE STUDIES

After the Japanese Red Army terrorist massacre at Israel's Lod Airport in 1972, killing twenty-six and wounding almost one hundred, the terrorists then shot each other or blew themselves up with hand grenades. The LTTE issues black cyanide capsules for its Black Tiger suicide terrorist teams and expects them to use these if captured. The two North Korean intelligence agents who placed a bomb on a Korean airline that killed 115 people attempted to commit suicide by taking cyanide capsules when captured. One agent died; the other survived and confessed to the attack. The Kurdish PKK uses female suicide bombers, usually a lone female with two hand grenades.

Martyrdom attack: This technique is used by religious extremist ter-rorists who believe that they will attain a special place in their next life or "heaven" if they die while killing their enemies. This attack is guided and delivered by a human being who has absolutely no intention of returning from the mission alive. In fact, returning alive may be a dis-grace. Many people who are motivated, on a personal level, to conduct a martyrdom attack are capable of carrying out acts we would think crazy and impossible. In September 1999, a thirty-nine-year-old man, tacitly associated with the Egyptian Moslem Brotherhood, attacked President Mubarak with a knife, knowing full well that U.S. Secret Service-trained bodyguards would gun him down. He did it with little planning, saw an opportunity to commit martyrdom, and died in the attempt. The UBL, Hezbollah/IJO, Islamic Army of the Caucasus, Hamas, and PIJ generally use male bombers in martyrdom attacks. The Sri Lankan LTTE's Black Tigers, Palestinian al-Aqsa Martyr's Brigade, and Turkish PKK have used female martyrdom bombers.

- **HG suicide/martyrdom explosives — manual delivery**: The delivery of an explosive device carried in a bag or wrapped around the body of a bomber. The bomber will blow up with the device.

- **HG suicide/martyrdom bomb — Vehicle Delivery, Land (aka suicide car bomb or truck bomb):** This is an attack using a car or truck driven into or near the victim by a terrorist operative who explodes the bomb, killing the driver and destroying the target. The suicide attack on the U.S. Marine barracks in Beirut killed 241 Americans. Between 1983 and 2002, numerous suicide car bombs were launched against American embassies in the Middle East and Africa, killing more than four hundred.

Hamas marytrdom bombers Mukhtar Abdul Fattah (left), Bassem al-Takrouri (center), and Fuad Jawad al-Qawasmeh (right).

MARYSE BELIVEAU/AUTHOR

Suicide bomb vehicle attack pattern.

- **Vehicle delivery, maritime:** The LTTE and al-Qaeda use small high-speed boats as floating human-guided bombs that explode once they reach their target. The October 2000 attack on the American destroyer USS Cole (DDG-67) in Yemen was a classic example of maritime martyrdom bombing. The Sri Lankan LTTE may be the world master of maritime suicide attacks: It has destroyed dozens of Sri Lankan navy ships with high-speed explosive boats driven by the "Sea Tigers."

- **Vehicle delivery, skyjacking/aircraft as weapons system** use an aircraft as a human-guided explosive device or improvised cruise missile. These attacks have been feared for decades. In 1973, Israeli air force fighters shot down a Libyan Airlines 727, Flight LN 114 over Sinai, believing it was a terrorist-hijacked aircraft preparing to crash into Tel Aviv. It was in fact lost in a sandstorm and suffering a navigational error. All 113 passengers aboard were killed. In December 1994, Algerian Islamic extremists hijacked an Air France flight from Algiers to Marseille. Intelligence gained on the ground revealed that the aircraft was refueling to fly to Paris and crash into the Eiffel Tower. French GIGN commandos then stormed the aircraft and killed the hijackers. The September 11, 2001, skyjackings in America were the first successful use of this tactic in terrorism.

- **Light infantry weapons suicide/martyrdom attack:** This is a terrorist attack in which the attackers use military firearms and hand grenades against a knowingly hardened position where death is almost guaranteed. In June 2002, Palestinian Islamic Jihad operatives started a wave of successful two- and three-person martyrdom attacks on Israeli settlements in the face of overwhelming firepower. The attackers are invariably killed after they have killed as many victims as possible. On July 4, 2002, an Egyptian gunman conducted an armed attack on an El Al ticket counter at Los Angeles Airport. He fired from two weapons and then used a knife, trying to kill as many Israelis as possible until gunned down by El Al security officers.

Aviation Attacks

Aviation attacks are planned missions attacking passengers, aircraft, airports, or air facilities of the victim society. The most common type of aviation attacks are skyjackings and in-flight bombings.

- **Skyjacking—mobile hostage taking:** The skyjacking of an aircraft creates a mobile hostage barricade. The skyjackers seize the aircraft for ransom of passengers or as a

Pan Am Flight 103.

human-guided weapon system. This type of operation can take place in flight or on the ground. Extortion and violent intimidation are used in an effort to have the skyjackers' demands met. Often victims are paraded and executed before the news cameras. During the 1970s, some aircraft were symbolically blown up for television at the end of the operation. If the aircraft is disabled or forced to remain on the ground, the operation becomes identical to a hostage barricade (see page 263).

- **Airport facility attack:** Obvious indicators include a gateway ruckus, storming the jetway, fence loitering, storming flight lines, and vehicle ramming.
- **Skyjacking—aircraft as weapons system:** See the previous section on martyrdom attacks.
- **Aircraft bombing—dropped or delivered device:** These attacks can be done in flight or while the aircraft is grounded.

- **In-flight bombings:** These attacks have been numerous and have killed thousands since the first in-flight bombing in 1949. The 1985 Air India 747 bombing destroyed the aircraft over the Atlantic Ocean, killing 329 passengers. The bomb was placed in checked baggage by a passenger who never boarded the flight. This was proven when another bag checked by the same Sikh terrorist exploded at Narita Airport in Japan. It was destined for another Air India 747. The 1989 bombings of Pan Am Flight 103 over Lockerbie, Scotland, and UTA Flight 772 over the Tenere Desert in Chad were carried out by three Libyan intelligence agents who never boarded the aircraft and an agent who got off at an intermediate stop. All of these bombing occurred when the passenger who checked the bags never boarded the flight—a key clue. The 1993 World Trade Center bomber Ramzi Yusef was convicted of plotting to simultaneously blow up twelve airlines over the Pacific Ocean using bombs placed under seats. A different technique was used by the so-called al-Qaeda–associated "Shoe Bomber" Richard Reid, who attempted to light a fuse linked to explosives hidden in his shoe. An explosion of this sort over the main fuel tank would have blown up the aircraft over the Atlantic.

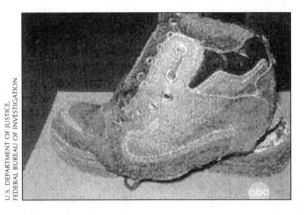

Richard Reid's shoe bomb.

- **On-ground bombings:** In Rome on December 17, 1973, Palestinian terrorists rushed through the airport gate security area, shooting. They then stormed the passenger area firing machine guns, and paused only to throw an incendiary bomb onto a loaded American Airlines 707. The explosion and fire killed all of the twenty-nine people aboard and destroyed the aircraft. The terrorists continued the attack by skyjacking a Lufthansa airliner and later escaped.

In other incidents, bombs that were to have exploded in the air have blown up instead on the ground. In 1986, such a bomb exploded in Sri Lanka while an airliner was taxiing, killing sixteen passengers and wounding forty-one.

- **Small-arms ground-to-air attack:** Armed gunmen with machine guns and rifles have attacked aircraft while taxiing on the ground for takeoff, with intent to damage or blow up the aircraft's full fuel tanks. One such incident occurred in Zurich, Switzerland, in 1969 when gunmen behind the perimeter fence fired AK-47 rifles on El Al Flight 432. The attack was stopped when an Israeli air marshal jumped off the plane and opened fire on the terrorists.

- **Rocket or missile ground-to-air attack (MANPAD/SAM):** A rare attack is the use of an unguided rocket such as an American M-72 light anti-armor weapon (LAAW) or Russian-built RPG-7 rocket launcher to blow up an airliner on the ground. In April 1985, a terrorist fired a Russian RPG-7 rocket at a taxiing Jordanian airliner. The rocket struck the aircraft but failed to explode. A successful attack could have been catastrophic had the rocket hit the fuel tanks.

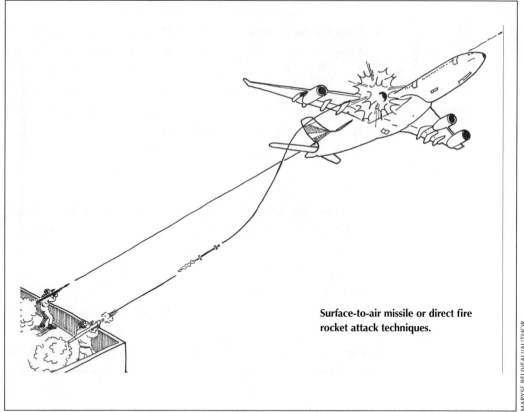

Surface-to-air missile or direct fire rocket attack techniques.

MARYSE BELIVEAU/AUTHOR

- **MAN portable air defense (MANPAD) missile (aka surface-to-air missile or SAM):** This attack employs a sophisticated missile designed to shoot down aircraft and helicopters by damaging the engines and starting a fire. More than thirty incidents of the use of MANPAD missiles have been documented since 1970, killing well over four hundred passengers.

Many of the attacks were in sub-Saharan Africa (Angola). In 1973, five terrorists were arrested in Rome with two missiles as they prepared to shoot down an Israeli airliner. In 2002, an al-Qaeda-owned SA-7 missile missed a U.S. Air Force E-3 Sentry aircraft taking off from an airbase in Saudi Arabia. On November 28, 2003, al-Qaeda terrorists fired two SA-7 missiles at an Israeli airliner taking off from the Mombasa, Kenya, International Airport. Both missiles missed.

- **Detection:** The MANPAD is a very long system that creates a distinct silhouette when an operator places the long tube atop a shoulder. The terrorist generally must test the heat-seeking acquisition system before the missile can be launched. This means the terrorist will test it days or hours before the attack. If this silhouette is seen, it must be assumed that an attack is imminent.
- **Look for the launcher!** A MANPAD missile cannot be easily smuggled into a residence. It resembles a green pipe more than five feet long and in its shipping case is over seven feet. That means it cannot be easily transported from place to place. Shipping cases are also heavy and require two people to carry. In the 2002 attack in Mombasa, Kenya, the launch tubes were painted light blue in order to look more like PVC piping and not military weapons.

Maritime Attacks

Maritime terrorism first evokes the image of piracy at sea. This is a common crime, but the seas have been increasingly a location for terrorism. There are many examples of terrorists seizing vessels and using them later as suicide platforms. They have abducted crews from oil platforms and dive boats with tourists, as well as hijacking arms shipments to be used in later operations. Terrorists also run shipping companies to legally generate funds. Vessels can be pirated (marjacked) to act as floating weapons of mass destruction that can ram vessels, or be used to create explosive devices. Flammable fuel carriers such as oil tankers, natural gas carriers, or even grain transporting ships are subject to seizure and detonation without authorities knowing until the last moment.

Maritime attack—marjacking: This is the seizure and commandeering of a vessel to be used as a floating hostage barricade or for other purposes.

- **Cruise ships:** In 1961, a group called the Junta of Liberation seized a cruise ship in the Caribbean with more than 550 hostages. In 1985, the Italian cruise liner *Achille Lauro* was seized off of the

coast of Israel after a terrorist onboard had been discovered preparing for a suicide attack on the next destination, Ashdod, Israel. In Colombia, Russia, Sri Lanka, and the Philippines, ferries full of passengers have been marjacked for ransom.

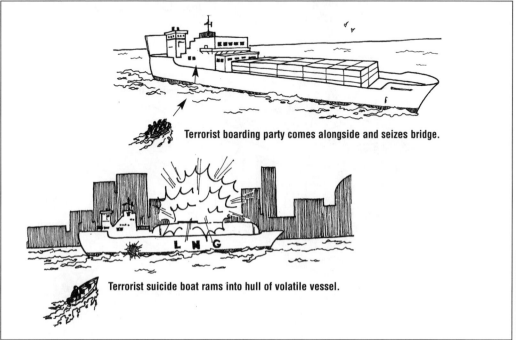

Terrorist boarding party comes alongside and seizes bridge.

Terrorist suicide boat rams into hull of volatile vessel.

- **Merchant vessels** have also been seized by terrorists.
- **Gas oil platforms (GOPLATS):** Hostage takings have occurred on GOPLATS off the West African oilfields. Terrorists have yet to destroy a GOPLAT, but a successful attack could create a major ecological disaster.

Maritime attack—light infantry weapons attack from sea: Also known as amphibious assault. Terrorists use small craft to come ashore and make direct armed assaults on targets. Terrorist commando groups have conducted amphibious assaults using small rubber boats such as the Zodiac to land ashore and infiltrate or attack a nation's shores. In the 1970s and 1980s, Israeli forces stopped Palestinian amphibious commando raids along the Israeli coast. Zodiac rubber raiding craft were launched from merchant vessels (mother ships) in the eastern Mediterranean Sea and were to motor ashore. In a March 1978 raid, eleven Palestinian terrorists landed on a Haifa beach, killed an American citizen, and hijacked a passenger bus. The subsequent rescue attempt by the army killed twenty-five passengers and nine terrorists. Seventy other civilians were wounded.

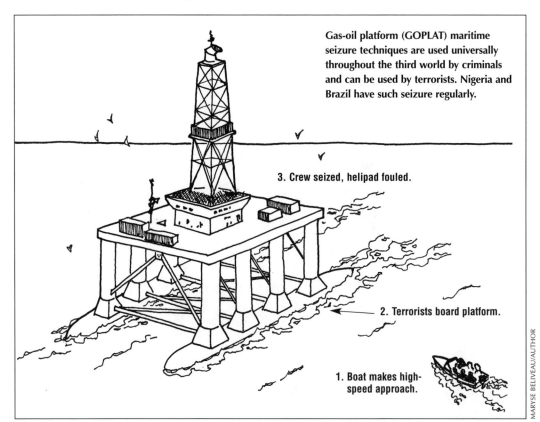

Gas-oil platform (GOPLAT) maritime seizure techniques are used universally throughout the third world by criminals and can be used by terrorists. Nigeria and Brazil have such seizure regularly.

3. Crew seized, helipad fouled.

2. Terrorists board platform.

1. Boat makes high-speed approach.

MARYSE BELIVEAU/AUTHOR

Maritime attack—light infantry weapons assault from shore: This is a simple attack that could be effective against poorly guarded gates and perimeters near ships or ports. In July 1988, terrorists from the Abu Nidal Organization conducted a LIWA attack by storming the pier at the port of Piraeus after a car bomb, designed to breach the security perimeter, prematurely detonated. Two of the assault teams were killed in this explosion. The remainder of the cell assaulted down the pier and seized the passenger ship *City of Poros*. The terrorists sprayed the passengers with machine-gun and rocket fire, killing nine and wounding ninety-eight.

Maritime attack—combat swimmer or diver: The use of swimmers or scuba divers who carry explosives or weapons and use the sea, rivers, or waterways as an approach to mask their operations. The LTTE uses divers to attack Sri Lankan navy and commercial harbors.

Maritime attack—vessel as a weapons system: A form of suicide/martyrdom attack. More details can be found on page 266.

Vehicle Commandeering (Hijacking) and Theft

Truck or car hijackings can provide terrorists a surveillance platform, an infiltration vehicle, an explosives weapons platform, a weapon of mass destruction (with chemicals or fuels), a sniper hide, a mortar carrier, an anti-aircraft gun mount, a resupply vehicle, an escape transport, or a lucrative source of financing.

- **Highjacking for weapons system:** A vehicle is stolen or hijacked to be converted into a bomb or other weapons platform.
- **Escape platform hijacking:** A vehicle is stolen specifically to transport the terrorist group to and from the attack site.
- **Transportation hijacking:** The vehicle is stolen to move people, equipment, or hostages to and from safe locations.

Industrial and Infrastructure Attack

Industrial and infrastructure attack includes conventional weapons, plausible accidents, or improvised devices used to destroy chemical plants, petroleum refineries, electrical grids, road systems, rail, or bridges, or to block transportation.

Domestic terrorists use this strategy often to bring pressure onto a government through the discomfort of the people. The terrorist group may decide to knock out large segments of services that a government provides to the public, to demonstrate to the people that they cannot

POLICE NATIONALE, MINISTRY OF THE INTERIOR, REPUBLIQUE DE FRANCE

gain comfort or be protected in the most basic acts such as driving safe-
ly on the highway, or be provided with consistent power and water supplies, fuel or oil revenues, or uninterrupted communications.

Groups could also attack infrastructure to cause a release or activation of a weapon of mass destruction. For example, four members of
the True Knights of the Ku Klux Klan were convicted of planning an
armored car robbery in Wise County, Texas, but intended to explode
diversionary bombs at a natural gas processing/storage facility to cover
the robbery. They believed the facility contained lethal gases that could
create a disaster.

Detection: The simplest methods of detection should always be considered first. Techniques of destruction include chopping down an
electrical pole, pulling up rail lines with crowbars, or removing bolts
from the base of the electrical towers. An infrastructure attack could
involve:

- **Rail or subway attack:** Power lines, rails, and vehicles could be
  attacked with different types of weapons to stop the lines of communication. Attacks could range from explosives to weapons of
  mass destruction in subways, stations, or rail lines.

- **Communications, power, water, and energy attack:** Terrorist attacks on these services are designed to inconvenience a population and make the government appear helpless. In April 1990, the Earth Night Action Group knocked out power to 95 percent of Santa Cruz County, California, by toppling large power lines. Another group targeted power lines for a nuclear reactor in an effort to shut it down.
- **Road interdiction:** These would be attacks and roadblocks on major highways. They may also be combined with abductions or ambush attacks.
- **Transportation facilities attack:** Bus stations, train stations, truck stops, and other transportation hubs are critical nodes, and attacking them brings fear to passengers who will seek other methods of transportation if they feel they are not safe.

Physical Intimidation or Maiming

Terrorists often use maiming to express a point related to loyalty within the organization or to punish uncooperative civilians. Victims may be beaten or maimed instead of assassinated by terrorist supporters as a symbolic gesture. These types of attacks may yield intelligence about operatives in the country, because they may come into contact with the police and hospital systems. Officers may learn good information from maimed terrorists or supporters about other members of the terrorist group.

Psychological Threat

Nonspecific credible threats such as bomb scares, death threats, and warning graffiti raise the level of pressure on individuals and degrade security measures. Hundreds of bomb scares are usually mimicked after real terrorist bombings, and this keeps the fear level high. Death threats are specific threats against an individual. Should a death threat be received from a group that has clearly assassinated people in the past, the personal level of fear can be debilitating. Weapons of mass destruction hoaxes claiming to contain anthrax or other biological weapons have become a way of life for American family planning clinics. After the real September 17 anthrax attacks, hundreds of envelopes with various kinds of anthrax-like powders and anthrax threats were received by these clinics from anti-abortion terrorists.

This mural is a classic example of terrorist Psychological Operations.

U.S. DEPARTMENT OF DEFENSE

Detection of psychological threats requires stopping them before they are sent. Searches could yield large quantities of threatening letters and envelopes with inert powders or agents prepared for insertion.

Improvised or Offensive Chemical Weapons Attack

Chemical weapons are a weapon of mass destruction. Any combination of hazardous materials can be used to form chemical weapons such as phosgene gas. Deliberately weaponized chemicals like mustard gas can be seen as wafting clouds. Lethal or nonlethal choking agents, such as CS (tear gas) or OCP (pepper spray), could be used as part of a conventional weapons attack scenario to disable unprepared personnel.

Biological Terror Weapons Attack

As weapons of mass destruction, bioweapon attacks disperse air-, cuteanous-, or bloodborne pathogens that introduce a disease into human beings or animals. The disease can be introduced through deliberately tampering with food or water supplies, by mail or by aerial spraying. Bioweapon attacks could occur without warning.

Biological terror weapons generally are created to strike in three ways:

1. As antipersonnel weapons.
2. As anti-animal weapons (see the next section).
3. As anti-agriculture weapons (see the next section).

Delivery and transmission of a bioweapon: The manual or oral dispersement of a bioweapon requires either a fine dispersal device a person deliberately sent to infect others. Aerosol sprays fixed on crop dusters could infect a mass of people. However, weaponized dispersal agents could be delivered by spilling infected powders in a confined area. A suicide/martyrdom attack could involve a person who has been deliberately infected with the disease and travels extensively in crowded locations and sneezes, spits, or simply breathes normally.

Detection: Due to the insidious nature of a terrorist-introduced infectious disease, detection before an attack may be difficult. Some equipment can appear to be routine drug paraphernalia. Caution should be taken if experienced counternarcotics officers find that the atmosphere is incorrect for real narcotic production operations. Look for:

- Needles.
- Vials with identified medical agents.

- Unidentified powders.
- Powder milling machines.
- Documents that threaten bioweapons attack.
- Medical materials.
- Terrorist connections with infectious disease doctors.
- Arrested victims attempt to spit or breathe on you.

Standoff delivery of bioweapons: The anthrax attack of September 2001 was delivered in a standoff manner—through the mail. Any agent or disease that is delivered away from the source is a standoff delivery. Look for:

- Powdery substances in mailings that should not have powders.
- Documents with residue of saliva or body fluids.
- Nonexplosive dispersal devices built for mortars, grenades, or rockets. Chemically treated smoke grenades are a good example.

Vehicle delivery of bioweapons: An agent or disease that is spread through spraying from a car, airplane, or vessel may offer a wider initial area of infection and expands the chances of a mass medical crisis.

Agro-Terrorist Attack

Agriculture attack: An attack using biological or conventional tactics on farming, arable land, or livestock is designed to inflict long-term economic impact. A deliberately introduced farm animal disease such as hoof-and-mouth could devastate the entire meat industry. Detection of these attempts is almost identical to detecting biological weapons (see above).

Anti-animal illnesses: The International Organization of Epizootics (OIP) is responsible for setting international animal health standards. It maintains an A-list of "transmissible diseases" that have the potential for very serious and rapid spread, irrespective of national borders; that are of serious socioeconomic or public health consequence; and that are of major importance in the international trade of animals and animal products.

Diseases That Primarily Affect U.S. Cattle, Swine, and Poultry

- **Foot-and-mouth disease:** Affects cattle, swine, horses. A vaccine exists. It's transmitted through aerosols, or by direct and indirect contact.

- **Vesicular stomatitis:** Affects cattle, swine, and horses. A vaccine exists. It's transmitted by direct contact and insect vectors.
- **Swine vesicular disease:** Affects swine. No vaccine is available. Transmitted through ingestion of infected meat.
- **Rinderpest ("cattle plague"):** Affects cattle, sheep, goats. A vaccine exists. Transmitted through direct contact and airborne droplets.
- **Contagious bovine pleuro-pneumonia:** Affects cattle. A vaccine exists. Transmitted though inhalation of droplets of infected animal secretions.
- **Lumpy skin disease:** Affects cattle. A vaccine exists. Transmission through insect vectors.
- **Valley fever:** Affects cattle. A vaccine exists. Humans are susceptible, and the disease can be fatal. A human vaccine exists. Transmission through insect vectors or direct contact.
- **Bluetongue:** Affects sheep, cattle. A vaccine exists. Transmission through insect vectors.
- **African swine fever:** Affects swine. No vaccine is available. Transmitted through direct contact, aerosols, insect vectors, and infected meat ingestion.
- **Classical swine fever (hog cholera):** Affects swine. A vaccine exists. Transmission by direct and indirect contact.
- **Highly pathogenic avian influenza ("fowl plague"):** Affects chickens and turkeys. A vaccine exists. Transmission by direct contact and aerosols.
- **Newcastle disease:** Affects poultry and wild birds. A vaccine exists. Transmission by direct contact, contaminated feed, and water.
- **Bovine spongiform encephelopathy (BSE or "mad cow disease"):** Affects cattle. No vaccine is available. Transmitted by foods containing infected meat and bone meal.

Crop Diseases of Concern

- **Stem rust of wheat:** Affects wheat, barley, and rye. This is a fungus, transmitted through airborne spores.
- **Stripe rust of cereals:** Affects wheat, barley, and rye. A fungus, transmitted through airborne spores.
- **Powdery mildew of cereals:** Affects wheat, barley, and rye. A fungus, transmitted through airborne spores.

- **Corn blight:** Affects corn. Bacteria, transmitted through water-borne cells.
- **Rice blast:** Affects rice. A fungus, transmitted through airborne spores.
- **Rice blight:** Affects rice. Bacteria, transmitted through waterborne cells.
- **Rice brown-spot disease:** Affects rice. A fungus, transmitted through airborne spores.
- **Late blight of potato:** Affects potatoes. A fungus, transmitted through airborne spores.

Nuclear Systems and Radiological Materials Attack

Nuclear Fission Attack

This is the ultimate terrorist weapon—the explosion of a purpose-built device, popularly known as an atomic bomb, that creates great power though the splitting of the atom. Depending on the size of the weapon, the force can kill or vaporize hundreds of thousands of people in a split second, fatally injure tens of thousands more, and contaminate thousands of square miles with radioactive particles.

Radiological Dispersal Device or Explosive Dispersal of Radioactive Materials (RDD/EDRM— aka "Dirty Bomb")

This is a conventional explosion using some form of explosive but is wrapped with highly radioactive material. The explosion disperses radioactive materials over a wide area. It is a psychological weapon for the terrorist, because the word *radioactive* evokes fear and uncertainty. Radioactive materials make the cleanup of the attack site extremely difficult.

Detection: This device can only be detected with the discovery of the planning, the actual device or bomb factory. Handling and storage equipment for radioactive materials are not as extensive as for a fission device. It could also be medical waste marked with radiological warnings or labeled as radiological equipment (such as X-ray machine parts). The easier the material is to acquire in general, the less damage it would do. As little as a measuring cup worth of material could be used.

Contamination radius: The purpose of the device is to disperse the radioactive material into the surrounding area and effectively make cleanup difficult. At a minimum, the affected area will need to be decontaminated. At worst, if the material is highly radioactive, buildings in the area may have to be torn down because of radioactive material embedded in them. For example, a highly radioactive RDD/EDRM device detonated in downtown Manhattan would not cause much physical damage to either lives or property. But areas contaminated by the direct blast and dust that drifts downwind would have to be evacuated, potentially costing hundreds of millions of dollars in decontamination costs, structural demolition fees, and lost revenues. The cost in fear is priceless.

Health risks:

- **Short-term risk:** The majority of casualties will come from the explosion of the device. Radioactive materials will not cause immediate risks at the time of detonation.

- **Long-term risk:** Radiation may cause some sickness and death depending on its amount. In all likelihood, the explosion itself will ultimately cause more deaths than the radiological material.

Personal Radiological Attack

This is an attack in which radioactive equipment or metals are placed near the victim over a period of time, and progressively exposing the victim to long-term, potentially fatal radiation sickness. There is a documented case of a university student placing highly radioactive materials on a professor's desk in an effort to kill him. Look for:

- Strange heavy metals that cannot be identified.
- Unusually heavy containment vessels.
- Devices with radioactive warning or handling markings.

Ecological Attack

This tactic can be used with any of the other destructive terrorist tactics (bombing, infantry attack, and many more) to create a large-scale ecological disaster, and specifically to destroy the natural environment, as opposed to immediately affecting the local people. This could include disasters created by spilling large quantities of toxins or scattering hazardous materials, even sewage. It can be used to redirect resources away from physical security and toward securing the ecological hazard. This category does not include attack by ecological groups or agro-terrorism; ecological attack is a tactic unto itself. Types of ecological attack could include:

U.S. DEPARTMENT OF ENERGY

- Oil spills (includes ships, refineries, storage facilities, and gas oil platforms).
- Toxic waste dispersal.
- Chemical dumping in waterways.
- Oil well fires.
- Dam or levee destruction and flooding.

Cyberattack

Public information as well as military and governmental command, control, communications, computers, and intelligence (C4I) are all vulnerable to attack via computer pathways. Broad virus distribution, harassment attacks, e-mail bombs, and maliciously written codes can all slow or degrade information sharing systems and communications. However, terrorists use the simplest method of attack, so a cyber- or communications attack via the Internet or other methods of systems connection may just be a diversion for another, more conventional operation. Knocking down the telephone or the computers in a city's 911 emergency call center is just as potentially effective as pinning down all the police.

In September 2000, the first "Cyber War" broke out between the government of Israel and supporters of the Palestinian uprising (the

Intifada) in Lebanon, Iran, and Saudi Arabia. The supporters started wide-scale attacks on Israeli government systems and Web sites. This was called the "Electronic Jihad." One of the terrorists hacking Israeli government Web sites told the *Jerusalem Post* that their strategy was, "The more money they lose in fixing and strengthening their systems means less money to buy bullets and rockets for use against our children. . . . Maybe you can't hold a gun and fight, but you can contribute to the struggle."

Who and Where They Are:
A List of Active Terrorist Groups

Transnational Terrorist Groups—Light Grey Bar
International Terrorist Groups—Dark Grey Bar

Acronym	English Name	Foreign-Language Name	Country	Area of Operations
AA	The Partisans' League	'Asbat al-Ansar	Lebanon	National
ABB	Alex Boncayao Brigade		Philippines	National
ACCU	Peasant Self-Defense Group of Cordoba and Uraba		Colombia	National
ADF	Allied Democratic Forces		Uganda	Transnational
AF	Eagle	al Faran	India/Pakistan	Transnational
AF	Sword of al Fatah	al-Fatah/Al-'Asifa	Israel/Palestine	Transnational
AH	Iron	al Hadid	India/Pakistan	Transnational
AIAI	Ethiopian Islamic Union	al-Ittihad al-Islami	Ethiopia	National
AIAI	Somali Islamic Union	al-Ittihad al-Islami	Somalia	National
AIS	Islamic Salvation Front	Armee Islamique du Salut	Algeria	National
AISSF	All India Sikh Student Federation		India	National
ALIR	Army for the Liberation of Rwanda	Interahamwe	DR Congo	National
AN	Aryan Nations		United States	National
ANO	Abu Nidal Organization		Israel/Palestine	Transnational
AQ\UBL	World Islamic Front for Jihad Against the Jews and Crusaders	al-Qaeda	Afghanistan	International
ARGK	People's Liberation Army of Kurdistan		Turkey	National
ARIF	Arakan Rohingya Islamic Front		Myanmar	National
ASG	Abu Sayyaf Group	Abu Sayyaf	Philippines	Transnational
ASP	Anarchist Street Patrol		Greece	National
ATTF	All Tripura Tiger Force		India	National
AUC	United Self-Defense Forces/Group of Colombia		Colombia	National
AUM	Aum Supreme Truth	Aum Shinrikyo	Japan	Transnational
AVC	Alfaro Lives, Damn It	Alfaro Vive, Carajo	Ecuador	National
AWB	Afrikaaner Resistance Movement	Afrikaaner Weestand Beweeging	South Africa	National
BK	Babbar Khalsa		India	National
BLA	Bavaria Liberation Army		Austria	National
BLT	Bodo Liberation Tigers		India	National
BOF	Brethren of the Faithful (Islamic Change Organization cover name)		Saudi Arabia	National

Transnational Terrorist Groups—Light Grey Bar
International Terrorist Groups—Dark Grey Bar

Acronym	English Name	Foreign-Language Name	Country	Area of Operations
BSF	Bodo Security Force		India	National
CA	Conscientious Arsonists		Greece	National
CAC	Continuity Army Council		United Kingdom	National
CFF	Cambodian Freedom Fighters		Cambodia	National
CIRA	Continuity Irish Republican Army		United Kingdom	National
CNDD	National Council for the Defense of Democracy		Burundi	National
COES	Special Operations Commandos	Comandoes Operativos Especiales	Honduras	National
CON	Children of November		Greece	National
DFLP	Democratic Front for the Liberation of Palestine	Jebha Demorasi lil Tahrir al Filistin	Israel/Palestine	International
DHKP/C	Revolutionary People's Liberation Party/Front, Dev Sol	Devrimci Halk Kurtulus Partisi/ Cephesi, Devrimici Sol	Turkey	National
DK	Army of the Pure	Dal Khalsa	India	National
DKBA	Democratic Karen Buddhist Army		Myanmar	National
DPIK	Democratic Party of Kurdish Iran		Iran	National
DR	Tenth Regiment	Dashmesh Regiment	India	National
DRFLA	Democratic Revolutionary Front for the Liberation of Arabistan		Iran	Transnational
EIJ	Egyptian Islamic Jihad	al-Jihad	Egypt	International
EJI	Justice Army of the Defenseless People	Ejercito Justicia de los Indefensos	Mexico	National
ELA	Revolutionary Popular Struggle	Epanastikos laikos Agonas	Greece	National
ELN	National Liberation Army	Ejercito de Liberacion Nacional	Colombia	National
EPL	Popular Liberation Army	Ejercito Popular de Liberacion	Colombia	National
EPLF	Eritrean People's Liberation Front		Eritrea	National
EPR	Popular Revolutionary Army	Ejercito Popular Revolucionario	Mexico	National
ERNK	National Liberation Front of Kurdistan	Eniya Rizgariya Netewa Kurdistan	Turkey	National

Transnational Terrorist Groups—Light Grey Bar
International Terrorist Groups—Dark Grey Bar

Acronym	English Name	Foreign-Language Name	Country	Area of Operations
ETA	Basque Fatherland and Liberty	Euzkadi Ta Askatasuna	Spain	National
EZLN	Zapatista National Liberation Army	Ejercito Zapatistas de Liberacion Nacional	Mexico	National
F-17	Force 17		Israel/Palestine	National
FAA	Fighting Ansar of Allah (Islamic Change Organization cover name)		Saudi Arabia	National
FALN	Armed Forces of National Liberation	Fuerzas Armadas de Liberacion Nacional	United States	National
FAR	Revolutionary Armed Front	Frente Armadas Revolucionarias	Nicaragua	National
FARC	Revolutionary Armed Forces of Colombia	Fuerzas Armadas Revolucionarias de Colombia	Colombia	Transnational
FARF	Armed Forces of the Federal Republic	Forces Armées pour la Republique Federale	Chad	National
FDD	Forces for the Defense of the Democracy	Forces pour la Defense de la Democratie	Burundi	National
FGF	Fighting Guerrilla Formation		Greece	National
FIGL	Fighting Islamic Group in Libya		Libya	National
FLEC-FAC	Cabindan Liberation Armed Forces	FLEC—Forcas Armadas Cabindesas	Angola	National
FLEC-R	Liberation Front for the Enclave of Cabinda-Renovada	Frente de Libertacao do Enclave de Cabinda-Renovada	Angola	National
FLNC	National Liberation Front of Corsica	Front de la Liberation Nationale de la Corse	France	National
FNL	National Liberation Front	Forces Nationales de Liberation	Burundi	National
FNT	Chadian National Front	Front Nationale du Tchad	Chad	National
FNTR	National Front for the Renewal of Chad	Front Nationale pour le Tchad Renovée	Chad	National
FPMR/D	Manuel Rodriguez Patriotic Front	Frente Patriotico Manuel Rodriguez	Chile	National

Transnational Terrorist Groups—Light Grey Bar
International Terrorist Groups—Dark Grey Bar

Acronym	English Name	Foreign-Language Name	Country	Area of Operations
FRETILIN	Revolutionary Front for an Independent East Timor	Frente Revolucionaria Timorense de Libertacao e Independencia	Indonesia	National
FRF	Ricardo Franco Front	Frente Ricardo Franco	Colombia	National
FRUD	Front for the Restoration and Unity of Democracy	Front pour la Restoration d'Unite et Democratie—Dini	Djibouti	National
GAI/GI/IG	Islamic Group	al-Gama'a al-Islamiyya	Egypt	International
GAM	Free Aceh Movement	Gerakin Aceh Merdeka	Indonesia	National
GIA	Armed Islamic Group	Groupe Islamique Arme	Algeria	International
GRAPO	First of October Anti-Fascist Resistance Group	Grupo de Resistencia Antifascista Primero de Octubre	Spain	National
GSPC	Salafist Group for Call and Combat		Algeria	National
HAMAS	Islamic Resistance Movement	Hamas	Israel/Palestine	National
HIZB	Party of God	Hezbollah	Lebanon	International
HUJI	Movement of Islamic Holy War	Harakat ul-Jihad-i Islami	India/Pakistan	Transnational
HUJI/B	Movement of Islamic Holy War	Harakat ul-Jihad-i Islami/Bangladesh	Bangladesh	National
HUM	Movement of Holy Warriors	Harakat ul-Mujahideen	India/Pakistan	Transnational
IA	Islamic Amal		Lebanon	Transnational
IAA	Islamic Army of Aden		Yemen	National
IC	Islamic Call	al-Dawa al-Islamiya	Iraq	International
IFLB	Islamic Front for the Liberation of Bahrain		Bahrain	National
IJ	Islamic Jihad		Israel/Palestine	Transnational
IJH	Islamic Jihad in Hejaz		Saudi Arabia	National
IMC	Islamic Movement for Change		Libya	National
IMM	Islamic Movement of Martyrs		Libya	National
IMM	Islamic Martyrs Movement		Libya	National
IMU	Islamic Movement of Uzbekistan		Uzbekistan	National
INLA	Irish National Liberation Army		United Kingdom	National
INTERA	Interhamwe	Interahamwe	Rwanda	National

Transnational Terrorist Groups—Light Grey Bar
International Terrorist Groups—Dark Grey Bar

Acronym	English Name	Foreign-Language Name	Country	Area of Operations
IPMC-JW	Islamic Peninsula Movement for Change—Jihad Wing (Islamic Change Organization cover name)		Saudi Arabia	National
IRO	Islamic Revolutionary Organization		Saudi Arabia	National
JAA	Islamic Change Organization cover name	Jamaat al-Adala al-Alamiya	Saudi Arabia	National
JEM	Army of Mohammed	Jaish-e-Mohammed	Pakistan	Transnational
JIM	Islamic Group of Malaysia	Jemaah Islamiya	Malaysia	National
JMB	Jordanian Muslim Brotherhood		Jordan	National
JRA	Japanese Red Army	Nippon Sekigun	Japan	International
JVP	People's Liberation Front	Janatha Vimukthi Peramuna	Sri Lanka	National
KA	Karenni Army		Myanmar	National
KACH	Kach (Only Thus) Group	Kach	Israel/Palestine	International
KC	Kahane Lives!	Kachane Chai	Israel/Palestine/USA	International
KDP	Kurdistan Democratic Party		Iraq	Transnational
KLA	Kosovo Liberation Army		Yugoslavia	National
KLF	Khalistan Liberation Front		India	National
KMM	Malaysian Mujahideen of Kumpulan	Kumpulan Mujahidin Malaysia	Malaysia	National
KNLA	Karen National Liberation Army		Myanmar	National
KOMALA	Kurdish Communist Party of Iran		Iran	National
KR	Red Khmer	Khmer Rouge	Cambodia	National
LEO	Omar Forces	Laskar-e-Omar	Pakistan	National
LJM	Libyan Jihad Movement		Libya	National
LLA	Laos Liberation Army		Laos	National
LMAH	Legion of the Martyr Abduallah al-Huzaifi (Islamic Change Organization cover name)		Saudi Arabia	National
LNLF	Lao National Liberation Front		Laos	National
LRA	Lords Resistance Army		Sudan	Transnational
LT	Army of the Righteous	Lashkar-e-Tayyiba	Pakistan	Transnational
LTTE	Liberation Tigers of Tamil Eelam		Sri Lanka	National
LVF	Loyalist Volunteer Force		United Kingdom	National

Transnational Terrorist Groups—Light Grey Bar
International Terrorist Groups—Dark Grey Bar

Acronym	English Name	Foreign-Language Name	Country	Area of Operations
MAIB	Movement for the Self-Determination of the Island of Bioko	Movimiento para la Autodeterminacion de la Isla de Bioko	Equatorial Guinea	National
MEK/MKO	National Liberation Army of Iran	Mujahideen-e-Khalq	Iran	Transnational
MFDC	Casamance Democratic Movement Force	Mouvement des ForcesDemocratiques de la Casamance	Senegal	National
MFUA	United Azaoud Movements and Fronts	Mouvements et Fronts Unifies de l'Azaoud	Mali	National
MGF	Militant Guerrilla Formation		Greece	National
MIC	Movement for Islamic Change		Saudi Arabia	National
MILF	Moro Islamic Liberation Front		Philippines	National
MLB	Movement for the Liberation of Bahrain		Bahrain	National
MRTA	Tupac Amaru Revolutionary Movement	Movimiento Revolucionario Tupac Amaru	Peru	National
NDA	National Democratic Alliance		Sudan	National
NDF	National Democratic Front		Philippines	National
NDFB	National Democratic Front of Bodoland		India	National
NF	National Front		Iran	National
NIM	National Islamic Movement	Jumbish-i-Milli	Afghanistan	National
NIPR	Revolutionary Proletarian Initiative Nuclei		Italy	National
NLFT	National Liberation Front of Tripura		India/Pakistan	National
NPA	New People's Army		Philippines	National
NSCN	National Socialist Council of Nagaland		India	National
NTA	Anti-Imperialist Territorial Nuclei		Italy	National
OV	Orange Volunteers		United Kingdom	National
PAGAD	Qibla and People Against Gangsterism and Drugs		South Africa	National
PDF	People's Democratic Front		Chad	National
PFLP	Popular Front for the Liberation of Palestine		Israel/Palestine	National
PFLP-GC	Popular Front for the Liberation of Palestine—General Command		Israel/Palestine	National

Transnational Terrorist Groups—Light Grey Bar
International Terrorist Groups—Dark Grey Bar

Acronym	English Name	Foreign-Language Name	Country	Area of Operations
PFLP-SC	Popular Front for the Liberation of Palestine—Special Command		Israel/Palestine	Transnational
PIJ	Palestine Islamic Jihad		Israel/Palestine	National
PIRA	Provisional Irish Republican Army		United Kingdom	Transnational
PKK	Kurdistan Workers Party	Partiya Karkaren Kurdistan	Turkey	National
PLF	Palestine Liberation Front		Israel/Palestine	National
PLPH	Party for the Liberation of the Hutu People	Parti pour la Liberacion du Peuple Hutu	Burundi	National
PMOI	People's Mujahideen of Iran		Iran	National
PUK	Patriotic Union of Kurdistan		Iraq	National
PWG	People's War Group		India/Pakistan	National
RHD	Red Hand Defenders		United Kingdom	National
RIRA	Real Irish Republican Army		United Kingdom	Transnational
RN	Revolutionary Nuclei		Greece	National
RO-17	Revolutionary Organization of November 17	Epanastaiki Organosi 17 Noemvri	Greece	National
RSF	Revolutionary Subversive Faction		Greece	National
RSO	Rohingya Solidarity Organization		Myanmar	National
RUF	Revolutionary United Front		Sierra Leone	National
SAF	Sudan Alliance Forces		Sudan	National
SAIRI	Supreme Assembly for the Islamic Revolution of Iraq		Iraq	Transnational
SDA	Somali Democratic Alliance		Somalia	National
Sekihotai	Blood Revenge of the Partisan Volunteers for the Independence of the Japanese	Nippon Minzoku Dokuritsu Giyugun Betsudo Sekihotai	Japan	National
SL	Shining Path	Sendero Luminoso	Peru	National
SMB	Syrian Muslim Brotherhood		Syria	National
SNA	Somali National Alliance		Somalia	National
SNF	Somali National Front		Somalia	National
SNM	Somali National Movement		Somalia	National
SPLA	Sudan People's Liberation Army		Sudan	National

Transnational Terrorist Groups—Light Grey Bar
International Terrorist Groups—Dark Grey Bar

Acronym	English Name	Foreign-Language Name	Country	Area of Operations
SPM	Somali Patriotic Movement		Somalia	National
SSIM	Southern Sudan Independence Movement		Sudan	National
SSPA	Shan State Progress Army/Shan State Army		Myanmar	National
SURA	Shang United Revolutionary Army		Myanmar	National
TCG	Tunisian Combatant Group		Tunisia	National
TH	Turkish Hezbollah		Turkey	National
TOG	Tigers of the Gulf (Islamic Change Organization cover name)		Saudi Arabia	National
TP	Third Position	Terza Posizione	Italy	National
TYKB	Revolutionary Communists' Union of Turkey		Turkey	National
UFD	Union of Democratic Forces	Union des Forces Democratiques	Chad	National
UIFSA	United Islamic Front for the Salvation of Afghanistan		Afghanistan	National
ULA	Umma Liberation Army		Sudan	National
ULFA	United Liberation Front of Assam		India	National
ULNLF	United Lao National Liberation Front		Laos	National
UNITA	National Union for the Total Liberation of Angola	Uniao Nacional para a Independencia Total de Angola	Angola	National
UNRF	Uganda National Rescue Front		Uganda	National
USF	United Somali Front		Somalia	National
UVF	Ulster Volunteer Force		United Kingdom	National
VAPO	People's Extra Parliamentary Opposition		Austria	National
WNBF	West Nile Bank Front		Uganda	National

APPENDIX B

Explosives Components and Ingredients Checklist

Bomb and Improvised Explosive Device Components

- Container
- Arming switch
- Fuse
- Initiator
- Explosive filler
- Shrapnel or contaminant

Delay Mechanism Examples

- Alarm clock delay
- Candle delay
- Cigarette delay

Initiators

- Electric detonator
- Blasting cap
- Nonelectric blasting cap

Fuses

- String fuse
- Prim cord (det cord)
- Pressure fuse
- Pull fuse
- Delay fuse
- Time fuse
- Booby-trap fuse
- Chemical delay fuse
- Delay igniter fuse

Initiator—Action Firing Devices

- Fuse lighter
- Delay
- Pull
- Release
- Pressure
- Pressure-pull
- Percussion
- Trip mechanism
- Metal ball switch
- Altimeter switch
- Tension-release switch
- Blasting machine
- Mousetrap switch
- Pull-loop switch

Time Delay

- Watch switch
- Clock switches
- 7-day clock switch
- 50-day clock switch
- Long-delay clock
- Precision clock

Explosives and Ingredients Identification Checklist

Low Explosives

- Black powder
- Smokeless powder
- French ammonal

Primary High Explosives

- DDNP
- Lead azide
- Lead styphnate
- Mercury fulminate
- Tetracene

Secondary High Explosives

- ❏ Amatol
- ❏ Ammonal
- ❏ Ammonium nitrate
- ❏ Ammonium picrate
- ❏ Astrolite
- ❏ Blasting gelatin
- ❏ Composition "B"
- ❏ Composition C-4
- ❏ Cyclotol
- ❏ Dynamite, commercial
- ❏ Dynamite, military
- ❏ Flex-X
- ❏ Gun cotton
- ❏ HBX (Torpex)
- ❏ HMX
- ❏ Kinepak
- ❏ Minol
- ❏ Nitrocellulose
- ❏ Nitroglycerine
- ❏ Nitro-guanidine
- ❏ Nitro starch
- ❏ Octol
- ❏ PETN (Pentrite)
- ❏ Pentolite
- ❏ Picric acid
- ❏ Picratol
- ❏ Plastic explosive filler
- ❏ RDX
- ❏ Semtex
- ❏ Tetryl
- ❏ Tetrytol
- ❏ TNT
- ❏ Tritonol

Homemade Explosive Chemical Indicators

- ❏ Ammonium nitrate
- ❏ An-aluminum explosive
- ❏ Asprin tablets
- ❏ Battery acid
- ❏ Copper sulfate
- ❏ Carbon tetrachloride
- ❏ Double salts
- ❏ Lead picrate
- ❏ Mercury fulminate
- ❏ Methanol (same as above)
- ❏ Methyl nitrate dynamite
- ❏ Nitric acid
- ❏ Nitric acid-nitrobenzene explosive
- ❏ Potassium chlorate
- ❏ Petroleum jelly
- ❏ Potassium nitrate
- ❏ Red powder propellant
- ❏ Sodium chlorate
- ❏ Tetrachloroethlyene
- ❏ Tetrammine copper chlorate (ttcc)
- ❏ Urea nitrate explosive
- ❏ Urine
- ❏ White powder propellant
- ❏ Wood alcohol

Quick-Reference Chart: Homemade Explosives Chemical Precursors

Precursor	Use	Source
Acetic acid	HMX	Vinegar
Acetone	Acetone peroxide	Hardware store
Aluminum powder	Carbon-tet explosive	Paint store
Ammonium hydroxide	TACC	Ammonia, smelling salts
Ammonium nitrate	Fertilizer explosive	Farm/feed store, cold pack
Carbon tetrachloride (tetrachloroethylene)	Carbon-tet explosive	Pharmacy, fire extinguisher fluid
Citric acid	HMTD	
Copper sulfate	TACC	Insecticide, water purifying agent
Fuel oil/motor oil + gasoline	Fertilizer explosive	
Granular sugar	Sodium chlorate bomb	
Hexamethylenetetramine	HMTD	Drugstore (urotropine, hexamine, methenamine)
Hydrogen peroxide	HMTD, acetone peroxide	Drugstore
Lead monoxide	Lead picrate	
Mercury	Mercury fulminate	Thermometers
Methyl alcohol	Methyl nitrate dynamite	Methanol, antifreeze
Mononitrobenzene (nitrobenzene)	Hellhofite explosive	Drugstore (oil of mirbane), industrial solvent
Nitric acid	Hellhofite explosive	Improvised
Picric acid	DDNP, lead picrate	
Potassium chlorate	Plastic explosive filler	Medicine
Potassium nitrate	Black powder	Drugstore, soil
Sodium chlorate	TACC	Medicine, weed killer
Sodium hydroxide	DDNP	Lye
Sulfuric acid	Nitric acid precursor	Vehicle batteries
Tetracloroethylene	Carbon-tet explosive	Dry-cleaning fluid

Bomb-Making Accessory	Use
Absorbent (sawdust, shredded paper, etc.)	Explosive distillation
Alcohol (whiskey, rubbing, etc.)	Precursor
Aluminum foil	Explosive device
Bucket (w/ or w/o holes in bottom)	Explosive distillation
Clothespins	Explosive device
Fine woven cloth	Filter medium
Flat cans (tuna can, etc.)	Explosive device
Flour	Precursor
Heat-resistant containers (metal, ceramic, etc.)	Explosive distillation
Heat source	Explosive distillation
Measuring device (cups, tablespoon, etc.)	Explosive distillation
Narrow-neck bottles (wine, etc.)	Nitric acid distillation
Petroleum jelly	Plastic explosive filler
Pipes (iron, steel, heavy cardboard, etc.)	Explosive device
Protective gloves	Explosive distillation
Scale	Explosive distillation
Tape (paper, electric, masking—not cellophane)	Explosive distillation
Tubing (rubber, copper, etc.)	Explosive distillation
Window screening	Filter medium
Wires	Explosive device
Wood ashes	Potassium nitrate precursor
Wood boards	Explosive distillation
Wooden rods	Explosive distillation

Comparison Chart: Illicit Drug Precursors (DEA Monitored)

Precursor

Class 1

Anthranilic acid

Benzyl cyanide

Ephedrine

Ergonovine

Ergotamine

N-acetylanthranilic acid

Norpseudoephedrine

Phenylacetic acid

Phenylpropanolamine

Piperidine

Pseudoephedrine

3,4-Methylenedioxyphenyl-2-propanone

Methylamine

Ethylamine

Propionic anhydride

Insosafrole

Safrole

Piperonal

N-methylepherdrine

N-methylpseudoephedrine

Hydriotic acid

Benzaldehyde

Nitroethane

Class 2

Acetic anhydride

Acetone

Benzyl chloride

Ethyl ether

Potassium permanganate

2-butanone

Toluene

BATF Vehicle Bomb Explosion Hazard and Evacuation Distance Tables

ATF	VEHICLE DESCRIPTION	MAXIMUM EXPLOSIVES CAPACITY	LETHAL AIR BLAST RANGE	MINIMUM EVACUATION DISTANCE	FALLING GLASS HAZARD
	COMPACT SEDAN	500 Pounds 227 Kilos *(In Trunk)*	100 Feet 30 Meters	1,500 Feet 457 Meters	1,250 Feet 381 Meters
	FULL SIZE SEDAN	1,000 Pounds 455 Kilos *(In Trunk)*	125 Feet 38 Meters	1,750 Feet 534 Meters	1,750 Feet 534 Meters
	PASSENGER VAN OR CARGO VAN	4,000 Pounds 1,818 Kilos	200 Feet 61 Meters	2,750 Feet 838 Meters	2,750 Feet 838 Meters
	SMALL BOX VAN *(14 FT BOX)*	10,000 Pounds 4,545 Kilos	300 Feet 91 Meters	3,750 Feet 1,143 Meters	3,750 Feet 1,143 Meters
	BOX VAN OR WATER/FUEL TRUCK	30,000 Pounds 13,636 Kilos	450 Feet 137 Meters	6,500 Feet 1,982 Meters	6,500 Feet 1,982 Meters
	SEMI- TRAILER	60,000 Pounds 27,273 Kilos	600 Feet 183 Meters	7,000 Feet 2,134 Meters	7,000 Feet 2,134 Meters

BUREAU OF ALCOHOL, TOBACCO AND FIREARMS

BIBLIOGRAPHY

Publications

Adams, James. 1986. *The Financing of Terror.* New York: Simon & Schuster.

Agirre, Julien, and Solomon, Barbara Probst. 1974. *Operation Ogro: How and Why We Killed Carrero Blanco.* New York: Quadrangle/The New York Times Book Company.

Alexander, Yonah. 1994. *Middle East Terrorism: Selected Group Profiles.* Washington, DC: The Jewish Institute for National Security Affairs.

Alexander, Yonah, and Pluchinsky, Dennis A. 1992. *European Terrorism Today and Tomorrow.* Dulles, Virginia: Brassey's (US), Inc.

Alexander, Yonah, and Swetnam, Michael S. 2001. *Usama Bin Laden's al-Qaida: Profile of a Terrorist Network.* New York: Transnational Publishers, Inc.

Alexievich, Svetlana. 1990. *Zinky Boys.* New York and London: W. W. Norton and Company.

Alibek, Ken, with Handelman, Stephen. 1999. *Biohazard.* New York: Dell Publishing.

Anti-Defamation League of B'nai B'rith. 1988. *Extremism on the Right—a Handbook.* New York.

Auerbach, Ann Hagedorn. 1998. *Ransom.* New York: Henry Holt Company.

Bar-Zohar, Michael, and Haber, Eitan. 2002. *The Quest for the Red Prince.* Guilford, Connecticut: The Lyons Press.

Becker, Jillian. 1984. *The PLO.* New York: St. Martin's Press.

Bodansky, Yossef. 1999. *Bin Laden: The Man Who Declared War on America.* California: Forum of Prima Publishers.

Brackett, D. W. 1996. *Holy Terror: Armageddon in Tokyo.* New York: Weatherhill, Inc.

Campen, Alan, D., Dearth, Douglas, H., and Goodden, R. Thomas. 1996. *Cyberwar.* Fairfax, VA: AFCEA International Press.

Campen, Alan, D., and Dearth, Douglas. 1998. *Cyberwar 2.0.* Fairfax, VA: AFCEA International Press.

Cicippio, Joseph, and Hope, Richard W. 1993. *Chains to Roses.* Waco, Texas: WRS Publishing.

Cline, Peter. 1973. *An Anatomy of Sky Jacking.* London: Abelard-Schuman Limited.

Clutterbuck, Richard. 1978. *Kidnap and Ransom.* London: Faber and Faber.

Collins, Eamon. 1997. *Killing Rage.* New York: Granta Books.

Corbin, Jane. 2002. *Al-Qaeda.* New York: Thunder's Mouth Press/Nations Books.

Demaris, Ovid. 1977. *Brothers in Blood: The International Terrorist Network.* New York: Charles Scribner's Sons.

Derrer, Douglas S. 1992. *We Are All the Target*. Annapolis, MD: Naval Institute Press.

Dillon, Martin. 1990. *The Dirty War*. New York: Routledge Publishers.

Dobson, Christopher, and Payne, Ronald. 1982. *Counterattack: The West's Battle Against the Terrorists*. New York : Facts on File, Inc.

———. 1982. *The Terrorists, Their Weapons, Leaders and Tactics*. New York: Facts on File, Inc.

Drake, Richard. 1989. *The Revolutionary Mystique and Terrorism in Contemporary Italy*. Bloomington, Indiana: Indiana University Press.

Egendorf, Laura, K. 2000. *Terrorism: Opposing Viewpoints*. California: Greenhaven Press, Inc.

Ehrenfeld, Rachel. 1994. *Evil Money: The Inside Story of Money Laundering and Corruption in Government Bank and Business*. SPI Books.

———. 1990. *Narco-Terrorism*. New York: Basic Books.

Eliot, John D., and Gibson, Leslie K. 1978. *Contemporary Terrorism: Selected Readings*. Alexandria, Virginia: International Association of Chiefs of Police.

Emerson, Steven A., and, del Sesto, Cristina. 1991. *Terrorist*. New York: Villard Books.

Emerson, Steven, and Duffy, Brian. 1990. *The Fall of Pan Am 103*. New York: G. P. Putnam's Sons.

Ezell, Edward Clinton. 1986. *The AK 47 Story*. Philadelphia: Stackpole Books.

Gall, Carlotta, and de Wad, Thomas. 1997. *Chechnya*. London: Pan Books.

Guevara, Che. 1961. *Guerilla Warfare*. Lincoln, Nebraska: Bison Books.

Gunaratna, Rohan. 1987. *War and Peace in Sri Lanka*. Colombo, Sri Lanka: Institute of Fundamental Studies.

———. 1997. *International and Regional Security: Implications of the Sri Lankan Tamil Insurgency*. London.

———. 1998. *Sri Lanka's Ethnic Crisis and National Security*. Colombo, Sri Lanka: South Asian Network on Conflict Research.

———. 2002. *Inside Al Qaeda*. New York: Columbia University Press.

Hacker, Frederick J., MD. 1976. *Crusaders, Criminals, Crazies*. New York: W. W. Norton and Company.

Hammel, Eric. 1985. *The Root: The Marines in Beirut August 1982-February 1984*. Orlando, Florida: Harcourt Brace Jovanovich Publishers.

Harris, Robert, and Paxman, Jeremy. 1982. *A Higher Form of Killing*. New York: Hill and Wang.

Hart, Alan. 1984. *Arafat: Terrorist or Peacemaker?* London: Sidgwick & Jackson Ltd.

Hoffman, Bruce. 1998. *Inside Terrorism.* New York: Columbia University Press.

Huband, Mark. 1998. *Warriors of the Prophet.* Boulder, Colorado: Westview Press of Perseus Books Group.

Hubbard, David G., MD. 1986. *Winning Back the Sky.* Dallas, Texas: Saybrook Publishing Company.

Hudson, Rex A. 1999. *Who Becomes a Terrorist and Why.* Guilford, CT: The Lyons Press.

Israeli, Raphael. 1983. *PLO in Lebanon: Selected Documents.* London: Weidenfeld and Nicolson.

Jabar, Hala. 1997. *Hezbollah.* New York: Columbia University Press.

Jacquard, Roland. 2001. *His Name Is Osama Bin Laden.* Paris: Jean Picollec.

Jansen, C. H. 1979. *Militant Islam.* New York: Harper and Row.

Kaplan, David E., and Marshall, Andrew. 1996. *The Cult at the End of the World.* New York: Crown Publishers, Inc.

Katz, Samuel M. 1999. *The Hunt for the Engineer.* Guilford, CT: The Lyons Press.

Kegley, Charles W., Jr. 1990. *International Terrorism, Characteristics, Causes, Controls.* New York: St. Martin's Press, Inc.

Khomeini, Ayatollah Ruhollah. 1979. *Islamic Government.* New York: Manor Books, Inc.

Kobetz, Richard W., and Cooper, H. H. A. 1978. *Target Terrorism.* Alexandria, Virginia: International Association of Chiefs of Police.

Lacqueur, Walter, and Alexander, Yonah. 1987. *The Terrorism Reader.* Dobbs Ferry, NY: A Meridian Book—New American Library.

Lacqueur, Walter. 1999. *The New Terrorism.* New York: Oxford University Press.

Latham, Ronald, trans. 1958. *The Travels of Marco Polo.* London: Penguin Books.

Livingstone, Neil C., and Halevy, David. 1990. *Inside the PLO.* New York: William Morrow and Company, Inc.

Long, David E. 1990. *The Anatomy of Terrorism.* New York: The Free Press Publishers.

Marks, John, and Beliaev, Igor. 1991. *Common Ground on Terrorism.* New York: W. W. Norton and Company.

Martin, David C., and Walcott, John. 1988. *Best Laid Plans: The Inside Story of America's War Against Terrorism.* New York: Touchstone Publishers.

Martin, Mike. 1984. *Afghanistan: Inside a Rebel Stronghold.* Dorset: Blanford Press.

Meade, Robert C., Jr. 1990. *Red Brigades: The Story of Italian Terrorism*. New York: St. Martin's Press.

Miller, Abraham H. 1980. *Terrorism and Hostage Negotiations*. Boulder, CO: West View Press.

Miller, Judith. 1996. *God Has Ninety-Nine Names*. New York: Simon & Shuster.

Moyer, Frank A. 1983. *Special Forces Foreign Weapons Handbook*. Secaucus, NJ: Citadel Press.

O'Ballance, Edgar. 1979. *Islamic Fundamentalist Terrorism*. New York: New York University Press.

O'Neill, Bard, E. 1990. *Insurgency and Terrorism*. Dulles, VA: Brassey's (US), Inc.

Palmer, David Scott, ed. 1992. *Shining Path of Peru*. New York: St. Martin's Press.

Pipes, Daniel. 1983. *In the Path of God: Islam and Political Power*. New York: Basic Books.

Pynchon Holms, John, and Burke, Tom. 1994. *Terrorism*. New York: Pinnacle Windsor Publishing Company.

Ranstorp, Magnus. 1997. *Hizb'allah in Lebanon*. New York: St. Martin's Press.

Rivers, Gayle. 1986. *The War Against the Terrorists: How to Win It*. New York: Stein and Day Publishers.

Rosie, George. 1987. *The Directory of International Terrorism*. New York: Paragon House.

Sharma, Sanjay, and Mishra, Yatish. 1995. *Kashmir Tourism to Terrorism*. New Delhi: Sane Publications.

Scotti, Anthony J. 1986. *Executive Safety and International Terrorism: A Guide for Travelers*. Englewood Cliffs, NJ: Prentice-Hall, Inc.

Seger, Karl A. 1990. *The Anti-Terrorism Handbook*. Novato, California: Presidio Press.

Siino, Denise Marie. 1999. *Guerrilla Hostage*. Grand Rapids, MI: Fleming H. Revell.

Taylor, Peter. 1997. *Behind the Mask: The IRA and Sinn Feinn*. New York: TV Books, Inc.

Thackrah, John Richard. 1987. *Encyclopedia of Terrorism and Political Violence*. London and New York: Routledge and Kegan Paul.

Ullman, Harlan. 2002. *Unfinished Business*. New York: Citadel Press, Kensington Publicity Corp.

Villemarest, P. F. de, with Faillant, Daniele. 1976. *Histoire Secrete des Organisations Terroristes (Vols. 1, 2, 3, and 4)*. Geneva, Switzerland: Editions Famot.

Weaver, Mary Anne. 1999. *A Portrait of Egypt: A Journey Through the World of Militant Islam*. New York: Farrar, Straus & Giroux.

Weir, Ben, and Weir, Carol, with Benson, Dennis. 1987. *Hostage Bound Hostage Free.* Philadelphia: The Westminster Press.

Wright, Robin. 1985. *Sacred Rage.* New York: Simon and Schuster, Inc.

Government Documents

Department of the Air Force. *Coping with Violence Abroad: Personal Protection Pamphlet.* 1989, May 30. Headquarters, Department of the Air Force.

Department of the Army. *Field Manual 34-3 Intelligence Analysis.* 1990, March. Headquarters, Department of the Army.

———. *Medical Management of Chemical Casualties Handbook.* 1998, December. U.S. Army Medical Research Institute of Chemical Defense.

———. *Unconventional Warfare Devices and Techniques.* 1966, April. Department of the Army Technical Manual.

Department of the Navy. *Doctrine for Joint Special Operations.* 1998, April 17. Department of the U.S. Navy.

Department of the Treasury, Federal Law Enforcement Training Center, Office of General Training, Security Specialties Division BI. 1992. *Bomb Summary 1992.* U.S. Department of Justice.

Director of Central Intelligence. *Chemical/Biological/Radiological Incident Handbook.* 1998, October. Interagency Intelligence Committee on Terrorism, Community Counterterrorism Board.

Fainberg, A., and Bieber, A. M., Jr., for U.S. Nuclear Regulatory Commission. Revision to 1978 Edition. *Barrier Penetration Database.* Brookhaven National Laboratory.

FBI. 1993. *Bomb Summary 1993.* U.S. Department of Justice.

FBI Explosives Unit, Bomb Data Center. 1995. *General Information Bulletin: 1995 Bombing Incidents.* U.S. Department of Justice.

FBI. 2000. Project Megiddo_http:www.fbi.gov.

Federal Aviation Administration, FBI. *Bombs: Airport Security.* 1990, July. U.S. Department of Justice.

Fleet Aviation Specialized Operational Training Group, Pacific Fleet Naval Air Station, San Diego. *Survival Evasion Resistance Escape Advanced Sere Seminar E-2D-0047.*

Fleet Intelligence Training Center, Pacific. *Introduction to Terrorism Intelligence (U) K-3A-5033.* 1992, January. Department of the Navy.

International Association for Counterterrorism and Security Professionals. *Counterterrorism and Security Reports Vol. 8 No. 3.* 1999, November. IACSP.

Naval Civil Engineering Laboratory, Port Hueneme, CA. *Terrorist Vehicle Bomb Survivability Manual.* 1988, July. USACGSC.

Naval Explosive Ordinance Disposal Technology Center, Indian Head, MD, written by Petrousky, J. A. *Bomb Threat Awareness.* 1986, February 8. Office of the Chief of Naval Operations, Washington DC.

Pacific Fleet. Geneva Convention Relative to the Treatment of Prisoners of War, 12 August 1949, Including 1954 Geneva Accord (Vietnam). Fleet Aviation Specialized Operational Training Group, Pacific Fleet, San Diego.

Sniper Training and Employment. 1989, June. Headquarters, Department of the Army.

Countering Terrorism on US Army Installations. 1983, April. Headquarters, Department of the Army.

Defense Intelligence Agency. *SO 390 Counterterrorism Analysis (U)—Vol. 1.* Defense Intelligence College.

Special Edition: Terrorism, Early Bird: Current News. 1991, December. United States Department of Defense.

Terrorist Research and Analytical Center, Intelligence Division, FBI. *Terrorism in the United States.* 1991. U.S. Department of Justice.

———. *Terrorism in the United States 1982-1992.* 1991. U.S. Department of Justice.

The Joint Staff of Washington DC. *A Self-Help Handbook to Combat Terrorism: Service Members Personal Protection Guide (JS Guide 5260).* 1996, July.

U.S. Army Command and General Staff College, Fort Leavenworth, KS. *Field Circular on Individual Protective Measures Against Terrorism.* 1984, July 15. U.S. Department of the Army.

———. *Field Circular/Operational Handbook on Unit Terrorism Counteraction.* 1987, March 31. U.S. Department of the Army.

U.S. Army Military Police School, Fort McClellan, AL. *Field Circular 19-112 on the Use of Barriers (to Deny High Speed Approach) in Countering Terrorism Situations.* 1984, August. U.S. Department of the Army.

U.S. Centers for Disease Control and Prevention. *Biological Warfare and Terrorism: The Military and Public Health Response.* 1999, September 21. U.S. Department of the Army.

———. *Biological Warfare and Terrorism: Medical Issues and Response.* 2000, September 26. U.S. Department of the Army.

U.S. Department of the Navy, Office of Naval Intelligence. *Fundamentals of Naval Intelligence*. 1988. U.S. Department of the Navy.

———. *Joint Tactics, Techniques and Procedures for Anti-Terrorism*. 1998, March 17. U.S. Department of the Navy and U.S. Department of the Air Force.

U.S. Department of State. *Patterns of Global Terrorism: 1989*. 1990, April. U.S. Department of State Publication.

———. *Patterns of Global Terrorism: 1990*. 1991, April. U.S. Department of State Publication.

———. *Patterns of Global Terrorism: 1991*. 1992, April. U.S. Department of State Publication.

———. *Patterns of Global Terrorism: 1992*. 1993, April. U.S. Department of State Publication.

———. *Patterns of Global Terrorism: 1993*. 1994, April. U.S. Department of State Publication.

———. *Patterns of Global Terrorism: 1994*. 1995, April. U.S. Department of State Publication.

———. *Patterns of Global Terrorism: 1995*. 1996, April. U.S. Department of State Publication.

———. *Patterns of Global Terrorism: 1996*. 1997, April. U.S. Department of State Publication.

———. *Patterns of Global Terrorism: 1997*. 1998, April. U.S. Department of State Publication.

———. *Patterns of Global Terrorism: 1998*. 1999, April. U.S. Department of State Publication.

———. *Patterns of Global Terrorism: 1999*. 2000, April. U.S. Department of State Publication.

———. *Patterns of Global Terrorism: 2000*. 2001, April. U.S. Department of State Publication.

———. *Patterns of Global Terrorism: 2001*. 2002, April. U.S. Department of State Publication.

U.S. Department of State, Bureau of Diplomatic Security. *Significant Incidents of Political Violence Against Americans, 1990*. 1991, June. U.S. Department of State Publication.

———. *Significant Incidents of Political Violence Against Americans, 1991*. 1992, June. U.S. Department of State Publication.

———. *Significant Incidents of Political Violence Against Americans, 1992*. 1993, June. U.S. Department of State Publication.

INDEX

Centers for Disease Control
(CDC), 46, 154
types of anthrax infections,
161–62
Central Intelligence Agency
(CIA), xi
and Sept. 11 intelligence,
205–6
Chamchi, Buoabide, 250
Chatter, 216
Chemical weapons, 52,
139–53, 276
blood agents (cyanogens),
151
choking agents, 151–52
definition of, 147
dispersal systems for,
142–44
gas masks for, 139–40
indicators of incident, 153
nerve agents, 147–49
protective clothes/kits for,
140
testing equipment/storage
systems, 140–41
use of, 146
vesicants (blister agents),
149–50
why use, 145
Chile
fascism in, 54
Manuel Rodriguez Patriotic
Front-Autonomous
(FPMR/A), 48
China, Maoism in, 49, 53
Chlorine (CI), 152
Choking agents, 151–52
Cholera, 162
Christian Identity Movement,
56–57
Christianity, extremism in,
56–57, 58
Chun-Hyee, Kim, 11
CIA. See Central Intelligence
Agency (CIA)
City of Poros (ship), 273
Clothing
concealing weapons, 25
in intelligence profiling, 24
protective, 140
suicide/martyrdom indica-
tors, 35–36
Clouds, and chemical attacks,
153

Clubs, 120–21
Code Book, The (Singh), 113
Code(s)
names, 32, 76
written and ciphers, 113
Coke bottle bomb, 123
Colbern, Steven Garrett, 253
Collins, Michael, 47
Colombia. See also FARC
(Revolutionary Armed
Forces of Colombia)
AUC, 22
communism in, 20, 53–54
M-19 guerrillas, 88
skyjackers in, 187
Colonialism, and terrorism,
48
Combat training, 30
Command and control cell,
73, 78
Communications
between cells and leader-
ship, 76–77
computers, 112
secret, 113
voice, 113–14
Communism, 52–54
Computers
to analyze/integrate data,
4–5
attacks on, 281–82
use by terrorists, 112, 113
Concealment devices, 106
Contact procedures, 32–33
Corsican Army (AC), 22
Costs, of preventive measures,
xi–xii
Counterfeiting, 117
Counterterrorism (CT),
45–46
Countries, supporting terrorism, 65
financial support from, 115
schools, 29
Course of action (COA), 207
predicting, 208–9, 231
Covenant, Sword Arm of the
Lord (CSA), 22
Cover stories, 32, 183
Criminals/criminal activity
"cold hard cash" ideology,
59
drug trafficking, 51, 59
to finance terrorism, 116

and logistic cell, 103, 198,
240
sources of weapons,
119–20
and terrorism, difference
between, 44
Crop dusters, 111, 142, 276
Crops, diseases of, 278–79
Cuba
communism in, 53–54
state-supported terrorism,
17, 20, 29, 34
Culture
differences in, 227
profiling, 24
respect for, 8
terrorist survival skills in,
32, 181
Curcio, Renato, 65
Cutout system (communica-
tion), 77
Cyanogen chloride (CK), 151

D
Dahoumane, Abdulmajid, 16
"Dark Winter," 154
Daschle, Tom, 160
Data. See Intelligence analysis
Debris, unusual, 153
Decontamination kits, 140
Deductive analysis, 218–19
Defense Intelligence Agency,
67
DeJesus, Reinaldo A., 253
Denard, Robert, 19, 19, 59
Dennie, Cal, 107
Dept. of Energy Nuclear
Emergency Search Teams
(NEST), 46
Dept. of Homeland Security,
xi, 46
terrorism alert system, 234
Diniz, Albilio, 106
Di-Phosegene (DP), 152
Directional charges, 123
"Dirty bombs," 279–80
Diseases, of domestic animals,
277–78
Dispersal systems, 142–44
Distilled mustard, 149–50
Djindjic, Zoran, 126
Documents
false, use of, 32, 33–34
forging, for money, 117

Sea, infiltration by, 185,
190–91, 193
Sex, profiling, 24
Sharon, Ariel, 50
Sheik Mohammed, Khalid, 98
Shotguns, 130–31
Sikh extremism, 58
Simarro, Leirre Echevarria,
18
Singh, Simon, 113
Sinn Fein, 17
Skill levels, terrorists', 9–11
government-trained, 11–12
radical revolutionary,
16–19
religious extremist, 12–16
skills growth analysis,
222–23, 225
Skyjacking, 267
and key-word association,
5, 219–21
waves, 89
Sleeper cell, 15, 74
activation of, 197
Smallpox, 51, 157–59
"Dark Winter" exercise,
154
symptoms of, 159
Smith, Donald Lee, 253
Smuggling, 116
Sniper rifles, 126, 129, 130
Snipers, 37, 130, 259
Social Security card, 244
Soman (GD), 148
Sources, evaluating, 216–18
South Africa, African
National Congress, 48
South America, groups in, 14,
20, 22
Soviet Union, terrorist train-
ing in, 29
Spain
ETA and traffic stops, 249
fascism in, 54
Speculation, definition of, 208
Spencer, David, 106
Spikes (surveillance), 178
Spray, unusual, 166
Sri Lanka. See also LTTE
(Liberation Tigers of Tamil
Eelam), 17, 273
Stalin, Joseph, 53
Staphylococcal enterotoxin-B,
165

Stereotypes, 23
clothing, 24
of terrorists, 5–6, 7, 241
Storage systems, chemical
weapons, 141
Strategic value targets
(STRA-VT), 92
Strategies, terrorist, 85–93
execution time lines, 89–90
misdirection and deception,
87–88
selecting targets, 90–93
simplicity of, 85
strategic objectives, 86
tactical objectives, 87
wave strategies, 88–89
Submachine guns, 126, 127
Subway, attacks on, 274
Sudan, 29
Suicide/martyr candidate, 14
attacks by, 264–67
and biological weapons,
276
confronting, 36
in Israel, 50–51
preparation of, 34–35
Sulfur mustard, 149
Supplies, 100, 102–3
bomb-making accessories,
299
for logistics cell, 103–5
storage of, 106
Support
financing, 114–17
for logistics cell, 83
sources of, 65
Surveillance techniques,
173–80
and cell, 79
decision to attack, 196
detecting, 179, 180
discreet, 174–75
overt, 174, 177
still imagery, 176–77
studying surveillants,
173–74
and tactical ops cells, 198
technical, 178
video imagery, 177–78
visual, 176
who conducts, 174
Swine, diseases of, 277–78
Symbolic-value targets
(SYM-TGT), 93

Symptoms, of chemical/bio-
logical weapons, 153
anthrax, 160, 161–62
biological toxins, 164–66
blood agents, 151
choking agents, 151–52
mustard agents, 149
nerve agents, 147
smallpox, 159
viral hemorrhagic fevers,
164
Syria, 29

T
Tabun (GA), 147, 148
Tactical operations cell, 73,
81–83
activation/detection of, 198
executing attack, 199–200
final decision, 198–99
general threat questions,
228–29
move to target, 199
negotiation/debriefing,
202–3
regroup/exfiltration, 201–2
supplies for, 102
withdrawal, 200–201
Tactical-value targets (TAC-
VT), 92–93
Tanzim, 17
TAPIs. See Terrorist attack
pre-incident indicators
(TAPIs)
Targeteers, 90
Targets
general categories, 91–92
military personnel, 41–42
move to, 199
selecting, 90–91, 196–97
specific categories, 92–93
surveillance of, 176–78
target-related indicators,
215
"Technology judo," 7
Telephones, 113–14
Television, and surveillance,
178
Terrorism
availability of WMDs,
51–52
definition of, 39–42, 44–45
and drug trafficking, 51
education on, 3–4, 5

hijacking, 273
indicators at traffic stops, 243, 245, 246
infiltration by, 185, 188, 189
renting, 105, 108
used by terrorists, 108–9
Vesicants (blister agents), 149–50
Vest, suicide bomb, 35, 36
Victims. *See also* Targets
targeting, 90–93
of terrorism, 41–42
Videos, military, 31
Viral equine encephalitis, 164
Viral hemorrhagic fevers (VHFs), 164
Visas, 244
Voice communication, 113–14

W
Walking, across borders, 185
War
effectiveness of, 5–6
rules of, and terrorism, 42
Weaponization, 142
Weapons. *See also* Bombs; Chemical weapons;

Biological weapons; Guns
anti-tank rockets and guns, 132–33
armory, 98
bomb components/explosives, 121, 124
booby-trapped devices, 123
combat training in, 30
concealing with clothing, 25
grenade launcher, 122
indicators of training, 31
light infantry, 259, 260–61
man portable air defense systems, 136–37
manual, 120–21
mortars, 134–35
possession of, 26–27, 245
in safe houses, 98, 101, 107
selection of, 64
sources of, 119–20
surface-to-air missiles, 136
unusual purchases, 103–4, 105
Weapons of mass destruction (WMD). *See also* Chemical weapons; Biological weapons; Nuclear weapons
availability of, 51–52

Weather Underground, 48, 100
White Order of Thule, xii
Who Becomes a Terrorist and Why, 86
Williams, Kenneth, 206
Wiretaps, 178
Withdrawal plan, 200–201
World Trade Center
1993 bombing, 15
Sept. 11 attacks, xi, 16, 242, 248–49, 266
intelligence failure in, 205–6, 218–19, 233

Y
Yellow fever, 164
Yunez, Fuwaz, 46
Yusef, Ramzi, 202, 268

Z
Zabala-Muguirra, Jesús Maria, 8
Zawar Kili terrorist center, 46
Zionism, 57